Contract Law in Italy

Contract Law in Italy

Pier Giuseppe Monateri
Filippo Andrea Chiaves
Mauro Balestrieri

This book was originally published as a monograph in the International Encyclopaedia of Laws/Contracts.

Founding Editor: Roger Blanpain
General Editor: Frank Hendrickx
Volume Editor: Jacques Herbots

Wolters Kluwer

Published by:
Kluwer Law International B.V.
PO Box 316
2400 AH Alphen aan den Rijn
The Netherlands
E-mail: international-sales@wolterskluwer.com
Website: lrus.wolterskluwer.com

Sold and distributed by:
Wolters Kluwer Legal & Regulatory U.S.
7201 McKinney Circle
Frederick, MD 21704
United States of America
Email: customer.service@wolterskluwer.com

ISBN 978-94-035-2700-0

e-Book: ISBN 978-94-035-2701-7
web-PDF: ISBN 978-94-035-2702-4

The Authors

Prof. Avv. Dr. Pier Giuseppe Monateri was born January 15, 1958 and graduated in law at the University of Turin, Italy. He studied law in Cambridge, U.K., Harvard, U.S. and Berkeley, U.S. and conducted in-depth research in Somalia, Ethiopia, Djibouti, Cameroon, Israel, Eritrea, Vietnam, Australia and Japan. He is professor of Comparative Law at the University of Turin and is *professeur regulier* at the Faculté Internationale de Droit Comparé (Strasburg). Professor Monateri is an associate member of the International Academy of Comparative Law (Paris and New York), and has been Vice Chancellor and Jean Monet Professor at the University of Trento, Italy.

His works include La sineddoche. Formule e regole nel diritto delle obbligazioni e dei contratti, Milan, 1983; Il quantum del danno alla persona, 1st ed., Milan, 1984 and 2nd ed., Milan, 1989; Cumulo di responsabilità contrattuale ed extracontrattuale (Analisi comparata di un problema), Padua, 1989; Pensare il diritto civile (Dalle fonti all'interpretazione), Turin, 1995; Il modello di civil law, Turin, 1996; La responsabilità contrattuale e precontrattuale, Turin, 1998; La responsabilità civile, Turin, 1998. Il danno alla persona, Turin, 1998; Pensare il diritto civile, Turin, 2001; Methods of Comparative Law, Cheltenham, 2012; Geopolitica del diritto. Genesi, governo e dissoluzione dei corpi politici, Rome, 2013; I confini della legge, Turin, 2013; Classics in Comparative Law, Cheltenham, 2014; The Italian Legal System: An Introduction, Stanford, 2015; Comparative Contract Law, Cheltenham, 2017; Dominus Mundi: Political Sublime and the World Order, Oxford, 2017. Professor Monateri is a member of the board of editors of several law reviews, and coordinates the Cardozo Lectures in Law. He is the author of several papers, articles and case notes published in Italian and foreign reviews.

The Authors

Avv. Dr. Filippo Andrea Chiaves who graduated in law from the University of Turin, has been working in law firms in the United States and Italy. A Florence University comparative law doctorate lecturer having taught law and economics and comparative tort law at Milan's Bocconi University and in Bologna, he worked for Italian and U.S. law firms in Turin, Milan and Boston and was seconded to a leading Italian multinational bank. He is currently a litigation partner at Hogan Lovells in Milan assisting clients across wide-ranging industry sectors with particular focus on domestic and cross-border disputes, contentious insolvency and financial services litigation, combined with over fifteen years of experience as a full-time commercial litigator. He is the author of several case notes and coordinated the new CD-Rom edition of the Italian Digest of Private Law. His works include contributions to publications on bankruptcy law, financial services litigation, torts, product liability, and on copyright in advertising, and comparative advertising. His latest publications include *Transnational Insolvency Proceedings: Time for a Change in Europe*, 2017, INSOL World; the section on Italy of the contribution *Insolvency set-off in the reinsurance context in different jurisdictions*, March 12, 2018, INSOL World; *Le commissioni di massimo scoperto alla luce della sentenza delle Sezioni Unite n. 16303 del 20 giugno 2018, Dirittobancario.it*, June 20, 2018; *Manipolazione del tasso EURIBOR: contenzioso nazionale e rilievi comparatistici, Dirittobancario.it*, July 12, 2018; *Amministrazione straordinaria: contratti pendenti e contraenti in bonis, Dirittobancario.it*, November 11, 2018.; *La domanda di concordato preventivo è potenzialmente ammissibile anche dopo l'omologazione di un accordo di ristrutturazione dei debiti, Dirittobancario.it*, October 2019.

Dr. Mauro Balestrieri graduated in law at the University of Turin, and he is currently Research fellow in Comparative Law at the University of Turin—Department of Law. His research interests include Private Law, Comparative Law, Global studies, Law and Humanities and Methodologies of Comparative Law. He is the author of several essays and articles. Among his most recent publications are *La legge e l'arcaico. Genealogia comparata dell'ordine moderno*, Milan, 2017, and with P.G. Monateri, *Causazione e giustificazione del danno*, Turin, 2016.

Table of Contents

List of Abbreviations

A. Abbreviations of some Periodicals

Arch. civ.	Archivio civile
Banca, borsa	Banca, borsa e titoli di credito
Contratti	I contratti
Contratto e impresa	Contratto e impresa
Cor. giur.	Corriere giuridico
Corriere trib.	Corriere tributario
Danno e resp.	Danno e responsabilità civile
Digesto IV	Digesto delle discipline privati-stiche, IV Edizione
Dir. amm.	Diritto amministrativo
Dir. giur.	Diritto e giurisprudenza
Dir. giur. agrarian	Diritto e giurisprudenza agraria
Dir. ed econ. assicuraz.	Diritto ed economia delle assicurazioni
Dir. e giur. agr. Ambiente	Diritto e giurisprudenza dell'agricoltura e dell'ambiente
Dir. fallim.	Diritto fallimentare
Dir. ind.	Rivista di diritto industriale
Dir. lav.	Il diritto del lavoro
Dir. maritt.	Diritto marittimo
Dir. scambi internaz.	Diritto degli scambi internazionali
Dir. Trasporti	Diritto dei trasporti
Enc. dir.	Enciclopedia del Diritto
Enc. giur. Treccani	Enciclopedia giuridica Treccani
Foro amm.	Foro amministrativo
Foro it.	Il Foro Italiano
Foro pad.	Foro Padano
Giur. comm.	Giurisprudenza commentata
Giur. it.	Giurisprudenza italiana

List of Abbreviations

Giur. merito	Giurisprudenza di merito
Giur. pugliese	Giurisprudenza pugliese
Gius	Gius
Giust. civ.	Giusticia civile
Impresa	L'impresa
Mass. Foro it.	Massimario de Il Foro italiano
Mass. Giur. it.	Massimario di Giurispriudenza italiana
Notariato	Notariato
Not. giur. lav.	Notiziario giuridico del lavoro
NssDI	Novissimo Digesto Illustrato
Nuova giur. civ.	La nuova giurisprudenza civile commentata
Nuova rass.	Nuova rassegna di giursprudenza
P.Q.M.	P.Q.M.—Per Questi Motivi
Quadrimestre	Quadrimestre
Rass. Avv. Stato	Rassegna dell'Avvocatura dello Stato
Rass. dir. civ.	Rassegna di diritto civile
Rass. dir. tecnica doganale	Rassegna di diritto tecnica doganale
Rass. locazioni	Rassegna delle locazioni e del condominio
Rass. trib.	Rassegna del tribunale
Resp. civ. prev.	Responsabilità civile e previdenza
Riv. arbitrato	Rivista dell'arbitrato
Riv. crit. dir. priv.	Rivista e critica di diritto privato
Riv. dir. civ.	Rivista di diritto civile
Riv. dir. comm.	Rivista del diritto commerciale
Riv. dir. proc. civ.	Rivista del diritto processuale civile
Riv. dir. sport.	Rivista di diritto sportivo
Riv. giur. circolaz. e trasp.	Rivista giuridica di circolazione e trasporti
Riv. giur. edilizia	Rivista giuridica dell'edilizia
Riv. giur. polizia locale	Rivista giuridica di polizia locale
Riv. giur. sarda	Rivista giuridica sarda
Riv. not.	Rivista del notariato
Riv. trim. app.	Rivista trimestrale degli appalti
Riv. trim. dir. e proc. civ.	Rivista trimestrale di diritto e procedura civile
Società e dir.	Società e diritto
Studium iuris	Studium iuris
Temi Romana	Temi Romana
Vita not.	Vita notarile

B. Other Abbreviations

App.	Court of Appeals (used to identify decisions by the Court of Appeals)
c.c.	Italian Civil Code
c.p.c.	Italian Code of Civil Procedure
Cass.	Court of Cassation (used to identify decisions by the Court of Cassation)
Cass. S.U.	Court of Cassation in Plenary Session (used to identify decisions by the Court of Cassation in Plenary Session)
Cons. Stato	Consiglio di Stato (used to identify decisions by the Council of State)
Cons. Stato, Ad. Plen.	Consiglio di Stato in Plenary Session (used to identify decisions by the Council of State in Plenary Session)
Corte Cost.	Constitutional Court (used to identify decisions by the Constitutional Court)
Cost.	Constitution of the Republic
D. Lgs.	Government Delegated Decree (used to identify Decrees enacted by the Executive upon delegation by Parliament)
D.P.R.	Decreto del Presidente della Repubblica (used to identify Decrees enacted by the Executive and signed by the President of the Republic)
L.	Legge (used to identify a statute in citations)
M5S	Five Star Movement
Pret.	Pretura (used to identify decisions by the Pretura court)
R.D.	Regio Decreto (used for Royal Decrees enacted by the King)
TAR	TAR—Tribunale Amministrativo Regionale (used to identify decisions by this court)
Trib.	Tribunale (used to identify decisions by this court)

General Introduction

F. Chiaves

§1. THE GENERAL BACKGROUND OF THE COUNTRY

I. Geography

1. Italy is a 700-mile long peninsula stretching into the North-Central Mediterranean Sea, its territory also consisting of the two large islands of Sardinia and Sicily and smaller islands. Italy covers an area of 301,308 sq. km (116,289 sq. mi.)—slightly smaller than the State of California in the U.S.. Physically, it is characterized by four major regions: the Alps in the North, the North Italian Plain and Po river basin, the coastal plains of the peninsula, and the Apenines, forming its mountain backbone. Italy is bordered by France in the northwest, Switzerland and Austria in the north, Slovenia in the North East, and the Mediterranean Sea in the east, south and west, or specifically, clockwise from east to west, the Adriatic, Ionian, Tyrrhenian and Ligurian seas. The country had, in 2017, a population of 60,483,973 and a density of about 201 inhabitants per sq. km.

II. Cultural Composition

2. The population of Italy is remarkably homogeneous in religion, culture and language. The absolute majority of the population is Roman Catholic and speaks Italian or one of its numerous dialects or derived idioms. Linguistic minorities are just a small fraction of the population, and consist of Slovenian, German, French, Romansh, Albanian, Greek and Catalan groups. Slovenians are centered in the Friuli Venezia Giulia Region, German speaking people live mainly in the Upper Adige Valley, on the border with Austria, and French speaking people are concentrated in the Aosta Valley, near the French-Swiss border. The French and German minorities use their language in schools and official business.

III. Political System

3. Italy is a republic according to the Constitution approved by the Constituent Assembly in December 1946 and promulgated December 27, 1947. Despite its secular history, the country exists as a unified nation from 1861.

A. Historical Background of the Country

4. After the collapse of the Western Roman Empire in AD 476 under the weight of barbaric invasions, Italy suffered cultural decadence for over six centuries. Starting from the eleventh century, society evolved politically and economically and Italian city states emerged as separate political entities aside duchies and other feudal powers. In the Age of Absolutism in the seventeenth and eighteenth centuries, Italy was roughly divided into few major political entities such as the Kingdom of Piedmont, the States of Milan and the Republic of Venice in the north, the Papacy and the Grand-Duchy of Tuscany in the center, and the Kingdom of Naples and Sicily in the south, as well as in smaller principalities. When the French Revolution broke up, Italy was soon after invaded by Napoleon, who divided the country into few political entities under his control, except for the Papacy. Napoleon's defeat and the Vienna Congress of 1815 reestablished all preexisting crowns in their respective kingdoms. Starting in the late 1850s, the Kingdom of Savoy, Piedmont and Sardinia carried out the unification process by progressively annexing new states until 1871, when the Papal State capitulated. Italy's Savoy monarchy survived until World War II, when it was accused of excessive benevolence towards the defeated fascist *régime* and did not survive the June 1946 referendum whereby the people voted to abolish the monarchy and establish a republic. The Constitution of the Italian Republic was established 1948.

B. The Constitution

5. The Italian Constitution (*Costituzione della Repubblica*), promulgated on December 27, 1947 defines the basic structure and functions of the State granting the legislative power and control over the executive to the Parliament. The Constitutional Court (*Corte Costituzionale*), composed of fifteen judges appointed by the president, by the Parliament and by the highest courts, determines the constitutionality of all laws. For this purpose, it may only be seized by a lower court in the form of a prejudicial question. The Constitutional Court is also empowered to define the powers of the State, of the regions, to judge disputes between such institutions and to try the president and the ministers.

C. *The Legislative and Executive Powers*

6. The Parliament (*Parlamento*) consists of two houses with equal power and position: the Chamber of Deputies (*Camera dei Deputati*), composed of 630 deputies elected for five-year terms by universal and direct suffrage in a ratio of one representative for every 80,000 inhabitants, and the Senate (*Senato della Republica*), composed of 315 senators elected for five-year terms on a regional basis in a ratio of one senator for every 200,000 inhabitants. Citizens over eighteen may vote in all elections except senatorial elections, for which voters must be over twenty-five. All bills are passed only upon approval by both Houses of Parliament. Recent talks of Constitutional reform towards a federal-based system include diversification of tasks of the two Houses.

7. The President of the Republic (*Presidente della Repubblica*) is the Chief of the State, represents national unity and ensures respect of the Constitution. The president is elected for a seven-year term by a two-thirds majority of a joint session of the two Chambers of Parliament. The President of the Republic has the power to dissolve the Parliament except in his last six months in office. The president may nominate up to five eminent citizens as life senators, and he himself becomes one at the end of his term.

8. The executive power is held by the prime minister (*Presidente del Consiglio dei Ministri*) and by a chamber of ministers. All ministers including the prime minister are appointed by the President of the Republic and must be sustained by the majority of Parliament, although the defeat of a bill initiated by the executive does not force its resignation, as the cabinet can be removed from office only on a motion of censure voted by Parliament.

D. *Local Government*

9. For the purposes of local government, Italy is divided into twenty regions, each subdivided into provinces and then into municipalities. Elections laws as recently reformed now provide for each region, province and municipality to have popularly elected councils and executive committees headed by a chairman. Special constitutional provisions provide for wider powers and local autonomy to five regions and two provinces.

E. *Modern Politics*

10. Ever since the birth of the Republic in 1948, Italian politics were dominated by three parties, which constituted the expression of the Christian, communist and socialist ideologies. Since then, a succession of weak governments followed, all headed by the Christian Democratic party, often allied with the socialists and other minor moderate left wing entities (liberals, republicans, etc.) in order to barely achieve majority governments. The weakness of the cabinets, due to such varied composition, determined a chronic political instability which never achieved to balance the economic disparity between the rich, industrialized North of the country and its poor, depressed Southern part. Nevertheless, Italy's postwar rapid economic progress culminated in the 1960s and, after a long crisis, grew in the mid-1980s, making it the seventh most industrialized country in the world.

Internationally, Italy, which has been a member of the European Coal and Steel Community since 1951 and of the United Nations since 1955, joined the European Common Market in 1957, which later became the European Union. In the late eighties, major bribery and corruption scandals involving most government and opposition parties determined a virtual collapse of the political system, leading into a new scenario comprising two opposite factions, a right wing and a left wing coalition. Formally nonaligned parties include the communists and the Lega Nord separatists, seeking independence of the Northern part of the country. This dual coalition situation, although far from crowning a so-much-desired "Second Republic," has led to the formation of more stable cabinets, thus achieving long-term political and economic results such as entry into the European Monetary Union in 1998. At the same time, throughout the 1990s, Italy faced significant challenges as voters demanded political, economic and ethical reforms, approving substantial changes through referendums including moving from a proportional to a majoritarian electoral system and major political parties underwent far-reaching changes.

Since 1998, Italian politics experienced profound changes and radical transformations. In the national elections of 2001, the center-right coalition named "Casa delle Libertà," led and founded by the controversial figure of Silvio Berlusconi, received the absolute majority of the votes. The new government was in charge from 2001 to 2006 and it was composed by three main parties: Forza Italia, Alleanza Nazionale and Lega Nord. This period has been one of the most stable and cohesive in the history of modern Italian politics. However, in 2006, the center-left coalition "L'Unione" led by Romano Prodi defeated Berlusconi's party with a slight advantage of only 25,000 votes in the Chamber of Deputies. L'Unione, due to internal obstacles, remained in charge only for two years and in 2008 Berlusconi and his center-right coalition received again the political mandate from the people. Due to the downturn of economic growth caused by the global financial crisis of 2008, Italy underwent a period of acute political difficulties. The financial worries coupled with the global economic uncertainty influenced in turn the stability of the Italian institutional government. In 2011, after the resignation of Prime Minister Berlusconi, the technocratic government of Mario Monti promoted political, legal and institutional measures in order to ensure a more solid competitiveness for Italian economy. But from 2013 to 2017 a sort of stalemate ensued, followed by the emergence of the center-left coalition initially led by Pier Luigi Bersani and soon after by Matteo Renzi. The political program of the center-left union, however, did not obtain a positive reception in terms of popularity. The diffusion of nationalist and Eurosceptic positions, similarly as with other western countries, gave rise little by little to social and civil discontents which finally led to the emergence of a new political movement, the "Movimento 5 Stelle," led by the former comedian Beppe Grillo. In the general elections of 2018, Italy experienced the most radical institutional transformation since the end of the late century. The Movimento 5 Stelle became the leading group in Parliament, immediately followed by the Lega Nord; center-left parties, on the other side, appeared significantly reduced if compared to the previous years. What the last elections irrevocably testified is the end of political bipolarism as witnessed for decades in modern Italian history.

After a new electoral law came into force in 2016, following general elections in 2018 jurist Giuseppe Conte was appointed Prime Minister as the head of a coalition government between the antiestablishment victorious Five Star Movement (M5S) and the League party and, after the League filed in a motion of no-confidence, M5S and the center-left Democratic Party agreed to form a new coalition government with Conte remaining as Prime Minister in September 2019.

§2. Italian Law and the French Pattern

11. Survival of Roman law in Italy throughout the barbaric invasions was ensured by the Church, which jealously kept Roman legal textbooks in the libraries of its monasteries. Starting with the eleventh century, universities flourished and were active at rediscovering the *ius commune* as described in Justinian's *Corpus Iuris Civilis* and in other legal textbooks from Classical Rome. Schools of commentators of Roman legal materials such as those of the *Glossatores* and of the *Commentatores* adapted Roman rules to ongoing changes in fields such as commercial and maritime law as society evolved from a feudal to a more modern economy, and attempted to justify the rising of independent states in territories still formally controlled by the German Holy Emperor. In the age of Absolutism first and subsequently in the age of Enlightenment, ideas such as rationalism, natural law and division of powers made their way through the intellectual circuits of most Italian states. The French Revolution broke up and soon after Italy was invaded by Napoleon. All French approaches to law were imported at once in the country, first the idea of codification. Attempts to consolidate the sprawling mass of feudal, royal and canonic legal measures, regulations and court decisions had been carried out in the past but were usually limited to restricted areas of the law: collections such as the sixteenth and seventeenth century. French *Ordonnances* were enacted in several kingdoms in Italy in the 1700s, including Piedmont, Parma, Venice and Naples. However, the Napoleons codes were the first to really question the legal system itself by introducing principles of rationalism, equality and common rights and by sweeping away different legal treatment and privilege based on title, guild or social class.

In Italy Napoleon attempted to gain complete control over the sources of law by creating a single, authoritative body of laws enacted by the centralized state. The Italian translation of the French Civil Code of 1806 was imposed as law in all of Italy except for the Papacy.

12. The five French codes (civil code, criminal code, commercial code, civil code and criminal procedure code) survived Napoleon's defeat. In Italy alike in France, despite the return of conservatory *régimes*, the ideology of the French Revolution was not swept away and much of Napoleon's administrative legislation was maintained by the restored monarchies, except for Lombardy and Venetia which were reorganized under the Austrian Civil Code of 1811. Several states adopted codes based on the French model, notably Naples (1819), Parma (1820) and Tuscany (1853). The Kingdom of Piedmont, who was to carry out the unification process, adopted, between 1837 and 1854, codes being virtually identical to the Napoleons codes. After unification, they became the codes of the new Italian nation and were progressively extended to all conquered territories.

13. Early eighteenth century French legal tradition influenced Italian jurists and statutory law was worshipped as the only true source of legal regulation for a good thirty years, and the role of judges was limited to merely applying the law as granted by the State, not to construe it. Subsequently, Italian scholars were influenced by the Pandectists, whose theories on law organized a system based on elaborate legal definitions, dogmas and general concepts which contributed to the formation of the German Civil Code of 1900. This school of thought, as well as positivism, influenced the draft of the 1942 Italian Civil Code.

14. Most of the country's legislation underwent major reforms throughout Italy's post-World War II history: nevertheless, the basis of the legal system remains that of 1861 based on the French model. The quest for a major reform in the main centralized structure of the State has grown in the past decade years, leading all political entities in Parliament to set up a Reforms Committee to revise the 1948 Constitution introducing principles of federalism and decentralization in State politics, economics, finance and administration. After much preparation, the reform is taking shape and is expected to be enforced by the turn of the century.

§3. Primacy of Legislation

15. The Italian Constitution is the supreme law of the land which supersedes all and any other national rules. Article 10 provides for national law to comply with international treatises ratified by Italy. Below the principles set out in the Constitution, at least formally, statutory law as a body of rules enacted by the State is thought to be the primary and sole source of law. All other sources, such as custom, jurisprudence and scholars, are in some way secondary if not even subjugated to statutory legislation. This principle derives from the French post-Civil Code legal tradition, and is still felt today in Italy as one of the strongholds of the country's legal system. Therefore, as the Civil Code Preliminary Provisions state, in order to solve a legal problem, an Italian judge first seeks a solution in statutory laws by construing the provisions contained therein according to their literal, logical, or teleological meaning, with the aid of analogy and *travaux préparatoires*. Formally in Italy jurisprudence neither has a creative role in making the law, nor is there any system of precedent, although a judge with a legal problem certainly examines previous cases to solve a dubious question and especially considers decisions by the Court of Cassation and by courts of the major cities (Milan, Rome), whose views have practically become dominant in some areas of the law such as bankruptcy, copyright and commercial law. Scholars play a fundamental role as well, dominating legal education and influencing general legislative policies on a national scale.

16. Legislative measures are enacted by Parliament by means of statutes (*leggi*), and by the government in the form of urgent or delegated decrees (*decreti-legge, decreti legislativi*), which require approval by Parliament. Regions, provinces and municipalities may enact statutes in limited matters which have the same standing as national legislation. Parliament, government and all such entities also issue detailed regulatory measures (*regolamenti*) to integrate existing statutory provisions.

§4. The Position of the Judiciary

17. In Italy, decisions by the courts are neither formally considered a source of law nor is there a system of precedent whereby courts must follow previous decisions. However, court decisions play a significant role in construing statutes and decisions by the Court of Cassation are normally cited by lawyers in their complaints and pleas, and judges (although not forced to do so) very often decide along with previous cases.[1]

18. Separation of the Judiciary Power from the executive is achieved by means of a special Superior Council of the Judiciary (*Consiglio Superiore della Magistratura*), composed of law professors and members of the bench and bar, and headed by the President of the Republic. The Council independently appoints, assigns and removes all judges except those of the Constitutional Court. Judges are public officers and State employees. Becoming a judge implies passing a State exam and making a State career.

19. The Italian judicial system is headed by a Court of Cassation (*Corte di Cassazione*), which acts as the Supreme Court of the nation in questions of law in civil and criminal matters. It does not rule on the constitutionality of statutory provisions passed by the legislature. The Court of Cassation is not bound by its previous decisions and has changed views on several occasions on important questions of law. Lower courts often follow the Court of Cassation's latest position on a given legal question, or at least take it into consideration in the process of deciding a case. Very controversial issues are decided by the Court of Cassation in Plenary Session (*Corte di Cassazione a Sezioni Unite*): such decisions as well do not act as precedents, although their authority is deemed higher than ordinary Cassation decisions.

20. Following court reorganization legislation passed in 2011–2012, in civil and criminal matters Italy is currently divided into 26 Appeals Court districts (*Corti d'appello*) and 3 subdistricts, which are subdivided into 136 Tribunal districts (*Tribunali*, courts composed of three judges or headed by single judges). Since 1995,

1. *See* Bin, M., "Funzione uniformatrice della Cassazione e valore del precedente giudiziario," in *Contr. e impr.*, 1988, at 549 et seq.; Chiarloni, S., "Efficacia del precedente giudiziario e tipologia dei contrasti di giurisprudenza," in *Riv. trim. dir. e proc. civ.*, 1989, at 118 et seq. For a recent analysis, *see* Pellegrini, S., "Il contenzioso giudiziario in Italia tra mutamento e riforme," Giuffrè, Milan, 2008, at 7 et seq.

Justice of the Peace districts (*Giudici di Pace*), composed of semiprofessional judges, have the narrowest civil jurisdiction.

In addition, there are ninety-one Criminal Assize Courts (*Corti d'assise*) and twenty-four Criminal Assize Courts of Appeal (*Corti d'assise d'appello*), all of them composed of judges and several qualified jurors.

21. Public policy disputes arising between single citizens and the State (including regions, provinces, municipalities and other public bodies) are regulated by administrative law provisions. Since 1974, there have been twenty Regional Administrative Tribunals (*Tribunali Amministrativi Regionali, TAR*) who cover first degree administrative jurisdiction and whose decisions may be appealed before the Council of State (*Consiglio di Stato*), sitting in Rome.

§5. Distinction Between Public and Private Law

22. Private law is a set of provisions directly protecting rights and interests of individuals; public law is a body of rules regulating the general interests of a community.[2] Private law copes with legal relationships between individuals (human beings and corporate entities), and are generally governed by the civil code, which encompasses commercial and corporate law, family law, torts law. Public law copes with constitutional law, administrative law, civil and criminal procedure, criminal law, international law, taxation and local government.[3]

23. French law distinguishes between administrative and private contracts. A similar division exists in Italian law, whereas "private law contracts" are governed by the civil code and "public law contracts" are regulated by administrative law.[4] Public authorities and institutions as well as administrative bodies may of course enter into both kinds of contracts with individuals and corporations: for example,

2. *See* Martines, T., "Diritto costituzionale, Giuffrè," Milano, 1990, at 40 et seq.; Pugliatti, S., "Diritto pubblico e privato" in *Enc. Dir.*, XII, at 696 et seq.; Giannini, M.S., Istituzioni di diritto amministrativo, Milano, 1981, at 403; Pugliatti, S., "Gli istituti del diritto civile," Milano, 1943, at 24.
3. This traditional division between public and private law is contained in all basic academic textbooks (*see* Trimarchi, P., "Istituzioni di diritto privato," IX Ed., Milano, Giuffrè, 1991, at 26 et seq.; Torrente, A., Schlesinger, P., "Manuale di diritto privato," Milano, Giuffrè, 2011, at 22 et seq.; Pugliatti, S., "Diritto pubblico e diritto privato," in *Enc. Dir.*, XII, 1964, at 696 et seq.; Giorgianni, "Il diritto privato e i suoi attuali confini," in *Riv. Trim. dir. e proc. civ.*, 1961, at 391 et seq.) and is taught in first year law courses at the university, where students take exams in subjects such as private law, administrative law and constitutional law.
4. This principle is widely accepted by scholars and by courts. *See*: Garri, G., "La responsabilità civile della pubblica amministrazione," 1996, at 146–147; Sandulli, A., "Manuale di diritto amministrativo," Napoli, 1989, at 1167; Scognamiglio, R., "Responsabilità contrattuale ed extra-contrattuale," in *NssDI*, XV, at 670; Bortolotti, D., "Contratti della amministrazione pubblica," in: *Digesto IV*, Utet, Torino, 1989, at 37; Meloncelli, A., "L'informazione amministrativa," Rimini, 1983, at 282. Courts have stated this position as well: *see Soc. Dufrital v. Pref. Milano*, Cass. Jul. 29, 1987, n. 6547 (*Mass. Giur. It.*, 1987); *Soc. Sopin v. Univ. Studi di Roma*, TAR Lazio I, Nov. 18, 1988, n. 1613 (*Foro Amm.*, 1989, n. 2471; *Foro it.*, 1990, III, 32) and Cass., Aug. 9, 1977 (*Mass. Foro it.*, 1977, n. 3647). Courts have also claimed land expropriation plans set out by public bodies are governed by private law: e.g., *see* Cass., Mar. 28, 1987, 3027 (*Cor. Giur.*, 1987, 733, n. Lombardi).

principal-contractor-subcontractor agreements resulting from public bids, and, to a certain extent, public employment contracts are considered "public law contracts" governed by administrative law, which generally implies the predominance of the public party on the basis of the general idea that public interest must always prevail. On the contrary, a lease or a sale of goods agreement between an individual and a State agency shall be solely governed by private law, so that both parties are granted equal protection by the law and enjoy equal rights.

Employer-employee agreements as a result of collective bargaining are "private law contracts" with public elements, as they generally represent minimum wage and minimum working benefits and conditions which must be granted to workers according to Articles 36 and 39 of the Constitution.

Recently, the entire regulation of administrative and private contracts has been consolidated by the so-called *Codice dei contratti pubblici* (Legislative Decreelegislative No. 50 enacted April 18, 2016, amended and updated by Legislative Decree No. 56 of April 19, 2017), a single text in which all the legislation previously scattered and dispersed appears finally systematized and harmonized according to the most recent case law guidelines and to European legislation.[5]

24. Jurisdiction is organized accordingly with the distinction between public and private law.[6] Disputes arising from unfair treatment of individuals by the administration (example: violating legitimate expectations such as unlawfully eliminating a competitor's offer for a public bid) falls within jurisdiction of administrative courts, who only verify if the administrative measure was lawful or unlawful; whereas violations of legally protected rights and interests of individuals (such as a public agency's failure to pay a contractor for a bid) are examined by civil courts.

§6. The Merging of Civil and Commercial Law

25. In Italy commercial transactions are governed by rules expressed in the civil code.[7] No special jurisdiction exists for such transactions. Commercial law in Italy is entirely dealt with by the ordinary civil courts.[8] The formal distinction between civil and commercial law is of no particular importance and it is just a frame to arrange topics. The term "commercial law" usually regards legal rules on business transactions and implies areas of the law such as partnerships, agency, etc., statutes of limitation, all of which are regulated within specific sections of the Civil Code. Bankruptcy law, intellectual property law, copyright and patent law, and, to a certain extent, stocks, bonds, securities and negotiable instruments are governed by special statutes. Maritime law is governed by the Navigation Code.

5. *See* Perfetti, L.R., "Codice dei contratti pubblici—Commentato," Wolters Kluwer, 2017; De Nictolis, R., "I nuovi appalti pubblici. Appalti e concessioni dopo il d.lgs. 56/2017," Bologna, Zanichelli, 2017.
6. *See* Caringella, F., "Il riparto di giurisdizione," Milan, Giuffrè, 2008.
7. For an historical analysis, *see* Galgano, F., "Storia del diritto commerciale," Bologna, il Mulino, 1976, at 103.
8. *See* Galgano, F., "Trattato di diritto civile. Volume primo," Padova, CEDAM—Wolters Kluwer, 2014 at 76 et seq.

Introduction to the Law of Contracts

P.G. Monateri

§1. Formation of Contract

I. Definition of Contract

26. Contract is defined by the Civil Code as an agreement of two or more parties to establish, regulate or extinguish a "patrimonial"[9] legal relationship among themselves (Article 1321 c.c.). As a general rule, the parties to a contract can freely determine the contents of a contract within the limits imposed by the law (Article 1322 c.c.).[10]

27. Several contracts (such as bailment, sale of property, agency, loan, surety, etc.) are regulated by specific provisions in special sections of the civil code. However, as a general rule, other contracts may be conceived even if they are not specifically regulated by the law, provided the parties' interests are worthy of protection by the law (Article 1322, section 2, c.c.). In all such cases, contracts are regulated by the General Rules on Contracts contained in Title II of the Fourth Book of the Civil Code (Articles 1323–1324 c.c.).

II. Conditions for the Existence of a Contract

28. In order for an agreement to be defined as a "contract," four basic conditions must be met: (i) an agreement by the parties, (ii) a lawful *causa*, and (iii) a possible, lawful, certain or ascertainable object and (iv) compliance with formal requisites whenever it is provided by the law (Article 1325 c.c.).

9. The concept of "patrimony" as intended in Italian law is explained in VI below.
10. *See* Sacco, R., De Nova, G., "Il Contratto," Turin, UTET—Wolters Kluwer, 2016, at 87 et seq.

A. Agreement of the Parties

29. For a contract to be formed, there must be mutual assent.[11] Contract theory actually requires an actual "meeting of the minds" to form a contract, and implies the parties' intention to create legal relations. This implies problems of construing and interpreting the parties' intentions (*see* Introduction to the Law of Contracts, §9.).

B. Causa

30. The *causa*[12] is a Roman law concept which basically represents the reason for the agreement, and justifies the contractual obligations contained therein. Reference to the common law concept of "consideration," although not properly coinciding with that of *causa*, may help readers from common law based-systems to better understand this element of contract. In order for a contract to exist, there must be a lawful *causa* (Article 1418 section 2, c.c.) which is worthy of legal protection (Article 1322 section 2, c.c.). Examples: in a sales and purchase agreement, the *causa* is the transfer of goods in exchange for money; in employment contracts, the *causa* in the provision of work for a given salary; in a loan agreement, the *causa* is borrowing money in exchange for interest, etc.

C. Object

31. The object[13] of the contract must be "possible," thus achievable, provided that *ad impossibilia nemo tenetur*: therefore, if the object of the contract is not reasonably possible, the contract is void, the ground of such nullity being that the stipulation is *naturali ratione inutilis* (Article 1418 c.c.), which means that it must be *objectively* and *absolutely* impossible to perform the duties of that contract, as is the case for the sale of a sunken ship. Clearly, the party who knew about the impossibility before entering into the contract is liable for damages caused to the other party who relied on the validity of the contract (Article 1338 c.c.).

---

11. On the agreement of the parties, *see* Roppo, V., "Il contratto," Giuffrè, Milan, 2011, at 23 et seq.
12. On the *causa*, *see* Alpa, G., "Causa e tipo," in *Vita not.*, 1997, at 3; Sicchero, G., "Il contratto con causa mista," Cedam, Padua, 1995, at VIII-352; Alpa, G., "L'uso giurisprudenziale della causa nel contratto," in *Nuova giur. civ.*, 1995, II, 1; Sicchero, G., "Appunti sulla causa del contratto (nota a Cass. sez. II 15 luglio 1993, n. 7844, *Torresin* v. *Torresin*)," in *Giur. it.*, 1995, I, 1, 733; Ragusa Maggiore, G., "La scomparsa degli *idola fori*: la causa del contratto," in *Dir. fallim.*, 1995, I, 553; Marinelli, F., "La causa e l'oggetto del contratto nella dottrina civilistica italiana," in *Giust. civ.*, 1995, II, 327, *Rep. Foro it.*, 1995, "Contratto in genere," n. 131; Oberto, G., "Le cause in materia di obbligazioni," Giuffrè, Milan, 1994 (at XX-754); Battaglia, C., "Contratti innominati e causa atipica (nota a Cass. sez. I, 20 novembre 1992, n. 12401, *Soc. immob. turistica H.M.* v. *Ministero dei Trasporti*)," in *Giust. civ.*, 1993, I, 2761; Alcaro, F., "Causa del contratto: evoluzioni interpretative e indagini applicative," Giuffrè, Milan, 2016.
13. On the object of contract, *see* Marinelli, F., "La causa e l'oggetto del contratto nella dottrina civilistica italiana," in *Giust. civ.*, 1995, II, 327, *Rep. Foro it.*, 1995, "Contratto in genere," n. 131; Gabrielli, E., "L'oggetto del contratto," Giuffrè, Milan, 2015, at 5 et seq.

32. No contract for an unlawful object is valid.[14] There may be illegality as to formation, purpose, or performance of a contract. Nullity always arises from violation of statutory law or illegality on grounds of public policy, and affects the validity of the contract. Examples of void contracts bearing an unlawful object include contracts to commit crimes or wrongs, contracts affecting the State, contracts tending to pervert the course of justice, contracts in restraint of trade or generally violating commercial rules or regulations, and, generally speaking, contracts contrary to good morals.[15]

33. Finally, the object of contract must be "certain" or "ascertainable," which means it must be consistent and described in detail, not vaguely referred to and abstract: *id certum est quod certum reddi potest* (Articles 1346 and 1418 section 2, c.c.).[16] The object of a contract is "certain" when it is defined by the parties; it is "ascertainable" whenever the parties have only agreed upon the *method* to define it, such as when reference is made to the current market price of goods to be purchased.

34. Often the missing terms in contracts may be provided by statute or be filled by reference to the custom of the trade or to the course of dealings between the parties. The parties may also agree that some elements of the contract (such as the price of the goods) be determined by an arbitrator.[17] If, however, it can neither be objectively determined what the parties intended, nor can the gaps be ascertained elsewhere, then courts may be forced to conclude that lack of certainty militates against contractual validity.

D. Form

35. Under Italian law, the general rule is that contracts can be made informally.[18] In specific cases, the law provides for certain agreements to be valid and effective only if they are drawn in a certain form. This is the case, for example, for donations (Article 782 c.c.), wedding contracts, transfers of real estate ownership (*see* Articles 1350 and 1351 c.c.), leases lasting more than nine years (Article 1503 c.c.) and partnerships (Articles 2332 n. 2 and 2475 c.c.), all of which require written instruments and notarization. In all such cases, specifically defined in the Civil

14. *See* Lucchini Guastalla, E., "Il contratto e il fatto illecito. Corso di diritto civile," Milan, Giuffrè, 2015, at 155.
15. Examples include contracts promoting immorality or corruption in public life, agreements in the field of gaming and betting, contracts affecting the freedom or security of marriage, etc.
16. *See* Barenghi, A., "Determinabilità e determinazione unilaterale del contratto," Napoli, 2005, at 157; Alpa, G., "Appunti sulla nozione di oggetto del contratto," in *Vita not.*, 1981, at 815; Roppo, V., "Sugli usi giudiziali della categoria 'indeterminatezza/indeterminabilità dell'oggetto del contratto' e su una sua recente applicazione a tutela di 'contraenti deboli'," in *Giur. It.*, 1977, I, 1, at 146.
17. Should the arbitrator fail to perform this duty, or should his estimates be clearly unfair or mistaken, the court may be called to determine the required elements of contract (Art. 1349, s. 1, c.c.).
18. *See* Fazio, E., "Dalla forma alle forme. Struttura e funzione del neoformalismo negoziale," Milan, Giuffrè, 2011, at 37 et seq.

Code, form is an essential condition for the existence of the contract (form *ad substantiam*), which implies that contract is null and void if the formal requirements are not met.

36. The code also provides for cases in which a particular form is not required for the contract to be valid and effective, but is essential in order to prove its existence and contents (form *ad probationem*). Examples of this rule are scattered all over the code: a contractor may only prove in court that he was authorized by the owner to specific variations in a construction project, by producing a written authorization (Article 1659 c.c.). Compromise and settlement agreements and insurance contracts must also be proved by providing written evidence of the agreement (Articles 1967 and 1888 c.c.). In all such cases, the contract may never be proven by means of witnesses and no presumptions are operating (Articles 2725 and 2729 section 2, c.c.).

III. "Accidental Elements" to a Contract

37. Agreement of the parties, *causa*, object and form are essential elements that must be present for a contract to exist.[19] Furthermore, agreements may contain "accidental elements," such as conditions (*conditio*) and terms, which may affect execution of the contract by one or both parties.[20] The parties may for instance provide that some or all effects of the agreement be conditioned to a future event which may or may not occur (*conditio*, Article 1353 c.c.). Some contracts may not be conditioned in any way (as is the case for wedding contracts and other family law instruments, transferring shares and bonds and endorsing checks, etc.). If a contract contains unlawful conditions, the contract is void if the condition is essential (Article 1354 section 1, c.c.). If the condition only affects a clause of the contract, that clause is ineffective but the contract is valid (Article 1354 c.c.).

38. Terms are limitations in time to the effects of a contract (Article 1184 c.c.). Terms may be initial (example: the contract shall be effective starting May 3) or final (example: the contract shall last until May 3). A special condition is "*modus*."[21] *Modus* is a clause limiting the economic benefits of a beneficiary by imposing an obligation upon him, such as when money is granted to an institution to be employed for a specific research program. *Modus* differs from *conditio* because it implies an obligation and differs from the common law concept of consideration in that it applies only to gratuitous promises. Thus, it is quite similar to promises calling for an act.

---

19. *Conditio* and terms with reference to contracts are dealt with in Part I.—General Principles of the Law of Contract, Chapter 3, §3.
20. *See* Maggi, P., "La condizione, il termine ed il *modus*," in Fava, P., "Il contratto," Milano, Giuffrè, 2012, at 943 et seq.
21. *See* Marini, A., "Il *modus* come elemento accidentale del negozio giuridico," Milano, Giuffrè, 1976, at 189.

IV. Rights In Rem and Rights In Personam

39. Italian law adopts the widely known civilian distinction between rights in rem (*diritti reali*) and rights in personam (*obbligazioni*). Rights in rem, primarily consisting in property rights and other interests attached thereto, which are binding on any person claiming that property (*erga omnes*): therefore, a person entitled to property rights over a parcel of land has title of ownership which may not be questioned by anybody attempting to claim interest on that land. Rights in personam, also referred to as "obligations," are rights arising out of an agreement or out of tort, and therefore may only be imposed on the person or legal entity who is to perform an obligation. One may say that rights in rem are attached to things no matter who their owner is, whilst rights in personam are attached to persons.[22]

Contracts are agreements to create, dispose of, affect or cancel both rights in personam and rights in rem.

V. Obligations

40. An obligation is a duty relation between two persons whereby a party is bound to perform (or to refrain from performing) one act for the benefit of the other.[23] A duty is an obligation only if parties' interests at stake have an economic value which is appreciable in terms of money. The person having a duty to perform is conventionally called the "debtor," whilst the party entitled to the performance is referred to as the "creditor." These terms are not confined to money debt situations, but used for all obligations. With respect to performance, a creditor is therefore entitled to a right in personam which he may enforce only against his debtor.

41. According to Article 1173 of the Civil Code, obligations may arise from a contractual relationship (*viz.* duty to pay the sales price in a sales-purchase agreement), or from tort (duty to pay damages if held liable). Obligations may also derive from unilateral promises (*see* Article 1987 c.c.), from quasi-contracts (Articles 2028 et seq., c.c.: *negotiorum gestio*, unjust enrichment) and from several family relations governed by family law such as the duty to provide nourishment and education to one's children, or the duty to provide alimony in case of divorce, etc.

VI. The Concept of "Patrimony"

42. "Patrimony" may be defined as the set of all interests, assets and liabilities with an economic value, belonging to a person or corporate body.[24] A "patrimony" only includes rights and duties which may be appreciated in terms of money: for

22. On the general distinction between rights in rem and rights in personam, *see* Buckland W.W., McNair A.D., "Roman Law and Common Law: A Comparison in Outline," Cambridge, Cambridge University Press, 1952, at 89 et seq.
23. *See* Gambino, F., "Le Obbligazioni—Vol. I: Il rapporto obbligatorio," in *Trattato di Diritto Civile diretto da R. Sacco*, Torino, UTET—Wolters Kluwer, 2015, at 29 et seq.
24. Roppo, V., "Diritto privato," Torino, Giappichelli, 2014, at 91.

example, parental powers and other interests regarding family relationships (such as legitimacy or adoption) are not patrimonial rights or obligations. Usually an individual or a legal entity only has "one" patrimony for the purpose of the law. However, in particular circumstances, two or more patrimonies may be referred to the same person, such as when an heir accepts an inheritance "with benefit of inventory" (which means only after an evaluation of the inheritable assets), thus constituting a separate patrimony from his own (Article 490 c.c.). Similarly, in family law, as a general rule a married woman's personal patrimony is separated from the couple's common patrimony (*see* Articles 159 and 167 c.c.). In bankruptcy law, bankruptcy estates make up for a patrimony. Generally speaking, the creditors of a separate patrimony have priority in satisfying their debt with respect to the creditors of the person who is entitled to that patrimony: for instance, the creditors of the testator are to be satisfied prior to the creditors of the heirs on the estate of the deceased person (Article 490 c.c.).

VII. Unilateral Acts and Promises

43. In a unilateral act, one person makes a promise whereas the other party is never bound; nevertheless, the promise is enforceable. A will, for example, according to Italian law is a unilateral act. Resolutions by the board of directors of a company are unilateral acts as well. Some unilateral acts only affect the patrimony of the person who executed the instrument: for instance, granting a proxy or accepting an inheritance do not affect assets of third parties to the deal. Other times, unilateral acts may imply modifications in other people's patrimonies, may the outcome be positive (as is wavering a mortgage on another person's land) or, whenever the law so provides, negative (such as the act of requiring early termination of a contract, or the act of selling one's corporate shares).

44. Unilateral promises may be valid as unilateral acts in specific cases (Article 1987 c.c.).[25] The code only refers to two cases in which no acceptance is required for a promise to be binding: when an offer is made "to the world at large" (Article 1989 c.c.) and in the case of promissory notes. Beyond these cases, a promise requires acceptance to be effective; that is, the promisee must have in some way agreed to accept the promise. The rule is based on the principle that nobody's patrimony may be decreased or even increased against his intention. Gratuitous promises also, such as donations, require acceptance by the donee to be valid and effective (Article 782 c.c.). Finally, if the offer is made in the exclusive interest of the offeror (*viz.* the promise by the landlord to reduce the rent in a lease), acceptance is not necessary and the offer is immediately binding (Article 1333 c.c.).

25. *See* Camilleri, E., "Le promesse unilaterali," Milano, Giuffrè, 2002; Camilleri, E., "La formazione unilaterale del rapporto obbligatorio," Torino, Giappichelli, 2004; Gallo, P., "Contratti e promesse unilaterali: rilevanza attuale della distinzione," "In memoria di Ariberto Mignoli," 3, Bocconi legal papers, 2014, at 115 et seq.

§2. Historical Background of the Law of Contracts

45. In the standard ideology of the last century, contracts were essentially a matter of personal freedom, whereby every individual could regulate his relations with others and achieve his own, private goals. Freedom of contract within a system of economic competition was a milestone of eighteenth century capitalism in Europe. Economic theories of the time held that achieving private interests, resulting in a full exploitation of a country's economic resources, would have brought general advantages to the whole of society. Therefore, in order to guarantee full economic freedom and unlimited competition, the role of the State was to be limited to enacting few provisions defending the basic principles of capitalism. As a result, governments approved rules against contractual clauses limiting business transactions, and life-employment agreements were generally forbidden (Article 1780 *Code Napoléon*, Article 1628 of the Italian Civil Code of 1865), and in England non-competition agreements were strictly limited in time.

46. In Italy, the theory of freedom of contract collapsed with the turn of the century. *Laissez faire* was substituted by economic doctrines centered around the idea of active intervention by the State in the country's economy in order to protect the weaker classes and encourage economic development. Such a result was thought to be solely achievable by introducing limitations and controls over the private sector, limiting freedom of contract. Social security, public insurance, large State-owned companies affected the economy and developed throughout this century and well into Europe's post-World War II era. Labor unions became primary figures in collective bargaining, and protective legislation affected traditionally free areas of contract, imposing minimum wages, fixed prices on goods, superimposed clauses in public services and contracts, minimum duration and State-controlled lease fees, etc.[26]

47. Notwithstanding all of the above, although placed in an increasingly "social" dimension, modern Italian contract law is still centered upon the values of economic pluralism, capitalism and competition. The eighteenth century idea of "freedom of contract" has simply turned into limited, controlled freedom in light of public interest.[27]

In the last decades, as production of standardized goods and services developed, the latest trends in contract law have imposed simplifying contract formation procedures, leading companies to predefine contract model forms for consumers which leave no space for negotiation. As a consequence, European and national legislation was passed protecting consumers against exemption clauses and conditions of nullity enclosed in contract forms prepared by large enterprises, which may be excessively strict with respect to consumers.

---

26. *See* Monateri, P.G., "The Authoritarian Theory of Contract," in Monateri, P.G. (Ed.), "Comparative Contract Law," Cheltehnam, Edward Elgar, 2017, at 47 et seq.
27. On this point, *see also* Alpa, G., Conte, G., "Diritti e libertà fondamentali nei rapporti contrattuali," Torino, Giappichelli, 2018.

48. Another recent aspect of transactions and contractual relationships is that economically relevant business agreements are very often negotiated by individuals for and on behalf of corporate entities or public agencies, *not* for their own interests. Furthermore, transactions are very often negotiated by entire teams of experts who are acting on behalf of large companies. In other words, contracts are no longer the result of the "meeting of the minds" of two individuals as was in the eighteenth century.

§3. Classification of Contracts

I. "Typical" and "Atypical" Contracts

49. Italian law, as other civil law systems, provides many "blocks" of contracts to cover the most widely used transactions, such as sales, agency, bailment, surety, etc. These "blocks" are essentially sets of default rules. However, as a general rule, individuals may enter contracts which do not fit any "block," provided they cover interests which are worthy of legal protection by the law (Article 1322 c.c.).[28]

II. Contracts Based upon Consideration and Gratuitous Contracts

50. A contract is based upon consideration whenever each party suffers a detriment. Otherwise, the contract is gratuitous. In a sale agreement, for instance, the buyer pays the price but gains the object of the purchase, whereas the seller loses the object but gains the purchase price: thus, the contract is based upon consideration. Similarly, an insurer provides coverage for a risk but receives payment of the premiums. On the contrary, a donation is a gratuitous contract whereas a donor loses the object of the grant without receiving anything in exchange from the donee. Similarly, a loan is gratuitous if it is granted for no interest. Usually, in gratuitous contracts the grantor is offered wider protection: a donor may in several cases revoke his donation (Articles 800 et seq., c.c.) and general rules on construing contracts provide that whenever the meaning of a clause enclosed in a gratuitous contract is unclear, it should be construed so as to be as least burdensome as possible for the grantor.

III. Bilateral (Synallagmatic) and Unilateral Contracts

51. Bilateral contracts are agreements in which the duties and obligations to be performed by one party have a direct correspondence with those to be performed by the other: in a sale-purchase agreement, one party's duty to transfer ownership is directly related to the other party's duty to pay the sales price. The relationship, defined with the Greek term *synallagma*, implies each party may refuse to perform her duty unless the other party performs her own at the same time (Articles 1460 et

28. *See* Gazzoni, F., "Manuale di diritto privato," Napoli, ESI, 2003, at 762.

seq., c.c.).[29] Of course, this rule must comply with existing contractual usage and with any performance terms agreed-upon by the parties. Other consequences of the bilateral relationship include the right not to perform one's contractual duties in the case the other party's duties have become objectively impossible (Articles 1463 et seq., c.c.). Moreover, failure by one party to perform her contractual duties allows the other party to choose between demanding specific performance or termination of contract (Article 1453 c.c.).

52. In a unilateral contract only one of the parties agrees to perform a duty with respect to the other: *viz.* in a donation, only the donor grants (or agrees to grant) something to the donee; in a bailment, the bailee only is bound to keep the goods in custody and to return them upon the bailor's request. Finally, in a unilateral agreement whereby the owner promises to sell his property to the transferee if the latter decides to purchase it within a given deadline, only the owner is bound to execute his promise.[30]

IV. Partnerships and Societies

53. When two or more persons grant certain goods or services for a common goal, such as when establishing a partnership, there occurs no bargain and the parties do not mutually perform duties of any sort. Every party expects a benefit by the contract, but that benefit does not derive from performance of a duty by another party, but from participating to a common advantage or profit. Partnerships and societies are established by contract, and that contract is not bilateral.[31] Therefore, if one partner does not perform his duties (such as providing shareholder's contributions), the other partners still have to perform their own.

V. "Commutative" and "Aleatory" Contracts

54. Bilateral contracts may be "commutative" or "aleatory," depending on whether the entity and extension of any or all of the obligations relating to one of the parties depends upon future, uncertain events. In other words, if both parties' contractual duties are clearly defined and certain upon entry into the contract, we have a "commutative" contract; whereas one obligation implies assumption of a risk, we have an "aleatory" contract, as is the case for insurance and suretyships (Articles 1882 et seq., c.c.) or life annuities (Articles 1872 et seq. c.c.).

---

29. *See* Delfini, F., "Autonomia privata e contratto: Tra sinallagma genetico e sinallagma funzionale," Torino, Giappichelli, 2017, at 2 et seq.
30. About these distinctions, *see* Gallo, P., "I contratti, le promesse unilaterali, l'apparenza," Torino, Giappichelli, 2017, at 509 et seq.
31. On this point, *see* Galgano, F., "Trattato di diritto civile," vol. 4, CEDAM—Wolters Kluwer, 2014, at 4.

VI. Duration Contracts

55. In some cases, execution of one's contractual duties may imply an ongoing performance which continues in time (such as lease, employer-employee relationships, hire of work and skill, energy or water supply, surety, trademark license agreements, agency, partnerships, etc.).[32] The duties relating to such contracts are single, periodical duties and do not constitute a single obligation: this explains why in all such cases early termination of the contract has no effects on all previously performed duties (Articles 1458, 1373 section 2, c.c.). Usually, these kinds of agreements last for an unlimited time period, and may therefore be terminated by any one party upon prior notice to the other.

VII. "Consensual" Contracts, "Solemn" Contracts, "Real" Contracts

56. "Consensual" contracts require acceptance of the offer for the agreement to be binding, regardless of the form in which acceptance is expressed. Most contracts care "consensual" provided that, as seen above, the general rule of the Civil Code (Articles 1321 and 1322, c.c.) is that no particular form is required for a contract unless the law specifically provides so.[33]

57. On the contrary, "solemn" contracts require a given form in order to be valid and effective.[34] Generally speaking, preliminary agreements and contracts regarding the transfer of interests and rights in land, buildings and immovable assets may be notarized and must be executed in writing (Article 1350 c.c.). The same rule applies to leases lasting more than nine years, to all and any contracts entered into by public governmental agencies and to transfer agreements regarding investment bonds (*see* Article 18 *ter* of Act No. 216 of June 7, 1974). Checks, promissory notes and bonds must also be expressed in writing. Formal requisites may imply strict procedures: corporations may only be established in writing by means of a notarized document (*see* Articles 2332 n. 2 and 2475 c.c.), and the same instrument is to be executed for donations (Article 782 c.c.), except for donations of worthless movable things (Article 783 c.c.). Wills may be enclosed in a notarized document or else may be written by the testator and kept secret in the hands of a notary: in any case, they must be expressed in writing. Finally, the law provides for certain clauses contained in contracts to be specifically approved in writing and signed in order to be valid and effective (*see* Articles 1341, 1342 and 1469 *bis* et seq., c.c.).

58. "Real" contracts require delivery of a good to be binding.[35] Such is the case in donations of movable things with a moderate value, which do not require acceptance and may be executed by simple delivery (Article 783 c.c.). Debate over this

32. *See* Granieri, M., "Il tempo e il contratto: itinerario storico-comparativo sui contratti di durata," Milano, Giuffrè, 2007, at 217 et seq.
33. *See* Iorio, G., "Corso di diritto privato," Giuffrè, Milano, 2016, at 338.
34. *See* Modica, L., "Vincoli di forma e disciplina del contratto. Dal negozio solenne al nuovo formalismo," Giuffrè, Milano, 2008, at 69.
35. *See* the seminal study of Natoli, U., "I contratti reali," Milano, Giuffrè, 1975.

problem was traditionally focused on loans, which in Roman law were binding upon delivery of the loaned things or money to the beneficiary. Modern doctrine mostly believes that a loan is binding even before delivery if the parties have reached an agreement, while those who disagree define predelivery meeting of the minds as a simple preliminary agreement.

Therefore, loans are "real" contracts as defined by Article 1813 of the Civil Code: "Loans are agreements whereby one party delivers a given amount of money or other consumable goods to the other party, who becomes the owner of the goods and is bound to return an equal quantity of money or goods of the same kind."

Although loans are binding upon delivery of the loaned goods, however, a promise to loan is binding for the promisor without any delivery having been performed.

Bailments require delivery of the bailed goods as well for the contract to be binding (Article 1766 c.c.). There is no transfer of ownership of the goods which are to be later returned, except in case of bank deposits, whereas the bank becomes the owner of the bailed amount and is bound to return an equal amount of money (Article 1782 c.c.).

59. Commodate agreements (Articles 1803 et seq., c.c.) are real contracts as well as they become binding upon delivery of the borrowed goods. Commodates differ from loans whereas goods are borrowed gratuitously for the sole benefit, use and accommodation of the borrower. The borrower does not become owner of the goods, and must return the same, specific, borrowed goods to the owner.

§4. Contract and Torts

60. Recovery for damage wrongfully caused to any third person, which is referred to in Italian law as "non-contractual liability,"[36] is regulated in a special section of the Civil Code (Articles 2043 et seq.). Violations of contractual duties by the parties to an agreement are generally disciplined by the Civil Code in the section dedicated to contracts (Articles 1321 et seq.) and are known as rules of "contractual liability."[37] Rules on contractual liability are analyzed throughout the Selected Bibliography in sections 2–3. In some instances, a person may be held liable both under contract law and under tort law, as is the case when a person rents

36. On non-contractual liability, *see* Alpa, B., "La responsabilità civile," Milan, 1976; Alpa, B., "Atipicità dell'illecito," Milan, 1977 and Franzoni, M., "L'illecito," Milano, Giuffrè, 2004.

37. On contractual liability, *see* Monateri, P.G., "La responsabilità contrattuale e precontrattuale," Turin, 1998, and *inter alia* Mengoni, L., "La responsabilità contrattuale," in *Enc. Dir.*, vol. XXXIX, Milan, 1988; Visintini, G., "La responsabilità contrattuale," Padua, 1984; Bianca, M., "Dell'inadempimento delle obbligazioni," in "Commentario del codice civile" diretto da Scialoja e Branca, Bologna-Rome, 1979 and further editions, Giorgianni, M., "L'inadempimento," Milan, 1975. *See also* Costanza, M., "Il danno contrattuale," Zanichelli, Bologna, 2014 and Moro, P., "La responsabilità contrattuale. Atti giudiziali commentati," Giuffrè, Milano, 2014.

a defective product from the producer and the product causes damages. As no concurrence of claims in contract and tort would be possible, the injured person may choose to file claims under contract law or under tort law.[38]

61. Italian statutory law encompasses few, very general provisions on torts which may be better defined as principles, rather than rules.[39] The basic norm is encompassed in Article 2043 of the Civil Code, which provides that "Whoever causes unjust damage to another person must compensate that person for that damage." Other provisions are limited to Articles 2044–2059 c.c., which in very general terms provide for:

(1) liability for parents and tutors for damages caused to any third person or thing by infants, persons of unsound mind or pupils under their custody, unless they prove they took any possible step to prevent damage (Articles 2047–2048 c.c.);
(2) liability of masters and employers for damages caused to any third person or thing by their employees when performing their work (Article 2049 c.c.);
(3) liability of entrepreneurs performing dangerous business for damages caused to any third person or thing by the conduct of such business, unless they prove they had taken any possible existing measures to prevent damage (Article 2050 c.c.);
(4) liability for owners of animals or things for damages caused to any third person or thing by their property (Articles 2051–2052 c.c.);
(5) liability for owners of buildings for damages caused to any third person or thing by collapse of their buildings, whenever damages were due to maintenance failures or construction defects (Article 2053 c.c.);
(6) liability for drivers and owners of vehicles for damages caused to any third person or thing by the circulation of such vehicles (Article 2054 c.c.).

In many of such cases (as for employers or owners of animals, and especially with regards to sellers of defective products), the doctrine of strict liability, *viz.* liability without fault, applies. Thus, in all such cases, persons are held liable regardless of their actual negligence.[40]

---

38. *See* Cass. Civ. May 14, 1987, n. 4441 and Cass. Civ. Jun. 26, 1984, n. 3739. On the contrary, several court decisions have held that victims may file applications under tort law and under contract law *at the same time*, and that every action will have its due course regardless of the other: *see* Cass. Civ. Sep. 22, 1983, n. 5638 (*Rep. Giust. Civ.*, 1982, 3947, n. 90); Cass. Civ. Aug. 7, 1982, n. 4437 (*Rep. Giust. Civ.*, 1982, II, 3453, n. 60); Cass. Civ. Mar. 13, 1980, n. 1696 (*Giur. It.*, 1980, I, 1, 1460). *See* Anzani, G., "Il concorso di responsabilità contrattuale ed extracontrattuale," in *Resp. civ. prev.*, 1, 2018, at 278 et seq.
39. On contractual liability, *see* Monateri, P.G., "La responsabilità contrattuale e precontrattuale," Utet, Torino, 1998.
40. On strict liability, *see* Trimarchi, P., "Rischio e responsabilità oggettiva," Milan, 1961; Comporti, "Esposizione al pericolo e responsabilità civile," Naples, 1965; Martini, D., "Responsabilità per danni da attività pericolosa e responsabilità per danni nell'esercizio di attività pericolosa," in *Giur. it.*, 1973, I, 2, 963 et seq.; Mazzon, R., "Responsabilità oggettiva e semioggettiva," UTET—Wolters Kluwer, 2012.

62. As a very general rule, damage recovery requires proof that there was a direct relation between the defendant's behavior and the event which caused the damages incurred by the plaintiff. This theory, known as the theory of direct causation,[41] also provides that the defendant is not held liable for any damages which the plaintiff would presumably have incurred regardless of the action by the defendant,[42] and that there is no redress for damages which were not *directly* caused by another person's unlawful behavior. Furthermore, any additional damages caused by the damaged person's reckless behavior after damages, are not recoverable (*see* Articles 2056 section 1 and 1227 section 2, c.c.). Finally, if damages were caused by two or more people, all of them are jointly liable (Article 2055 c.c.), and if the damages were also caused by negligence on the part of the damaged person, damage recovery is proportionally reduced (*see* Articles 2056 and 1227 section 1, c.c.).

63. Tort law and contract law may be compared as for what regards tortious liability and contractual liability.[43] Both imply recovery for violations of duties or obligations: contractual liability rules preserve the interests of parties to an agreement against violations by any other party of their contractual duties (or duties deriving out of any other promise). Tortious liability rules seek protection against violations of the general duty to refrain from causing damages to third parties (*neminem lædere*).

In the torts section of the Civil Code, Article 2056 directly extends application of contractual liability rules provided for in Articles 1218 et seq. Thus, tortious liability and contractual liability are generally governed by the same rules regarding damage recovery.[44] However, they differ under five basic aspects, first as a matter of burden of proof, where the rules take opposite directions. Tort law applies the general rule according to which one must prove the grounds of one's claim (Article 2697 c.c.), requiring the damaged person to prove that damages were caused by the defendant's fault. On the contrary, contract law requires the debtor (and not the injured party) to prove that failure to perform was not due to his fault (Article 1218 c.c.). Second, tort law provides for a total recovery of any damages incurred, while under contract law an injured party may only seek to recover damages which could have reasonably been predictable when the parties agreed on performance (Article

41. *See, inter alia* Prisco, D., "Concorso di colpa e responsabilità civile," Naples, 1973, Realmonte, F., "Il problema del rapporto di causalità nel risarcimento del danno," Milan, 1967; Trimarchi, P., "Causalità e danno," 1967; Schlesinger, T., "Manuale di diritto privato," Giuffrè, Milan, 1978, at 652 et seq., Trimarchi, P., "Istituzioni di diritto privato," IX ed., Milan, 1991, at 164 et seq. *See also* Monateri, P.G., Gianti, D., Balestrieri, M., "Causazione e giustificazione del danno," Giappichelli, Torino, 2016.
42. This rule dates back to a court decision of 1939: Cass. civ. Jul. 17, 1939 (*Resp. civ. prev.*, 1939, 461).
43. *See* Scognamiglio, R., "Responsabilità contrattuale ed extracontrattuale," in *NSSDI*, XV, 1968, at 670 et seq.; Trimarchi, P., "La responsabilità civile: atti illeciti, rischio," Giuffrè, Milano, 2017.
44. For instance, both under contract law and under tort law recovery includes incurred damages and lost profits (Art. 1223 c.c.), and if the plaintiff fails to determine the exact amount of damages, the court may decide to liquidate a reasonable amount (Art. 1226 c.c.). Damage recovery includes interest (Art. 1284 c.c.).

1225 c.c.). Finally, the statute of limitations for tort claims[45] runs out after five years (Article 2947, two years for car accidents liability) while as a general rule claims for violations of contractual duties must be brought to court within ten years from discovery of the violation (Article 2946 c.c.).

§5. Contract and Quasi-Contract

64. As we have previously said, transfers of rights which are appreciable in terms of money usually require a valid *causa* in order for a contract to be binding and effective. Thus, delivery of a good by the seller to the buyer, as well as transfer of money from the buyer to the seller are justified by a common *causa*, which is the sale and purchase agreement. Transfers of rights may lack a valid *causa* whenever they are a consequence of unlawful behaviors or torts. However, unfair transfers of rights may also occur without there being an unlawful behavior, as is the case when one person mistakenly pays a certain amount of money to another person, or when one person uses things owned by another person in good faith. In all such cases, performance by one party lacks a valid *causa* and generates an unjustified enrichment in favor of another party (Articles 2033 et seq.).[46]

65. As a general rule, the law provides that these situations of unjustified performance by one party be "balanced" by forcing the other party to perform an equivalent obligation, thus creating a semi-contractual relationship where each party performs a duty in exchange for something. This is why these situations, referred to as "unjust enrichment" issues, were traditionally called quasi-contracts (*see* Part II, Chapter 13).

66. *Negotiorum gestio* occurs whereby one person conducts another's business without being entrusted to do so, generally in the absence of that other person. For instance, a person who makes urgent repairs to his neighbor's property whilst the latter is away. Generally, the law requires the beneficiary of *negotiorum gestio* to reimburse all expenses and costs sustained by the person who conducted business (Article 2031 c.c.).[47]

Payment of undue amounts and enrichment without *causa* occur whenever money is paid to another in the absence of an agreement between the parties or of

45. *See* Ottolenghi, M., "Prescrizione dell'azione per danni," Milan, 1975; Monateri, P.G., Costantini, C., "La prescrizione," UTET—Wolters Kluwer, 2009.
46. Suggested texts: Gallo, P., "L'arricchimento senza causa, la responsabilità civile," Giappichelli, Torino, 2018; Gallo, P., "Arricchimento senza causa e quasi contratti (i rimedi restitutori)," in *Trattato di diritto civile*, diretto da Sacco, R., Utet, Turin, 1996, at XII-276; Dell'Aquila, E., "L'arricchimento senza causa come correttivo dell'autonomia contrattuale," in *Riv. giur. sarda*, 1994, 849; Breccia, U., "La ripetizione dell'indebito," Milan, 1974; Barbiera, L., "L'arricchimento senza causa," Naples, 1964; Trimarchi, P., "L'arricchimento senza causa," Milan, 1962; Sacco, R, "L'arricchimento ottenuto mediante fatto ingiusto," Turin, 1959.
47. *See* Finazzi, G., "Ricerche in tema di *negotiorum gestio*. Requisiti delle *actiones negotiorum gestorum*," Cassino, Ed. dell'Universitá degli studi di Cassino, 2003.

a duty imposed by law. The person who provided payment is generally entitled to indemnification and the law provides a specific cause of action for recovery (Articles 2033 and 2041 c.c.).[48]

§6. CONTRACT AND THE LAW OF PROPERTY

I. No Distinction Between Legal and Equitable Ownership

67. Italian law belongs to the civil law tradition regarding property as an exclusive right of possessing, enjoying and disposing of a thing (*usus fructus et abusus*, Article 832 c.c.). Thus, no distinction between legal and equitable ownership can be found, whereas no tradition gave birth to two separate systems such as was the case for common law and equity in the English legal tradition. In Italy property is not merely seen as a set of interests, but as an absolute, abstract concept of full, total control over something.[49] The idea of property may be compared to a box containing a set of legal interests, including the right to use, dispose of, enjoy, manage a given thing. Under Italian law, the owner of the box may grant to third parties the right to use the thing, live in it, enjoy the goods produced by that thing, manage that thing, without losing his title to the box itself: the original owner still holds an abstract title, for he is a "bare" owner even if he has lost the right to dispose of or possess that thing.[50] In common law, if the person originally entitled to the box transfers all of those interests to third parties, he holds nothing as no box remains.

II. Property and Other Rights In Rem: Ownership, Usufructs, Easements, Surface Rights, Rights of Use, Habitatio, Emphyteusis

68. Another important distinction regards rights in rem, which are attached to things no matter who their owner is, and rights in personam which are attached to persons (*see* §1 above). All rights in rem regard property; there are six rights in rem which are strictly connected to "ownership" or "property" itself: usufruct, easements, surface rights, right of use, *habitatio*. Other rights in rem include mortgage and pledge, which are basically deposits of property as security for a debt: mortgage is a lien on land, buildings and other immovable assets, whilst pledge is a pawn

48. *See* Albanese, A., "Fatto illecito, fatto ingiusto e restituzione dell'arricchimento in assenza di danno," in *Resp. civ. prev.*, fasc. 2, 2004, at 538.
49. *See* Bessone, M., "Casi e questioni di diritto privato," vol. IV: "Proprietà e diritti reali," a cura di Alpa, G., et al., VII ed., Giuffrè, Milano, 1993, at 330 et seq.; Grossi, P., "Il dominio e le cose. Percezioni medievali e moderne nei diritti reali," Giuffrè, Milan, 1992. This idea has been inherited by the ancient Roman law tradition, where property rights (*ius proprietatis*) are defined as the right to use and abuse of something (*ius utendi et abutendi*).
50. *See* Chiodi, A., "Situazioni prodromiche in *common law* e in diritto italiano: uno sguardo comparativo su *reversion*, nuda proprietà e aspettativa reale," in *Quadrimestre*, 1992, 109; *Rep. Foro it.*, 1992, "diritto comparato," at 148; Benatti, F., "Le forme della proprietà: studio di diritto comparato," Milano, Giuffrè, 2010.

of personal, movable things to a creditor as security for some duty or engagement. Mortgage and pledge are dealt with in Part II, Chapter 9, below.

69. Usufruct is the right of using, enjoying and receiving the profits of the property of another.[51] The features of the right vary with the nature of the things which may be the object of the right, such as consumables or non-consumables. For instance, an owner may agree to grant somebody the right to use, enjoy and dispose of his dwelling; usually, the usufructuary of a dwelling is entitled to any profits such as rents, freights and revenues from annuities. Similarly, an owner may agree that a third party be entitled to pick the fruits from the trees of his garden, thus executing a usufruct on natural profits. In all such cases, the original owner transfers the right to dispose of his property, but still holds title as "bare" owner. The usufructuary must manage the property as any careful owner would do, and must pay ordinary maintenance and repair costs (gross repairs and costs are to be paid by the "bare" owner).

Usufructs regard property and therefore imply agreements made in writing whereas this right is granted in exchange for money, and the instrument is very often notarized and registered.

70. Easements or "servitudes" are other kinds of rights to use the property of another. They include rights in the owner of one parcel of land (the dominant estate) to use the land of another (the servient estate) for a special purpose not inconsistent with a general property in the owner (Articles 1027–1099 c.c.).[52] The easement is a right in rem in that it is always for the benefit of an adjoining land, not for the benefit of an individual: thus, a person is entitled to the right as long as he has title on the land, and title transfer implies transfer of the right. Easements are granted by contract, usually in exchange for money. They may not be granted for an unlimited time, and may never be granted to persons who are not holders of the dominant or servient estate.

71. Some easements are imposed by the law. Otherwise, they may result from agreements which must be made in writing and require notarization in order to be

51. On usufruct, *see* Guarnieri, A., Tessera, D., "Dell'usufrutto, dell'uso e dell'abitazione. Artt. 978-1026," Giuffrè, Milano, 2017; Musolino, G., "L'usufrutto," Bologna, Zanichelli, 2011; De Tilla, M., "Il diritto immobiliare. Trattato sintetico di giurisprudenza ragionata per casi. Vol. II—le servitù, l'usufrutto, l'uso e l'abitazione," Giuffrè, Milan, 1996, at VI-1166; Rossi, G., "*Duplex est usufructus*: ricerche sulla natura dell'usufrutto nel diritto comune," Cedam, Padua, 1996, at VIII-388; De Tilla, M., "Sui rapporti tra affitto, locazione ed usufrutto (nota a Cass. sez. III, 28 gennaio 1995, n. 1051, *Laudani* v. *Carciola*)," in *Rass. locazioni*, 1996, 287; Bigliazzi Geri, L., "Usufrutto, uso e abitazione," in *Enc. giur. Treccani*, "Diritto civile," Rome, 1994, vol. XXXII; De Cupis, A., "Usufrutto (diritto vigente)," in *Enc. dir.*, vol. XLV, Giuffrè, Milan, 1992, at 1111; Mogorovich, S., "L'usufrutto di azienda," in *Impresa*, 1992, 2825.

52. On easements, *see* Spanò, G., Caruso, S., "Le servitù prediali," Giuffrè, Milano, 2013; Musolino, G., "Uso, abitazione e servitù irregolari," Zanichelli, Bologna, 2012; De Tilla, M., "Il diritto immobiliare. Trattato sintetico di giurisprudenza ragionata per casi. Vol. II—le servitù, l'usufrutto, l'uso e l'abitazione," Giuffrè, Milan, 1996, at VI-1166; Colletti, R., "Le servitù e la cessione di cubatura," in *Nuova rass.*, 1996, at 68; Palazzolo, S., "Servitù coattive," in *Enc. giur. Treccani*, Rome, 1992, vol. XXVIII; Gasparrelli, V, "La proprietà immobiliare. Diritti, limitazioni, servitù prediali," Maggioli, Rimini, 1992, at 441 et seq.

registered. Traditionally, the permitted kinds of uses include rights of way (such as the right of ingress and egress to and from the premises of a lot owner to a street appurtenant to the land of the lot owner), flowage easements (such as the right of lower land to allow water from higher land to flow across it, or the right to take water from a stream owned by another), light and air easements (which imply forcing a neighboring land owner to refrain from obstructing light and air by constructing a building or structure on his own property), etc.

72. Rights of use and *Habitatio*[53] are special easements which are very seldom granted in modern times. The "right of use" implies, like usufruct, the right to use, enjoy and receive the profits of the property of another, but limited to the needs and custom of one's family, to be determined according to his welfare (Article 1021 c.c.). *Habitatio* implies the right to live in a dwelling according to one's needs and the needs of his family (Article 1024 c.c.). Right of use and *Habitatio* are not transferable rights: they may not be the object of lease agreements (Article 1024 c.c.), and are not subject to attachment or seizure.

73. Surface rights (*superficies*)[54] are rights of easement enabling the grantee to dispose of the surface of land owned by the grantor, thus to construct buildings and permanent installations on premises which remain the property of another (Article 952 c.c.). Surface rights may be granted by the owner of the land to enable a third party to build on his premises; the owner of a parcel of land with a building attached thereto may choose to sell the building but not the land, thus granting surface rights to the purchaser of the building. Surface rights may be limited to the top of a building, thus allowing the holder of such rights to build on top of a building owned by another person.[55] Surface rights may also be granted for buildings placed below another person's land, so that the grantee becomes the owner of constructions present under premises owned by another (Article 955 c.c.). The typical example is with garages, which are often owned by persons not owning the land or the buildings above.

If the holder of surface rights constructs a building on or under the relevant premises, he automatically becomes the owner of that building. If the building collapses, he still holds surface rights on the land, but if the building is not

53. On rights of use and *Habitatio see* De Tilla, M., "Il diritto immobiliare. Trattato sintetico di giurisprudenza ragionata per casi. vol. II–L'usufrutto, l'uso e l'abitazione," Giuffrè, Milan, 2017, at VI-1166 et seq.; Bigliazzi Geri, L., "Usufrutto, uso e abitazione," in *Enc. giur. Treccani*, "diritto civile," Rome, 1994, XXXII.

54. On surface rights, *see* Guarneri, A., "La superficie," Giuffrè, Milano, 2017; Catti, S., "Costituzione del diritto di superficie, donazione e riserva d'usufrutto," in *Vita not.*, 1997, 1040; De Tilla, M., "Il diritto immobiliare. Trattato sintetico di giurisprudenza ragionata per casi. Vol. II—Il diritto di superficie," Giuffrè, Milan, 1996, at VI-1166; Guarneri, A., "Superficie (sintesi d'informazione)," in *Riv. dir. civ.*, 1996, II, 507; Chianale, A., "Il diritto di superficie: epitomi giudiziarie ed occasioni perdute (nota a Cass. sez. II, 13 febbraio 1993, n. 1844, *Sgroia* v. *Gaudieri*)," in *Giur. it.*, 1994, I, 1, 1851; Bessone, M., Di Paolo, M., "Superficie (diritto civile)," in *Enc. giur. Treccani*, Rome, 1993, vol. XXX; Salis, L, "Proprietà superficiaria e proprietà separata (nota a Cass. sez. II, 13 febbraio 1993, n. 1844, *Sgroia* v. *Gaudieri*)," in *Riv. giur. edilizia*, 1993, I, 1026.

55. *See* Cass. civ. Jun. 15, 1971, n. 1674, and Cass. civ. Oct. 8, 1962, n. 2874, in *Giust. civ.*, 1963, I, 565.

reconstructed for twenty years, under the statute of limitations his right automatically shifts back to the owner of the land (Article 954, section 3, c.c.).

74. Emphytheusis[56] (from the Greek word meaning "to grow the products of soil") is the right to exploit, enjoy and use land owned by another for a monthly rate. Emphyteusis survived as the last feudal institution whereby the lord, holding an abstract title to property (*dominium eminens*) granted the rights to his land to a tenant who was entitled to use the property and exploit it (*dominium utile*). *Emphyteusis* is similar to the ancient hierarchical system of holding lands known in England as tenure. The holder of the right may practically behave like an owner on the land for very long periods of time (usually, twenty years). He may choose to pay a monthly rent (which may consist of a sum of money or a fixed quantity of produce) or to capitalize it by paying the entire sum in a single installment and thus becoming full owner of the land (Article 972 c.c.).

Traditionally speaking, *emphyteusis* contracts concerned agricultural territories and were reserved for land used for farming, agriculture or breeding, although the law allows *emphyteusis* to be granted on urban premises as well. In the sixties and seventies, statutory legislation was enacted to discourage *emphyteusis* and to facilitate termination of existing contracts.[57] As a result, *emphyteusis* has nowadays practically disappeared.

75. Mortgage and pledge are basically deposits of property as security for a debt. Mortgage (Articles 2808 et seq., c.c.) is a conveyance or conditional fee of land or other immovable assets by a debtor to his creditor intended as a security for the repayment of a loan or performance of a duty. A pledge (Articles 2784 et seq., c.c.) is a lien or contract that calls for the transfer of personal property (movable assets) only as security. Pledges and loans are characterized by being rights in rem, in that security is attached to the thing regardless of its owner: if an owner having a mortgage on his land sells that land, he also transfers the mortgage (unless he pays his debt and cancels the mortgage).

III. Modern Conveyancing

76. Traditionally, property law distinguishes between "movable" and "immovable" assets. "Immovable" assets include land, soil, airspace and buildings attached

---

56. On *emphyteusis*, *see* Francisetti Brolin, M.M., "Enfiteusi e devoluzione. Profili ricostruttivi," Napoli, ESI, 2016; Morsillo, G., "In tema di affrancazione di fondo enfiteutico (nota a Trib. Roma 25 maggio 1995, *Bartolazzi* v. *Bartolazzi*)," in *Dir. e giur. agr. ambiente*, 1997, 139; Lipari, M., "Il capitale di affrancazione dell'enfiteusi: si accentua il contrasto tra proprietà ed impresa agricola (nota a Corte Costit. 23 maggio 1997, n. 143, *Calenda* v. *Parrocchia Brignano*)," in *Dir. e giur. agr. ambiente*, 1997, 392; Ludovici, R., "I canoni di natura enfiteutica previsti dalla vigente normativa in materia di usi civici, loro revisione ed affrancazione," in *P.Q.M.*, 1996, fasc. 2, at 104; Caterini, E., "Enfiteusi tra lavoro e proprietà (nota a Corte Costit. 9 dicembre 1991, n. 441, *Battaglia* v. *Denaro*)," in *Giur. costit.*, 1991, 3698.
57. Rent revision every ten years was abolished, rents were thoroughly reduced and capitalization of the rent for full ownership was encouraged (*see* Emphyteusis Act No. 607 of Jul. 22, 1966, Emphyteusis Act No. 1138 of Dec. 18, 1970 and Emphyteusis Act No. 270 of Jun. 14, 1974).

thereto; all other tangible or intangible things are "movable" assets (Article 812 c.c.). The original owner of both movable and immovable assets may transfer any rights in rem connected to his property by contract (Article 922 c.c.).[58]

77. Generally speaking, contracts for the transfer of proprietary interests in movable assets do not require particular forms, as long as there is an agreement bearing a possible, lawful, certain object supported by a lawful *causa*. For instance, buying a bottle of milk in a supermarket is a contract made orally, its object being the transfer of a movable asset, its *causa* being the sale of goods in exchange for a given amount of money. Exceptions include automobiles, boats, ships, aircraft and other vehicles (referred to as "registered movable assets"), which require registration and may therefore be sold or disposed of only by written agreement (Articles 1350 and 1351 c.c.). The contract must be notarized in order to be registered in the Vehicle Records.

78. Conveyance and transfers of interests in immovable assets, such as land and buildings, must be expressed in writing (Article 1350 c.c.). The law does not require notarization for the contract to be binding between the parties; however, as we have already pointed out,[59] for title transfer to be fully enforceable to the world at large (the outcome being binding to all who may claim title on that property), the transfer must be formally recorded in the Public Registries (Articles 2643 et seq., c.c.). As registration requires notarization, for only notarized documents or documents made by public officers may be entered into the Public Registries, contracts for the transfer of interests on land or other immovable assets are generally executed by a notary in order to be fully enforceable.

79. In Italy, the conveyance of any existing estate, interest or charge in or over land or other immovable assets, and the creation of new legal interests, are made by contract, and notarization is basically required for registration. Modern real estate conveyancing practices generally comprise of three distinct phases.[60] First, the parties to the deal reach a preliminary agreement, whereby the seller promises to convey the property and the buyer promises to purchase it.[61] This agreement *must* be made in writing, as the law imposes that preliminary agreements regarding real estate be made in the same form as final contracts (Articles 1350–1351 c.c.). Subsequently, the parties negotiate the price and all other relevant elements of the deal. When all basic clauses are defined and the parties have drafted a final agreement,

58. Other indirect ways to acquire ownership of land or immovable assets include taking things which are not owned by anybody ("occupation" of *res nullius*) and incorporating improvements in the property of another (known as "accession").

59. *See* above, Introduction to the Law of Contracts, §1, III, D and further, Part 1, Chapter 1, Formation, §2, I, B, 1.

60. Gambaro, A., Morello, U., "Trattato dei diritti reali. Vol. 1: Proprietà e possesso," Giuffrè, Milano, 2008; Mattei, U., "La proprietà immobiliare," II ed., Giappichelli, Turin, 1995; Tamborrino, F., "La compravendita di appartamenti, uffici e negozi," II ed., Giuffrè, Milan, 1995, at 112; Tosi, E., "Il sistema delle garanzie nel contratto di compravendita," in *Società e dir.*, 1994, 714; Lepri. A, "La compravendita immobiliare," Giuffrè, Milan, 1993, at XVI-974 et seq.

61. *See* Serrao, E., "Il contratto preliminare," Padova, CEDAM, 2011, at 184; Bellini, L., "Il contratto preliminare di compravendita immobiliare," in *Corriere trib.*, 1997, ins. 11.

they finalize their deal by formally executing the contract in front of a notary. It is generally the notary's duty to record the notarized, sealed instrument in the Land Registry.

80. Donations regarding the release or gift of an interest in land are also made by contract, provided that the donee must accept to receive the interests in land conveyed by the grantor.[62] Donations regarding interests in land *must* be made in writing and *must* be executed before a notary.

§7. Contract and Trust

81. Trust belongs to the common law tradition, and no matching fiduciary relationship exists in Italian law. However, Italy was the only civil law country to ratify the Hague Convention on Trusts of July 10, 1985 recognizing trusts governed by any foreign law.[63] Thus, foreign trusts are perfectly operative in Italy, as long as they do not violate the general legal principles of the land which are protected by the Constitution.[64] Italy does not have specific rules regulating trust, which is traditionally considered incompatible with the existing system of law. Article 6 of the Hague Convention provides that the settlor of the trust may choose his trust to be governed by any law, and the Italian Civil Code provides that this rule generally applies to contracts.[65] Some authors regard Article 6 of the Hague Convention as an advantage for Italy,[66] as it implies that the country really does not need specific legislation on trust (which would require drastic changes in the general outline of the law), provided that settlors simply may refer to developed legislation of countries where trust is a traditional, commonly used instrument. The simplest way to prove the existence of a trust is to notarize the document establishing that trust under foreign law. All other elements are governed by foreign law.[67]

82. Traditionally, trusts were considered incompatible with the Italian system of law, because they violated the general definition of ownership and property based

62. On donations, *see* Torrente, A., "La donazione," Giuffrè, Milano, 2016.
63. *See* Contaldi, G., "Il trust nel diritto internazionale privato italiano," Giuffrè, Milano, 2005; Carbone, S.M., "Trust interno e legge straniera," in *Trusts*, 2003, at 333; Albisinni, F., Gambino, R., "The Italian Civil Law System and the Hague Convention on Trusts," in 2 *Journal of International Planning* (1993) 73 at 86.
64. *See also* Capaldo R., "Atto pubblico di *trust*," in *Notariato*, 1997, 176; Lenzi, R., "Operatività del *trust* in Italia," in *Riv. not.*, 1995, 1379; Piccoli, P., "Possibilità operative del *trust* nell'ordinamento italiano. L'operatività del *trustee* dopo la convenzione de L'Aia (dal Convegno di Treviso del 18–19 novembre 1994 sul tema 'Esercizio di poteri gestori nel contesto internazionale. Profili delle varie forme di rappresentanza e intermediazione')," in *Riv. not.*, 1995, 37; Ponzanelli, "Gli enti *non profit* in Italia. Associazioni, fondazioni, volontariato, *trust*, fondi pensione," in *Rep. Foro it.*, 1994, "diritto civile," 54; Lupoi, M., "Il *trust* nell'ordinamento giuridico italiano dopo la Convenzione de L'Aia del 10 luglio 1985," in *Vita not.*, 1992, 966.
65. Article 25 Preliminary Provisions of the Civil Code.
66. Lupoi, M., "Introduzione ai *trusts*. Diritto inglese, Convenzione dell'Aia, diritto italiano," Milan, Giuffrè, 1994, at 158 et seq.
67. *See* Santoro, L., "Il trust in Italia," Giuffrè, Milano, 2009, at 109 et seq.

on the Roman law model, creating an atypical right in rem[68] and thus violating the general principles of property law. However, an in depth analysis of trust shows it is a unilateral act and not an agreement, and that the trustee is always considered the "owner" of the estate, even if the settlor and the beneficiary hold specific interests regarding that estate.

§8. Good Faith and Fair Dealing

83. In business transactions as in all other legal relationships between human beings, the law imposes parties to behave in "good faith."[69] Good faith is an intangible and abstract quality with no precise statutory definition. It encompasses the concepts of loyalty, correctness, honesty of purpose, absence of malice and honest intention to abstain from defrauding or seeking advantage by damaging one's counterpart. Good faith in contract law implies freedom from intention to defraud, full and complete disclosure of information, cooperation with one's counterpart, honesty in the conduct of negotiations and faithfulness to one's duty or obligation as provided for in a given agreement.

§9. Style of Drafting

84. Drafting a contract very much depends on the type of agreement that needs to be prepared: a short-term lease, although bearing a similar structure, deeply differs from a stock option agreement, and so on. Most contracts (except for notarized documents) are prepared by professional lawyers for their clients. All contracts usually represent initial headings bearing the names of the parties, a "Whereas" section, and general clauses regarding the object, consideration, terms and conditions of payment, termination, duration, governing law, and governing language of the agreement, as well as the date and signature of the parties, and often includes other specific clauses and exhibits. Notarized agreements (such as those regarding real estate conveyancing) must usually meet certain standards of form imposed by statutory law.

85. Drafting a contract in Italy implies relying on words whose basic definition is encompassed in the Civil Code or in other legislative measures. Thus, contracts (alike statutes) are generally shorter and less detailed than their common law counterparts. The use of very general terms with wide meanings is often the case: for instance, the use of the term "man" to identify both men and women is a settled concept and does not require any specific clause defining the term in detail.

---

68. *See* above, Introduction to the Law of Contracts, §1, IV.
69. Piraino, F., "La buona fede in senso oggettivo," Giappichelli, Torino, 2015; Uda, G.M., "La buona fede nell'esecuzione del contratto," Giappichelli, Torino, 2004.

86. The style of drafting is very much connected with existing rules on contract interpretation.[70] Like for statutes, Italian law provides specific rules of construction of clauses enclosed in contracts (Articles 1362–1371 c.c.).[71] These rules also apply to unilateral acts and promises (Article 1324 c.c.) and are to some extent similar to those provided for wills. The rules are to be employed according to a hierarchy: only if the first does not prove satisfactory, the second applies, and so on.

The first basic criterion for construing contracts requires to seek the common intention of the parties (if there was such a common intention). Whenever there was a common understanding and the parties agreed for a certain meaning of the words contained in a clause, that common meaning is essential and binding, regardless of the literal sense of the words contained therein (Article 1362 c.c.). Thus, the common intention of the parties must prevail over the common sense of the words.[72] The meaning of a clause may be understood only by analyzing the general *context* of the agreement (Article 1363 c.c.), which implies examining the parties' behavior during negotiations, upon execution of the contract and with respect to performance of the contract (Article 1362 section 2, c.c.).[73]

If the parties insist on opposite or different interpretations of the same contractual clause, the rules seek to find the most reasonable interpretation. First of all, no such rules apply if one of the parties claimed a different meaning of a clause in bad faith. Otherwise, a clause is first to be interpreted so as to have some effect, whereas the meaning which would render it ineffective is to be rejected (Article 1367 c.c.). If yet no reasonable interpretation may be reached, the court must construe the words according to the general practices in that specific field of business (Article 1368 c.c.). If the clause is contained in model forms of contract prepared by one of the parties in advance,[74] any dubious clause is to be interpreted in the most favorable way for the other party (Article 1370 c.c.). If all other criterions have not provided a satisfactory meaning to a clause, the words are to be interpreted so as to equally balance opposite interests in the deal (Article 1371 c.c.).

---

70. *See* Monateri, P.G., "L'interpretazione del contratto," in P.G. Monateri, "Manuale del nuovo contratto," Bologna, Zanichelli, 2007, at 277 et seq.; Sangermano, F., "L'interpretazione del contratto: profili dottrinali e giurisprudenziali," Giuffrè, Milano, 2007; Brutti, M., "Interpretare i contratti: La tradizione, le regole," Giappichelli, Torino, 2017.
71. *See* Irti, N., "Testo e contesto. Una lettura dell'Art. 1362 c.c.," Cedam, Padua, 1996, at VIII-196; Fonsi, G., "L'interpretazione del contratto in giurisprudenza e in dottrina (Art. 1362 e 1363 c.c.)," in *Vita not.*, 1993, 1624; Morace Pinelli, A., "*In claris non fit interpretatio*: un brocardo che non trova asilo nel nostro ordinamento giuridico (nota a Cass. sez. II, 23 dicembre 1993, n. 12758, *Marino* v. *Soc. coop. Iliade*)," in *Giur. it.*, 1994, I, 1, 1163.
72. *See* Cass. civ., May 21, 1983, n. 3526; Cass. civ., Mar. 26, 1983, n. 2152.
73. *See* Cass. civ., Apr. 21, 1965, n. 575.
74. This rule only applies whenever the contract model form was prepared for an undefined number of future contracting parties: *see* Cass. Oct. 30, 1969, n. 620; Cass. Jun. 14, 1966, n. 1542.

§10. SOURCES OF THE LAW OF CONTRACTS

I. Legislation

87. Contract law is basically statutory law. Most rules on contracts are contained in the Civil Code (Articles 1321 et seq., c.c.), providing a general set of regulations which may be applied to all forms of agreements. Special sections of the Civil Code are dedicated to specific kinds of contracts such as agency (Articles 1703 et seq., c.c.), lease (Articles 1571 et seq. c.c. and Urban Leases Act No. 392 of July 27, 1978), sale of goods (Articles 1470 et seq., c.c.), lease (Articles 1571 et seq., c.c.), surety (Articles 1882 et seq., c.c.), pledge and mortgage (Articles 1784 et seq., c.c.), partnerships (Articles 2247–2550, c.c.), carriage agreements (Articles 1678 et seq., c.c.), building contracts (Articles 1664 et seq., c.c.), hire of work and skills (Articles 2094 et seq., c.c.), banking transactions (Articles 1834 et seq., c.c.), professional services (Articles 2222 et seq., c.c.), mediation (Articles 1754 c.c.), loans (Articles 1813 et seq., c.c.), warranties (Articles 1936 et seq., c.c.), etc.

88. Legislation was enacted throughout Italy's post World War II history in all major fields of law. The main statutes may be listed as follows:

- *Administrative Procedure Act* (L. 2248 of March 20, 1865, "section E").[75]
- *Public Expropriation Act* (L. 2359 of June 25, 1865).
- *Tax Revenue Acts* (R.D. 639 of April 14, 1910 and No. 636 of October 26, 1972).
- *State Finances Act* (R.D. 827 of May 23, 1924).
- *Penal Code* (of 1930).
- *Legal Services Act* (R.D. 578 of November 27, 1933).[76]
- *Promissory Notes and Bills of Exchange Act* (R.D. 1669 of December 14, 1933).
- *Checks Act* (R.D. 1736 of December 21, 1933).
- *Patents and Inventions Act* (R.D. 1127 of June 29, 1939).[77]
- *Citizenship Act* (R.D. 1238 of July 9, 1939).
- *Code of Civil Procedure* (R.D. of October 28, 1940).
- *Courts Act* (R.D. 12 of January 30, 1941).[78]
- *Copyright Act* (R.D. 633 of April 22, 1941).
- *Civil Code* (R.D. 262 of March 16, 1942).
- *Bankruptcy Act* (R.D. 267 of March 16, 1942).
- *Trademarks Act* (R.D. 929 of June 21, 1942).
- *Building Acts* (L. of 1150 of August 17, 1942 and L. 865 of October 22, 1971).
- *Constitutional Court Act* (Constitutional L. 1 of February 9, 1948).[79]

75. Amended by R.D. 1054/1924, 177571933, 654/1948, by L. 103471971, by D.P.R. 214/1973, and by L. 186/1982, L. 391/1988 and L. 241/1990.
76. Amended by R.D. 37/1934, by Statues No. 794/1942 and No. 31/1982, by D.P.R. 392/1990 and by L. 183/1993.
77. Amended by R.D. 244/1940, No. 1354/1941 and No. 360/1994.
78. Amended by L. 30/1989, No. 35371990, No. 477/1992 and by D.P.R. 105/1994.
79. Amended by Constitutional L. 1 of Mar. 11, 1953, by L. 87/1953 and by the Constitutional Court's Resolution of Mar. 16, 1956.

– *Elections Act* (D.P.R. 570 of May 16, 1960).[80]
– *Automobile Insurance Act* (L. 990 of December 24, 1969).[81]
– *Employment Act* (L. 300 of May 20, 1970).[82]
– *Divorce Acts* (L. 898 of December 1, 1970 and L. 74 of March 6, 1987).
– *Land and Building Permits Act* (L. 10 of January 28, 1977).
– *Social Welfare Act* (L. 180 of May 13, 1978).
– *Rents Act* (L. 392 of July 27, 1978).[83]
– *Petty Offenses Act* (L. 689 of November 24, 1981).
– *Adoptions Act* (L. 184 of May 4, 1983).
– *Criminal Procedure Code* (L. of October 24, 1989).
– *Bank Credit Act* (D.P.R. 385 of September 1, 1993).
– *Finance Investments Acts* (L. 96 of January 25, 1994 and L. 415 of July 23, 1996).
– *Privatization of Public Companies Act* (L. 474 of July 30, 1994).
– *Products Safety Act* (D.P.R. 115 of March 17, 1995).
– *International Private Law Act* (L. 218 of May 31, 1995).
– *Competition in Public Services Act* (L. 481 of November 14, 1995).
– *Privacy Act* (L. 675 of December 31, 1996).
– *Electronic Data Processing Act* (D.P.R. 513 of November 10, 1997).
– *Finance Mediation Act* (D.P.R. 58 of February 24, 1998).
– *Commerce Act* (D.P.R. 114 of March 31, 1998).
– *Intellectual Property Code* (D.lgs 30 of February 10, 2005).
– *Consumers Code* (D.lgs 206 of September 6, 2005).
– *Code of Private Insurance Companies* (D.lgs 209 of September 7, 2005).
– *Antimafia Act* (D.lgs 159 of September 6, 2011).
– *Jobs Act* (D.lgs. 22 of March 4, 2015 and D.lgs 23 of March 4, 2015).
– *Code for Public Procurement* (D.lgs 50 of April 18, 2016).
– *Same Sex Marriage Act* (L. 76 of May 20, 2016).

II. Case Law, Periodicals, Revues and Scholars

89. Beyond legislation, much of modern Italy's rules and regulations of contracts are a result of the fundamental role played by judicial courts (*see* General Introduction, §3). Although precedent is not binding in Italian law, jurisprudence has in fact played a fundamental role in defining and completing major fields of law regulated by statute. Thus, it is hardly surprising that lawyers frequently make reference to cases in their complaints and courts base their decisions on cases previously defined by the Court of Cassation, by the Council of State, as well as by *Tribunali* or Appeals Courts.

---

80. Amended by L. 1147/1966, by D.P.R. 223/1967 and by L. 108/1968 and L. 18/1979.
81. Amended by D.P.R. 857/1976 and D.P.R. 576/1978 and D.P.R. 45/1981, and by the Foreign Vehicles Act (L. 242 of Aug. 7, 1990).
82. *See also* Public Employment Act (L. 70 of Mar. 20, 1975).
83. Amended by D.P.R. 9/1982, D.P.R. 708/1986 and D.P.R. 551/1988.

90. Case law is basically published through periodicals and reviews, which also contain opinions and comments by scholars. Scholars play a very important role in the education of lawyers and judges, as they practically dominate law schools. Commentaries are another widely used instrument for lawyers. Much like the German *Kommentar*, a commentary is an updated collection of comments and decisions offering an article-by-article analysis of current positions by courts on single statutory provisions. A lawyer basically refers to reviews and commentaries to follow the latest trends in the law. Commentaries and collections of statutes are now available on CD-Rom, providing an efficient, quick instrument of reference.

Part I. General Principles of the Law of Contract

Chapter 1. Formation

F. Chiaves

§1. AGREEMENT

I. Offer

91. A contract is formed where and when the offeror has notice of the acceptance by the offeree (Article 1326 c.c.).[84] In order to have an offer there must be intention to create legal relationships. This intention must be clearly expressed.[85]

92. Offers may be revocable or irrevocable. Usually, an offeror is allowed to legally revoke his offer at any time before the contract is formed;[86] however, if the offeree has begun performance of his contractual duties in good faith before having notice of the revocation, the offeror is bound to indemnify the offeree for all and any expenses or losses incurred in beginning performance of that contract (Article 1328 c.c.). Also acceptance of an offer can be withdrawn by the offeree, provided that his intention to revoke is notified to the offeror before the offeree's own acceptance reaches him (Article 1328, section 2, c.c.).[87] Offers may be irrevocable for a given time limit which must be expressed in the offer (otherwise, it is considered revocable).[88] In case of an irrevocable offer, the offeror's death or supervening incapacity does not deprive the offer of such effect, unless the nature of the transaction or other circumstances preclude such effect (Article 1329 c.c).

---

84. *Barda v. Averni*, Cass. Jul. 3, 1990, n. 6788 (*Foro it.*, 1991, I, 511). *See also* Cass. Civ., sez. II, 13/06/2018, n. 15503.
85. *Adotti v. Soc. immob. Santa Maria della Mole*, Cass. Dec. 15, 1982, n. 6922 (*Mass. Giur. it.*, 1982); Cass. Civ., sez. II, 22/09/2000, n. 12575; Cass. Civ., sez. lav., Dec. 5, 2018, n. 28164.
86. *Ermeti v. Soc. Terme Crodo*, Cass. Feb. 9, 1985, n. 1072 (*Mass Giur. it.*, 1985); Cass. Civ., sez. un., 28/06/2011, n. 14319.
87. Cass. Civ., sez. III, 03/04/2001, n. 4888.
88. *Lanzilao v. Lanzilao*, Cass. Oct. 11, 1983, n. 5910 (*Mass. Giur. it.*, 1983); Cass. Civ., sez. II, Aug. 29, 1991, n. 9229.

93. Irrevocable offers are to be distinguished from options (*opzioni*). In an option both parties agree that one of them shall place an irrevocable offer which the other party is free to accept or reject within a given time limit (Article 1331 c.c.).

94. Other peculiar forms of offer include offers for a unilateral contract, where the offeree is ordinarily not bound as he never promised anything. In Italian law, whenever the offeror only is bound to perform contractual duties (*contratto con obbligazioni del solo proponente*), the offer becomes irrevocable whenever it is notified to the offeree, who may reject the offer within a given time limit, after which the contract is formed upon implied acceptance (*see* Article 1333 c.c.). Examples include letters of patronage[89] and contracts to procure business, whereas the agent is paid by the commissioner regardless of the fact that he has actually procured any business transactions.

95. Offers may be directed "to the general public," as is the case for priced goods stacked in supermarkets. Such offers are effective as long as they contain the essential elements of the contract: for instance, exposing goods bearing the price in a shop window constitutes an offer.

Such offers must be revoked in the same way the offer was proposed or in equivalent forms in order for revocation to be effective with regards to the general public (Article 1336 c.c.).

II. Acceptance

96. Acceptance of an offer is usually made by a communicated promise. The promise may be implied in fact by the promisee's conduct, or by an act designated by the offeror to signify acceptance, and, in some situations, silence.

97. When acceptance is made by a communicated promise, generally acceptance must reach the offeror within the time limit set by the offeror himself or within the time which is reasonable according to actual circumstances (Article 1326, section 2, c.c.). Acceptance is deemed to be known by the offeree when it reaches his address (registered mail is the commonest piece of evidence), regardless of his effective knowledge,[90] unless the offeree proves it was impossible for him to have notice of it and that such impossibility was not due to his fault (Article 1335 c.c.).[91]

89. *CARIPLO v. Soc. Selle Aquila*, Cass. Sep. 27, 1995, n. 10235 (*Giust. civ.*, 1996, I, 3007; *Banca, borsa*, 1997, II, 396); Cass. Civ., sez. III, 03/04/2001, n. 4888; Cass. Civ., sez. I, 09/02/2016, n. 2539.

90. *See* Cass. 744/65.

91. *See also* Cass. Civ., sez. II, Apr. 6, 1981, n. 1944.

98. If the offeror has set a time limit for acceptance, late acceptance is generally not effective. However, the offeror can treat late acceptance as effective provided that he immediately informs the offeree of such decision (Article 1326, section 3, c.c.).[92]

99. Offers may call for acceptance by performance. In sale of goods contracts, beginning performance is a reasonable mode of acceptance and, therefore, the contract is formed whenever performance begins. For instance, in an offer to buy goods for prompt or current shipment, shipment of conforming goods is an acceptance implying formation of a contract for the sale of goods (Article 1327 c.c.).[93] In all such cases, the purchaser becomes the owner of the goods whenever performance has begun, which implies that any risk deriving from shipment of the goods is borne by the purchaser and not by the seller (*see* Part II, Chapter 4.).

Offers calling for acceptance by performance without prior notice of acceptance to the offeror imply that notice of performance must be promptly given to the offeror; failure to do so makes the offeree liable for damages (Article 1327 c.c.).

100. As a general rule, silence of an offeree does not constitute acceptance.[94] However, the parties to a contract may have previously agreed that inaction constitutes acceptance of an offer. Furthermore, silence constitutes acceptance whenever the law provides so, as is the case for offers to unilateral contracts (Article 1333 c.c., above). Silence also constitutes acceptance whenever the offeree, by her own prior words or conduct, has given the offeror reason to interpret in good faith silence as acceptance or whenever usage and current business practices regard silence as acceptance.

101. Acceptance may be conditional or qualified, or an offeror may furthermore require a specific form of acceptance: in all such cases, acceptance is ineffective if given in a different form or in case of non-occurrence of condition (Article 1326, section 4, c.c.).

102. In order for a contract to be formed, acceptance however expressed must fully comply with the offer. Clearly, an acceptance which does not match the offer is an offer (Article 1326, section 5, c.c.).

103. Usually, revocable offers and acceptances made by individuals become ineffective upon the death of the offeror or of the acceptor, or upon their supervening incapacity before the contract is formed (Article 1329 c.c.). However, the law provides that offer and acceptance remain effective if the offeror or offeree are entrepreneurs and die or become incapacitated, unless it otherwise appears from the nature of the transaction or other circumstances (Article 1330 c.c.). This rule does not apply to "small" entrepreneurs as defined by Article 2083 of the Civil Code.

---

92. Corte App., Roma, sez. II, Apr. 26, 2018, n. 2786.
93. *See* Cass. Civ., sez. un., Jun. 9, 1997, n. 5139.
94. Cass. Civ., sez. III, May 14, 2014, n. 10533.

III. Consideration

A. *Consideration Is Not a Requirement in Italian Law*

104. Consideration in common law-based systems is an essential element that is generally required to make a promise binding and to make an agreement enforceable as a contract. Consideration represents the element of bargaining to indicate that each party agrees to surrender something in return for what it is to receive.[95]

105. Consideration is not a requirement in continental civil law countries based on the French legal tradition.[96] Under Italian law a contract is formed whenever the parties reach an agreement bearing a specific, possible, lawful, certain or ascertainable object, a lawful *causa* and if the agreement is expressed through a proper form. No bargain element is required for a contract to be fully enforceable.

B. *Gratuitous Promises*

106. Under Italian law, gratuitous promises are binding if they are accepted by the promisee, thus forming a contract. The rule is based on the principle that rights may not be transferred without the transferee's consent.

Gratuitous agreements are contracts even though only one of the parties is bound to contractual duties and nothing of value is given in return for her performance.

107. The object of the promise may consist in transferring goods or money (donations) or in executing a task, such as: a gratuitous promise to pay or to guarantee payment of a debt; an agency relationship whereas the agent acts gratuitously on behalf of the principal; a gratuitous bailment, etc.

Donations imply an increase in the promisee's assets and a decrease in the promisor's assets. Donations under Italian law are classified as contracts, and thus require the donee's acceptance to be enforceable (Article 782 c.c.).

108. As a general rule, expressions used by the parties in gratuitous agreements are to be given the most favorable interpretation for the promisor or to be construed so as to imply duties which are as less burdensome as possible (Article 1371 c.c.).[97]

Furthermore, gratuitous agreements usually imply a lower degree of contractual liability with respect to the promisor. Thus, a donor is lawfully entitled to revoke a donation for ingratitude (Article 800 c.c.). Similarly, in commodate agreements if the owner urgently needs to dispose of the given goods, he may require the beneficiary to return them immediately at any time (Article 1809 section 2, c.c.).[98]

---

95. In American law, *see* for instance Restatement (Second), Contracts, §71(1) (1981).
96. The civil law doctrine of the *causa* has been often misleadingly identified with the common law doctrine of consideration, whereas the *causa* is the basic reason why an agreement was formed, the immediate scope for entering into a contract.
97. Cass. Civ., sez. III, Jul. 15, 2016, n. 14432.
98. *See* Introduction to the Law of Contracts, §3.

C. Natural Obligations

109. Natural obligations are duties which are valid and binding in conscience and according to natural justice but are not enforceable by law as they are not recognized by the law as adequate to set in motion the machinery of justice. Paying a prescripted debt is a natural obligation. As a general rule, under Italian law natural obligations are not enforceable, the obliged party thus being exempted from legal liability (Article 2034 c.c.).[99]

§2. Formal and Evidential Requirements

I. Formal Requirements

A. No Contracts under Seal in Italian Law

110. For centuries before the doctrine of consideration was developed, contracts under seal were enforced in the common law tradition as sealed instruments requiring writing and delivery. In modern English and American laws contracts under seal constitute the only way to implement a binding promise without consideration. Contracts under seal today do not require a legal consideration provided they are implemented by a deed, i.e., that they are signed and drafted in writing. All other traditional formal requirements have practically disappeared: the seal may be merely recited by the words "seal" or L.S. and delivery may be implied from a party's words expressing his/her intention to enter into the contract. Deeds need not be prepared by notaries or specialized lawyers.

111. There are no contracts under seal in Italian law, there being no such equivalent in civil law systems to what are referred to as *actes authentiques* in French law, as *öffentliche Urkunde* in German law or as "public acts" (*atti pubblici*) in Italian law. Whilst common law systems require a *special form* in order for an agreement or a promise without consideration to be binding and effective as a contract, special formal requirements are imposed in civil law systems for two basic purposes: to ensure "certainty" in business transactions (provided that written, recorded documents keep better track of title to rights and interests), and to lead individuals to think carefully before disposing of their assets, which explains why notarization is a requirement in real estate conveyance, wills and generally in all transfers of ownership or other interests regarding land and other immovable assets.

99. *See* Cass. Civ., sez. II, Feb. 12, 1980, n. 1007.

B. Solemn Contracts

112. In modern Italian law it is a basic rule that in legal transactions one's intentions may be expressed in any form, except whereby a special form is required by the law.

Several legislative provisions impose specific formal requirements, which must be substantially met for an agreement to be binding and effective (form *ad substantiam*) or simply for that agreement to be supported by evidence (form *ad probationem*).

Substantial requisites are examined below, whereas evidentiary requisites are analyzed in the following section dedicated to the law of evidence.

1. Kinds of Formal Requirements

113. The Civil Code requires any preliminary or final agreements regarding real estate conveyance and transfer of ownership or interests in immovable assets to be executed in writing (Articles 1350–1351, c.c.). Similarly, lease agreements exceeding nine-year terms are to be expressed in a written form, and the same rule applies to negotiable instruments.[100] All agreements entered into by government agencies and other public bodies must be done in writing,[101] as well as door-to-door contracts for the sale of investment bonds,[102] and agreements regarding the management of assets.[103]

114. In Italy as in other civil law systems, the law imposes that certain transactions and agreements be effective only if enclosed in a formal, solemn document, drafted by a notary or by other government officers, known as an "authentic act" or a "public act" or a "notarial act."[104]

Conveyancing and transfers of interests in immovable assets do not require notarization to be binding between the parties; however, for title transfer to be fully enforceable the world at large, *viz.* with respect to third parties, the law requires that the transfer be formally recorded in the Public Registries. As only notarized, solemn documents or private agreements legalized by a notary may be included in such registries, all transfer agreements regarding land and immovable assets must be executed by a notary form in order to be fully enforceable.

115. Notarization is mandatory for establishing corporations and limited liability companies (Articles 2332 n. 2 and 2475, c.c.), for pledges (Article 2787 c.c.) and

100. *See* Arts. 1, 83, 88, 99, 103 and 109 of the Checks Act (R.D. 1736 of Dec. 21, 1933) and Arts. 1 and 100 of the Promissory Notes and Bills of Exchange Act (R.D. 1669 of Dec. 14, 1933).

101. *See* Art. 95 of the State Finances Act (R.D. 827 of May 23, 1924).

102. Article 18 *ter,* L. 216 of Jun. 17, 1974.

103. Article 8 s. 1 (a) L. 1 of Jan. 2, 1991.

104. *See* Marmocchi, E., "L'atto pubblico fra tecniche di redazione e forme di comunicazione," Giuffrè, Milan, 2006; Chianale, G., "L'atto pubblico. Contributo allo studio dei costi transattivi," Giappichelli, Turin, 1992; Crisci, G., "Atto pubblico (diritto civile)," in *Enc. dir.*, IV, Giuffrè, Milan, 1959; Brugi, B., "Atti pubblici," in *NSSDI*, I, sez. II, Utet, Turin, 1958.

mortgages (Article 2821 section 1, c.c.) and for donations (Article 782 c.c.), except for donations of moderate value which require simple delivery. In common law systems, donations are solemn contracts because they are promises without consideration, thus requiring special forms to be executed. Under Italian law, formal requirements are imposed for donations only in order to induce the donor to thoroughly meditate before deciding to dispose of his assets, and to ensure that heirs and creditors of the donor are informed of the donation through the public records.

Wills are valid and effective only if expressed in writing by the testator's own hand, or dictated to a notary, or notarized.

116. The law may furthermore impose other formal requirements, such as elements that must be included in an agreement for that agreement to be fully enforceable: thus, for instance, when conveying a building, the written contract must contain information on the building permit granted for construction on those premises.[105] Other compulsory formal requirements include words that must be present in a document in order for an agreement to be binding and effective: for instance, the word "Check" or "Promissory Note" must be included in the bond in order for such negotiable instruments to be valid.[106]

117. Finally, the law imposes that certain clauses contained in standardized model forms for contracts entered into by individuals with enterprises be specifically signed for approval in writing, whenever such model forms are prepared and provided by the enterprise (Article 1341 c.c.).

2. Notaries

118. In Italy, notaries are professionals who carry out a public duty and are therefore classified as public officers. Notaries basically have a monopoly over drawing legal instruments in the fields of corporate, family and property laws, recording them and keeping their custody.[107]

Notaries may legalize existing private documents or prepare new, solemn deeds. An official document is prepared by the notary in the presence of the parties to the deal and their witnesses, and the document is signed by all such persons and finalized with the notary's seal.

---

105. *See* Arts. 17 and 18 ss. 2, 3 and 4 of Act No. 47 of Feb. 28, 1985.

106. *See above*, note 1.

107. For a general overlook on notaries in Italy, *see* Di Fabio, M., "Manuale di notariato," Giuffrè, Milan, 2014; Mazzola, M., "Notaio e notariato," in *Digesto IV*, vol. XII, Utet, Turin, 1993; Barone, R., "Campo d'azione del notaio. Limiti, differenze, analogie, prospettive," in *Riv. not.*, XLVI, Giuffrè, Milan, 1992; Guasti, F., "I notariati francese e italiano di fronte all'Europa: problemi e scelte," in *Riv. not.*, XLV, Giuffrè, Milan, 1981; Di Fabio, "Manuale di notariato," Giuffrè, Milan, 1981; Ferrari, E., "L'atto notarile," Giuffrè, Milan, 1977; Costamagna, G., "Alle origini del notariato italiano," Consiglio Nazionale del Notariato, Rome, 1975; Casrnelutti, F., "La figura giuridica del notaro," in *Riv. dir. proc. civ.*, Cedam, Padua, 1950; Boero, P., "Autenticazione," in *Digesto* IV, vol. I, Utet, Turin, 1995.

Notaries deal with establishing companies and drafting their bylaws, and attend Extraordinary Shareholders' Meetings. Real estate conveyance is also dealt with by notaries, as well as wills, donations and mortgages. Therefore, notaries pay a considerable role as trusted advisers in all such areas of the law, enjoying a high degree of respect and integrity. Other duties include legalizing powers of attorney, protesting negotiable instruments, attending public auctions, etc. In addition, notaries are usually appointed by courts to perform other duties such as community property division or drawing an inventory of the assets of a deceased person.

119. Notaries are organized under the Notaries Act No. 89 of February 16, 1913, which encompasses their functions, duties, professional organization and discipline. Notaries are selected on a national basis among law graduates with a two-year practice in the field. There exists a limited number of chairs to be covered for each notaries' district, so that no new notary can be effective until one of the existing posts remains vacant. The law provides for strict rules to be complied with by notaries in preparing deeds and legalizing existing documents, and thoroughly regulates a notary's code of conduct in his business. Any violations by notaries regarding their duties as public officers are sanctioned by the National Council of Notaries and by the Penal Code. Fees for advice and preparing formal documents are established in a special fees schedule and are in general considerably expensive.

II. Contracts and the Law of Evidence

120. The Rules of Evidence are embodied in Articles 2697–2739 of the Civil Code and in Articles 202–262 of the Code of Civil Procedure.[108] Probative matters are based on the general principle that presenting proof at the trial of an issue is generally a duty of the parties (and not of the judge, although there are exceptions).[109] Furthermore, Article 2697 of the Civil Code states the burden of proof rule, providing that a party who declares to have a right or claim in court has the burden to prove the grounds of her claims, i.e., to establish by evidence a requisite degree of belief concerning a fact; the other party may reject such allegations, but has a duty to prove the facts on which she bases her opposition.

A. Documentary Evidence

121. Civil law systems are characterized by a limited number of rules on evidence, whereas in common law systems the law of evidence plays a fundamental role in the handling of a trial in civil and criminal proceedings. As a general rule, evidence in common law trials is almost entirely elicited by witnesses, whereas

108. For a general overlook on evidence, *see* Taruffo, M., "La prova nel processo civile," Giuffrè, Milan, 2012; Verde, "Prova (diritto processuale civile)," in *Enc. dir.*, XXXVII, Giuffrè, Milan, 1988; Andrioli, "Prova (diritto processuale civile)," in *NSSDI*, XIV, Utet, Turin, 1967.
109. *See* Art. 115 c.p.c.

documentary evidence is usually not considered sufficient and requires confirmation by testimony. On the contrary, documentary evidence is a primary source of proof in civil law systems such as Italy, and evidence given by witnesses plays a secondary role which often needs to be further sustained by a document. Therefore, continental codes including the Italian ones have thoroughly regulated documentary evidence dedicating very few provisions to testimony.

122. Documentary evidence[110] regards private documents and notarized deeds. Notarized deeds are formal instruments drafted by notaries, signed by the parties and sealed by a notary. Due to the authority of the draftsman, the law assigns a very special probative effect to notarized deeds. These documents must be accepted by the court as establishing that the facts recorded therein were witnessed by the notary during the drafting procedure (Article 2700 c.c.). Therefore, notarized deeds do not provide full proof, for instance, that the allegations made by the parties to the notary and embodied in the document are true: they simply prove that the document was prepared by a specific notary on a specific date and that certain things were said and done in front of that notary. The same probative effect as notarized deeds is enjoyed by documents drafted by public officers (such as resolutions by agencies and other public bodies) and by court documents such as orders, decisions, depositions and transcripts of proceedings.

123. The establishing effect of this formal document may only be questioned through a criminal complaint alleging forgery, or by a special civil proceeding (*querela di falso*) claiming that the document was altered after it was executed and sealed by the drafting notary, or that the notary made a false statement. These proceedings really are a formalized version of those used to question private documents, and practically the same rules are applicable in discovery. However, they very seldom occur, as they imply questioning notaries, who enjoy a high degree of integrity in society, and impose a heavy burden of proof on the plaintiff.

124. "Private" documents include "any instrument signed by one or more individuals on which the expression of something is recorded by means of letters, figures, or marks" (Article 2701 c.c.). The text of the document may be drafted by any means and by any person, as long as it is directly signed by that or those individual(s) with his or their own hand(s).

125. As a general rule, private documents may only be used as evidence against those who signed them.

A private document which has been expressly or implicitly recognized by the party against which it is being used as evidence in trial, must be accepted by the court as establishing the facts set forth therein (Article 2702 c.c.). The establishing effect of the document may only be attacked through the same special civil proceeding provided for to question notarized deeds (*querela di falso*).

---

110. For Carnelutti's theories on the primary role of documentary evidence, *see*: Carnelutti, F., "La prova civile," Giuffrè, Milan, 2016; Carnelutti, F., "Documento (teoria moderna)," in *NSSDI*, VI, Utet, Turin, 1956; *Id.*, "Documento e negozio giuridico," in *Riv. dir. proc. civ.*, Padua, 1926.

A private document which has not been recognized by the party against whom it is being used in trial, must be proved to be true by the other party who is using it as evidence in trial. In order to prove that the document is true, that party is allowed to compare it with other documents and to provide additional evidence (Articles 214, 215 and 216 c.p.c.). The judge may also order the party who wrote or signed the document to handwrite in the presence of an expert. If the party refuses to do so, the documents may be recognized as true (Article 219 c.p.c.).

126. Dates and signatures in private documents have a lower probative effect than those contained in notarized deeds.

Generally speaking, the date of a private document is not presumed to be true. Certainty over a certain date may only be settled with reference to specific formal events which may have occurred, such as registration of the document by a notary or certified death of the person who wrote and/or signed the document. Postmarks on documents also provide certainty on dates (*see* Article 1704 c.c.).

127. A signature on a private document may be placed in front of a notary, who certifies that it has been truly placed on a given date. The notary's presence increases the probative effect of this document: in all such cases, the date and author of the document are presumed to be true in the same way as a notarized deed (*see* Articles 2702 and 2703 c.c.).[111]

128. Tax authorities may impose the use of stamped paper and registration for some documents. They are not formal requirements, as they do not affect the validity of the document. Failure to comply with registration or tax duty regulations may result in a fine but has no effect on the document itself, except in the case of checks and promissory notes. These instruments must bear a duty stamp in order to be enforceable.

129. Telegrams and faxes have the same probative effect as private documents, even if they do not bear a handwritten signature (Article 2705 c.c.).[112] Commercial books of account, household records, family account books and other unsigned statements are considered private documents as well.

130. Some documents do not have a full probative effect, although they provide likeliness of a fact. In all such cases, referred to as "beginning of written evidence," full probative effect may be reached by means of testimony. Thus, whenever a document expressed in writing deriving from the defendant is incomplete, the judge requires additional evidence (usually, confirmation by a witness) to support that document. Examples of "beginning of written evidence" include unsigned statements certainly coming from the defendant, letters[113] or notes[114] which clearly refer to the contents of a contract.

---

111. Cass. Civ., sez. un., Jun. 23, 2010, n. 15169.
112. *See* Cass. Civ, sez. II, Nov. 29, 2018, n. 30948.
113. App. Firenze, Mar. 14, 1950 (*Rep. Foro it.*, 1950, "Prova testimoniale," n. 44).
114. App. L'Aquila, Sep. 2, 1950 (*Rep. Foro it.*, 1950, n. 47).

B. Testimony

131. As in many other civil law systems based on the French legal tradition, Italian courts feel less comfortable with respect to evidence given by a witness than to evidence derived from writing, which may be summarized by the motto *lettres passent témoins.*

As a result, there are very few rules regarding testimony (*see* Articles 244–257 c.p.c.), which is generally regarded by courts as doubtful and suspicious, especially because witnesses may not have a clear memory of events after a certain period of time has elapsed between when a certain event has taken place and when the witness is being deposed on that event. Furthermore, testimony may be misleading because the description of a fact may be affected by numberless factors, including the intention to give a distorted version of the truth for one's personal interest.

132. Provided that agreements are often expressed in writing, as a general rule no testimonial evidence is accepted for contracts (or promises to pay monies) which are worth more than the equivalent of USD 3.00;[115] however, the court may require a witness to testify whenever it is deemed necessary according to the circumstances (Articles 2721 and 2726 c.c.) and whenever it is likely that further negotiation and additional, oral agreements have taken place between the parties after the written contract was signed (Article 2723 c.c.).[116]

Testimony may also be essential to prove a simulated contract, whereby no written statement may be used as reference (*see* Articles 1414 et seq., c.c.).

133. Furthermore, the judge *must* require evidence elicited from a witness in the case of "beginning of written evidence" (*see* previous section dedicated to documentary evidence), if the document was lost not because of recklessness, and whenever delivering a written statement would be materially or morally impossible for a contracting party (*see* Article 2724 c.c.).[117] Examples of material impossibility include fires, accidents and events which have caused destruction of the document. Moral impossibility relates to special relationships (mother and child, bride and groom) whereby business transactions are often not dealt with in writing.

134. Testimony is unquestionably forbidden with reference to compromise and settlement agreements (Article 1967 c.c.) and insurance (Article 1888 c.c.). The parties to any agreement may provide in writing that no testimonial evidence be accepted in the case of a future dispute in court. In this case, witnesses are admissible only in case the written agreement was lost not because of recklessness by the plaintiff.

135. Finally, according to Article 15 of the Hague Convention of July 1, 1964, ratified by Italy by Act No. 816 of June 21, 1971, testimony is always accepted for claims regarding international contracts for the sale of goods.

115. *See* Cass. Civ., sez. III, Mar. 21, 2013, n. 7122.
116. Cass. Civ., sez. II, 4 giugno 2015, n. 11597; Cass. Civ., sez. II, 19 settembre 2013, n. 21443.
117. *See* Cass. Civ., sez. II, 16 ottobre 2017, n. 24306.

C. Presumptions

136. Presumptions are conclusions which may be drawn by a known event with regards to an unknown event. Presumptions are usually based on experience and are envisaged whenever the burden of proof would be too heavy for one party.

Several presumptions are embodied in the civil code, such as: a newborn child conceived during matrimony is presumed to be the son of the mother's husband (Article 231). Most presumptions may generally be proved to be wrong (*praesumptio iuris tantum*): for instance, a tutor is presumed responsible for damages caused by an insane person, unless he proves he had properly looked after the insane person and taken any possible step to prevent him from causing the damages (Article 2047 c.c.).[118]

137. Clues are another form of factual presumption. A court may consider certain facts to be proved on the basis of clues: thus, in a car accident, the speed of a car may be approximated on the basis of the tracks left on the road by the braking wheels.

Clues are generally treated by courts like testimonial evidence, and are therefore subject to the relevant rules of procedure (Article 2729, section 2, c.c.). Their probative effect depends on the evaluation of the court, although the civil code imposes that only "heavy," "precise" and "coherent" clues be taken into consideration by courts.

D. Statements under Oath, Confession and Expertise

138. A party in trial may be requested by the other party to make a sworn statement in court with reference to a fact which is essential for the adjudication of a dispute (Articles 2737–2739 c.c. and 233–239 c.p.c.). The other party may choose to swear, in which case the judge must acknowledge full proof and that party wins on that specific count, but may be charged with perjury if the statement was false. As an alternative, that party may choose to lose on that specific point by refusing to swear, or may request that the other party make a sworn statement on the point.

139. A party may also be asked by a court to make a statement under oath whenever certain facts have not been fully proved (Articles 2736 n. 2 c.c. and 240 c.p.c.) or in order to provide an estimated value of things (Articles 241 et seq. c.p.c.).

140. Confession takes place whenever one party confirms the facts which form the grounds of the claims of the counterpart. Confession may be expressed through a formal admission made in court (Articles 228 et seq. c.p.c.), or orally to another person, or in writing. Hearsay is generally treated by the judge according to his discretion (Article 2735 c.c.), whilst the general rules on documents apply to written

118. Presumptions are also of particular relevance in cases concerning liability for defective products. *See* Cass. Civ., sez. III, May 29, 2013, n. 13458.

confessions. Admissions made to one's counterpart outside of court have full probative effect (*see* Articles 2733 section 2 and 2735 c.c.).

141. Experts may be appointed by the court to give technical advice on one or more issues (*see* Articles 191–201 c.p.c.). In all such cases, each party has the right to appoint an expert who is entitled to present a report as well. Experts appointed by courts may be called to make statements in court, although in most cases they simply prepare a written report. Reports do not have a binding probative effect, although courts very often consider them probative.

III. Burden of Proof

142. It is a general principle of the law of civil procedure that it is a duty of the parties to provide and present evidence to the judge (Article 115 c.p.c.). This rule is supported by another rule, according to which the duty of affirmatively proving a fact or facts in dispute is on the party having an interest at establishing a requisite degree of persuasion about that fact (burden of proof or *onus probandi*, Article 2697 c.c.). If the other party wants to object the grounds of that fact, it is her duty to prove her objection by evidence, and thus the burden of proof shifts to that party. As a result of this rule, whenever a court is deciding upon a given dispute, if an issue is not fully proven the court decides against the party whose burden it was to prove that issue.

143. Exceptions to the rule of the burden of proof include presumptions, whereby the burden of proof shifts to the party whose interests are conflicting with the presumption. Therefore, it is that party's duty to prove that the presumption is wrong in the specific case at issue.

144. Another relevant exception can be found in the field of contractual liability: the plaintiff simply must prove the defendant has failed to perform his obligations, whilst it is the defendant's duty to prove that his failure to perform was justified, for instance, by force majeure. This partial shift of the burden of proof rule applies to all contractual relationships where performance of one party consists of achieving a specific result (*obbligazioni di risultato*: such as is the case for a building contract, an agreement for the sale or supply of goods, or a commission to procure business). In all such cases, the plaintiff simply must show that the defendant has not achieved that result. The burden of proof does not shift when, on the contrary, performance simply consists of exercising reasonable care in achieving the purpose of the contract (*obbligazioni di mezzi*), as is the case for all agreements regarding the correct provision of services without there being a specific result (such as: employer-employee relationships, agency, agreements for professional services). In all such cases, where performance simply consists of rendering a service with one's best effort, the plaintiff's duty is more cumbersome, for he must prove that his counterpart's performance was lacking quality.

§3. NEGOTIATIONS AND PRE-CONTRACTUAL LIABILITY

I. Introduction

145. As a general rule, the parties to negotiation must negotiate in good faith (Article 1337 c.c.), i.e., with the common due diligence which men generally exercise in respect to their own concerns. This implies that unfair behavior by one party during deliberation, discussion or conference upon the terms of a proposed agreement entitles the other party to damages both in the case of subsequent breakdown in negotiations *and* if contract is finally executed.

Examples of incorrect, unfair, or disloyal behavior include failing to notify the other party about the intention to draw back from negotiations, or failing to duly inform the other party about the lack of an essential element making the contract void or unconscionable. It is also unfair to purposely drag on negotiations for many months in order to look for better occasions on the market, without informing the other party.

146. Pre-contractual liability may also arise out of unjustified breakdown of negotiations by one party. Negotiations may certainly be broken off whenever the parties fail to reach an agreement on one or more essential elements of the contract, but a party may be held liable for breaking off advanced negotiations without a serious reason or without warning. For instance, pre-contractual liability arises whenever one party claims that it is impossible to reach an agreement on a secondary element of contract, whereas all major elements are settled and the other party is willing to further negotiate. Another example is revocation of an offer before the contract is finalized but after the other party has started performance in good faith. As we have previously seen in Part I, Chapter I, if the party who started performance had not been previously informed by the other party of her intention to revoke the offer, she is entitled to reimbursement of all expenses incurred in starting performance (Article 1328 c.c.) and to damages for any other business occasions which she lost or gave up in order to start performance.

147. Pre-contractual liability implies restoring all damages incurred by the damaged party, including expenses and costs for carrying out negotiations and for starting performance (transportation, travel, planning, undertakings with banks, etc.), lost chances with other business transactions and partners, damages deriving from failure to finalize an agreement, etc.

II. Precontractual Liability

148. Preliminary negotiations can be defined to include any communication prior to acceptance of an offer.[119,120]

119. *See* Cass. Civ., sez. II, 14/03/2017, n. 6587; Cass. Civ., sez. III, Aug. 5, 2004, n. 15040; Cass. Aug. 30, 1995, n. 9157; Cass. May 11, 1990, n. 4051 (*Corriere giur.*, 1990, 832). *See also* Calzolaio, E.,

149. The rules on pre-contractual liability found in the Italian Civil Code of 1942 have been drafted after paragraph 242 of the German Civil Code of 1900 (B.G.B.). The B.G.B. highlights the importance of "good faith" in contractual relationships throughout several articles: under Article 1366 c.c., "Contract must be interpreted following good faith"; under Article 1375 c.c., "Contract must be executed in good faith"; under Article 1175 c.c., "Debtor and creditor must behave following the good faith and fair dealing rules," and, finally, according to Article 1337 c.c. "Parties must behave in good faith during the pre-contractual bargaining and contract drafting phase."

150. During preliminary negotiations, parties are under the duty of good faith and fair dealing. The relevant cause of action is in tort.[121]

III. Foundation of Pre-contractual Liability

151. Fair dealing obligations are designed to enforce a standard of conduct in preliminary negotiations.

The modern approach of Italian courts is to consider pre-contractual liability an appropriate cause of action especially in two classes of cases: knowledge of contract voidness and unjustified breakdown of negotiations.

IV. Knowledge of Contract Voidness

152. According to Article 1338 c.c., "He, who has or should have knowledge that contract is void and failed to disclose it to the counterpart, has to pay the damages suffered by the party who relied with no fault in contract validity."

153. Furthermore, a party is protected at law only if she relied on contract validity "without any fault." Generally, the party ignoring the rules set out by the law on transactions is deemed to be at fault.[122]

"La responsabilità precontrattuale dopo la riforma del *code civil* francese. Profili comparatistici," in *Riv. Trim. di Dir. e Proc. Civ.*, fasc.4, 2017, at 1301.

120. Alpa, G., "Italian Report to The XIIIth Congress International Academy of Comparative Law," in *Precontractual Liability*, Kluwer, 1991, at 165. *See also*, Benatti, F., "La responsabilità precontrattuale," ESI, Naples, 2012; Sapone, N., "La responsabilità precontrattuale," Giuffrè, Milan, 2008, at 51.

121. *See* Franzoni, M., "Il danno risarcibile," Giuffrè, Milano, 2010, at 102; Sacco, R., in Sacco, R., De Nova, G., "Il contratto," Turin, 1993, I, at 255; Cass. Civ., sez. II, Mar. 14, 2017, n. 6587; Cass. Oct. 4, 1948, n. 1667 (*Giur. it.*, 1949, I, 1, 29); and other nine decisions up to Cass. May 11, 1990, n. 4051 (*Foro it.*, 1991, I, 184); the opposite solution (similar to the German tradition but not established by judicial decisions) has been followed in Italy by Mengoni, in *Riv.dir. comm.*, 1956, II, 365.

122. *See* Cass., May 10, 1950, n. 1205, (*Foro it.*, 1950, I, 1307); Cass., May 27, 1960, n. 1358 (*Foro it.*, 1960, I, 1508); Cass., Jun. 27, 1972, n. 2199; Cass., Jul. 11, 1972, n. 2325.

V. Unjustified Breakdown of Negotiations

154. As a general rule, whenever during negotiations a stage has been reached where one party is relying on the execution of contract, the party deciding to unjustifiably abandon negotiations is liable for damages.

This is a typical situation whereby Article 1337 applies;[123] basically, this is the only common and frequent use of this rule.

Withdrawal implies liability only when it is "unjustified." "Justified" reasons include a more convenient contractual offer coming from a third person or any other circumstance making the deal less favorable. However, specific circumstances may imply different interpretation by courts. For instance, during negotiations for a lease agreement, if the prospective lessee requires the prospective landlord to pay for refurbishment of the space to be leased, such request may or may not be considered by a court as a commitment not to withdraw from negotiations.[124]

VI. *Culpa in Contrahendo* when a Valid Contract Has Been Completed

155. *Culpa in contrahendo* when contract has been completed is classified under Italian law as a "violation of the duty to disclose information."

Recent legislation following this trend includes regulating which kind of specific information a bank must render to the client (*see* L. 154 of February 17, 1992), or what standard of information is due to investors by stock exchange brokers (*see* L. 1 of January 2, 1991). Besides specific cases ruled by single statutes, a general duty to disclose information implies application of (a) Article 1439 c.c. on fraud or (b) Article 1337 c.c. on pre-contractual liability.

Article 1439 c.c. on fraud states that contract may be annulled when it was executed because of the tricks or fraudulent behavior (*raggiri*) by one party against the other. "Failure to act" once was not considered as a fraud. Today, this issue has become controversial.[125]

Tricky behavior must be intentional in order to be relevant.[126]

---

123. Cass. Civ., sez. II, Mar. 10, 2016, n. 4718. *See also* Cass. May 7, 1952, n. 1279, in *Foro it.*, 1952, I, 1638 and many similar decisions up to Cass., Mar. 5, 1992, n. 2704 (*Giur. It.*, 1993, I, 1, 1560).
124. App. Venezia, Jul. 6, 1955 (abridged in *Mass. Giust. civ.*, "App. Venezia," 1955, 97); App. Rome, May 20, 1955 (abridged in *Mass. Giust. civ.*, "App. Roma," 1955, 72).
125. The following decisions are favorable to the relevance of the "failure to act" fraud: Cass. Jul. 7, 1976, n. 2528; Cass. Jul. 24, 1976, n. 2961; Cass. Jan. 12, 1991, n. 257; Cass. Oct. 14, 1991, n. 10779 (*Giur. it.*, 1993, I, 1, 190); the opposite solution has been held by: Cass. Jan. 18, 1979, n. 363; Cass. Oct. 21, 1981, n. 5503; Cass. Oct. 18, 1991, n. 11038; Cass. Civ., sez. II, Mar. 15, 2005, n. 5549; Cass. Civ., sez. II, Mar. 31, 2011, n. 7468; Cass. Civ., sez. II, Jul. 4, 2012, n. 11191.
126. *See* Cass. Jul. 23, 1960, n. 2119; Cass., Jul. 4, 1981, n. 4383 (*Giust. civ.*, 1981, I, 2515); Cass. Civ., sez. III, May 25, 2006, n. 12424.

VII. Duty to Inform

156. Italian scholars,[127] as the French, set the violation of the duty to inform within the doctrine of "lack of consent," linking it to Article 1439 c.c. According to Article 1439 c.c., contract is void "[…] when deception employed by one of the contracting parties was such that, without it, the other contracting party would not have entered into the contract." The text is not very different from Article 1116 of the French Civil Code.

The duty to disclose information has been widened over time. Until recently, the only legal sources regulating this issue were the code articles on contracts annulled by mistake, fraud or violence (Articles 1427–1440 c.c.) and on rescission made under the threat of a danger or need (Articles 1447 et seq., c.c.).

In the last ten years, issues such as subliminal advertisement, corporate monopolies, "asymmetric" duty to disclose information or dominating position by one of the parties to contract and have been regulated by new legislation, mostly following European Community Directives.[128] The most remarkable example of this trend can be traced through the evolution of the *culpa in contrahendo* doctrine.[129] The Italian Civil Code bears a specific rule preventing bad faith in the pre-contractual bargaining process. Under Article 1337 c.c., "In preliminary negotiations, the parties shall behave in good faith."[130]

127. Several Italian authors have written on the subject. Liability arising out of failure to disclose is always dealt along with the pre-contractual good faith obligations. The latest works are by Benatti, F., "La responsabilità precontrattuale," ESI, Naples, 2012; Sapone, N., "La responsabilità precontrattuale," Giuffrè, Milan, 2008; Caruso, D., "La *culpa in contrahendo*. L'esperienza statunitense e quella italiana," Milan, 1993; Grisi, G., "L'obbligo precontrattuale di informazione," Naples, 1990; Nanni, L., "La buona fede contrattuale," Padua, 1988, at 1–143; Benatti, F., "Culpa in contrahendo," in *Contratto e impresa*, 1987, at 287 et seq.; Benatti, F., "La responsabilità precontrattuale," Milan, 1963; Cuffaro, V., "Responsabilità precontrattuale," in *Enc. dir.*, XXXIX, Milan, 1988, at 1265 et seq.; Ferrarini, G., "Investment banking, prospetti falsi e culpa in contrahendo," in *Giur. comm.*, 1988, II, at 585; Fusaro, A., "Fondamenti e limiti della responsabilità precontrattuale," in *Giur. it.*, 1984, I, 1, at 1199; Loi, M., Tessitore, F., "Buona fede e responsabilità precontrattuale," Milan, 1975; Rasi, S.A., "La responsabilità precontrrattuale," in *Riv. dir. Civ.*, 1974, at 496; Visintini, G., "La reticenza nella formazione dei contratti," Padua, 1972; Bessone, M., "Rapporto precontrattuale e doveri di correttezza," in *Riv. trim. dir. proc. civ.*, 1955, I, at 360.

128. *See* Gambaro, A., "Codice civile," in *Digesto IV*, Turin, 1988, on the relationship between the importance of the Civil Code and business transactions. The author points out how in modern times Civil Code rules are not apt to regulate the new deal of the world economy. A worldwide market is now prevailing over the internal one, and exchange of goods between individuals has been substituted by trade between economic groups, or between these groups and individuals, provoking a huge change in contractual relationships.

129. *See* Cass. Civ., sez. un., Feb. 1, 2019, (ud. Jan. 15, 2019, dep. Feb. 1, 2019), n. 3165 with explicit reference to EU Regulation n. 864/2007.

130. The role of *culpa in contrahendo* in Italy and in the United States are explained in the excellent work by Caruso, D., *ult. supra*.

EEC derived regulations are now offering a model of fairness in negotiations. According to such new rules, for instance, silence by itself does not mean fraud,[131] unless there was a fraudulent concealment of true facts or a violation of an explicit duty to speak enforced by the law.[132]

157. Article 1337 c.c. imposes a general duty to behave in good faith. The rule may also be read as imposing the duty on every party to inform her counterpart whenever she discovers the other party's mistake. Several recently enacted statutes deal with a new concept of good faith and fair dealing, imposing rules on openness, fairness and loyalty for door-to-door contracts,[133] sales of securities[134] and agreements to provide bank and financial services.[135] Other statutes require companies to provide additional information to the general public. Examples include legislation imposing corporate balance certification and publication,[136] or statutory law regulating the duty to print expiration dates on pharmaceutical and food products.

Legislation and scholars seem to be progressively detaching from the traditional German law standpoint on pre-contractual liability and heading towards solutions similar to modern German law on the *überraschende Klauseln*, and to American law invoking the *reasonable expectation* of the *unconscionable* party.

VIII. Damages

158. As a general rule, in case of "unjustified" withdrawal from negotiations, reliance damages are due (*interesse negativo*).[137] Reliance liability implies restoring all and any expenses sustained by the relying party. For instance, any costs sustained by a prospective landlord in restructuring the renting space in order to make it fit for the prospective lessee's requirements, must be refunded whenever negotiations are interrupted without a "justifiable" reason.[138] However, the amount of damages can never supersede the value of the prospective contract.[139]

131. This statement could be found in a 1948 decision of the court of Verona (Trib. Verona, Nov. 18, 1946, in *Foro Pad.*, 1947, 199): The sale of a truck, without disclosing that it was State-owned property, was considered fraudulent and avoided.
132. The Civil Code contains an explicit duty to disclose in Arts. 1892–1893 concerning insurance contracts.
133. *See* L. 216 of Jun. 7, 1974, D.L. 95 of Apr. 8, 1974, amended by EEC Directive 89/298, enacted in Italy by Dlg. 74 of Jan. 25, 1992, and L. 428 of Dec. 29, 1990.
134. *See* L. 1 of Jan. 2, 1991.
135. L. 154 of Feb. 17, 1992.
136. D.P.R. 136 of Mar. 31, 1975.
137. *See* T.A.R., Napoli, sez. I, Jun. 7, 2010, n. 12676; Cons. di Stato, sez. V, May 19, 2009, n. 3066; T.A.R., Roma, sez. II, Jul. 7, 2009, n. 6527.
138. *See* Trib. Roma, Sep. 25, 1973 (*Temi Romana*, 1974, 89).
139. *See* Cass. Feb. 12, 1982, n. 855 and Cass. Jan. 25, 1988, n. 582.

Chapter 2. Conditions of Substantive Validity

M. Balestrieri

§1. Capacity of the Parties

159. The capacity to hold rights, which is enjoyed by all persons according to Article 3 of the Constitution, must be distinguished from the *capacity to execute legal transactions*. Any person who has not been formally declared incapable at law may contract. Such matters are regulated in the Civil Code both in the section on Obligations (Articles 1190 and 1191 c.c. and Articles 1425 and 1426 c.c.), and in that dedicated to Persons and Family (Book I, Title XII, Articles 414–432).

160. The fundamental principle is that any legal transaction involving an incapable person must be executed by a statutory agent or guardian or tutor acting in his name or on his behalf. The agent's consent may be given *ex post*. The agent is generally controlled by courts, and specific authorization by the court is required for important transactions (Article 374 c.c.).

Italian law distinguishes between persons being wholly insane or partially unable to contract. Article 414 c.c. provides that persons under a permanent incapacity must be declared incapable thereof. A legal transaction or a contract is void when a person legally unable to contract (Article 1425 c.c.) has entered it. A contract or legal transaction executed by a person being *momentarily* under incapacity may be annulled by proving that such transaction or contract was entered under incapacity. The statute of limitations for the action runs out after five years (Article 428 c.c.).

I. Minors

161. A minor or infant is a person who has not reached the age of 18. Minors when married can require to be declared emancipated (*emancipati*) by filing a petition in court. Emancipated minors have full capacity to contract without supervision by a guardian for any business not exceeding ordinary management issues. For business considered "out of the ordinary" decisions are taken with the aid of a statutory agent under the court supervision (Article 394 c.c.).

162. Any payment made to a minor is not effective if the debtor does not prove that payment was provided with profit to the minor (Article 1190 c.c.). Due payment made by a minor cannot be revoked because of incapacity (Article 1191 c.c.).

163. The mere statement by a minor that he is of full age is no bar to rescission. On the contrary, an agreement with a minor is binding and enforceable although deriving from fraudulent behavior by the minor aimed at misrepresenting his or her age (Article 1426 c.c.).

II. Insanity

164. A contract is void if it was executed by a person legally unable to contract (Article 1425 c.c.).[140] Persons of unsound mind are often referred to as persons "under incapacity." Incapacity may be an irreversible, physiological condition or may be momentary. Persons under *momentary* incapacity may require a contract or legal transaction to be annulled by proving that execution occurred under temporary incapacity. The statute of limitations for this action runs out after five years (Article 428 c.c.). If a court has declared that a person is insane ("interdiction"), no further evidence of his or her incapacity is required, and any deeds by that person are considered void even if he or she were acting in lucid intervals.

The Civil Code provides a specific status for mentally disordered persons, prodigals or spendthrifts (*inabilitati*), who may be placed under the supervision of a counselor (Article 415 c.c.). Blind persons, deaf persons, drunkards and drug addicts are considered under the same status. Criminals undergoing sentences of a certain degree of severity are placed under "interdiction."

§2. Defects of Consent

165. According to Article 1427 c.c., contract may be annulled if consent was given only by error, or was extorted by violence or obtained by deceit.

I. Mistake

166. The rules of the Italian Civil Code on mistake (Articles 1427–1433) have been influenced by Austrian and Swiss law as well as by the decisions of the French courts.[141] The Italian Civil Code provides that "a contracting party whose consent was given by mistake … can require annulment of the contract when such mistake is essential (*essenziale*) and recognizable (*riconoscibile*) by the other contracting party" (Article 1428 c.c.).

167. The Civil Code deals with mistake in the following articles:

> Article 1428—Relevance of mistake. Mistake causes annulment of a contract when it is "essential" and "recognizable" by the other contracting party.
>
> *Article 1429—Essential mistake. Mistake is "essential":*
>
> (1) when it concerns the nature or the object of contract;
> (2) when it concerns the identity of the object of performance or a quality of said object which, according to common understanding or under the circumstances, should be considered essential for consent;

140. *See* Cass. Civ., sez. II, Jul. 4, 2012, n. 11191.
141. *See* Zweigert, K., Kötz, H., "Introduction to Comparative Law," Second Part, Oxford, 1990, I 101.

(3) when it concerns the identity or personal qualities of the other contracting party, so long as they were essential for consent;
(4) when the party was mistaken about the law and mistake was the only or principal reason for entering into the contract.

Article 1431—Recognizable Mistake.

Mistake is considered recognizable when, with respect to the content or circumstances of contract, or to the quality of the contacting parties, a person of normal diligence would have detected it.

168. The code provides a long list of cases whereby mistake can be considered "essential" (*essenziale*), requiring "recognisability" as a further condition: i.e., that the parties would not have been able to recognize the mistake by exercising reasonable and proper care (*errore riconoscibile*).[142] The difference in qualities of the parties can be a sufficient argument to allow the court to assert that mistake was "recognizable."[143]

A. *Mistake as to the Essential Substance*

169. Another way to annul the contract is to prove the lack of promised qualities in performance or in the object of contract. In sales contracts, the buyer must prove that the sold goods are unfit for purpose. This is a claim for lack of quality (*aliud pro alio*) in the object, ruled by Article 1497 c.c.[144]

170. Moreover, when the goods being sold lack the qualities promised or those essential for the use for which the goods are normally intended, the buyer is entitled to obtain resolution of the contract according to the general provisions on Resolution for Non-Performance (Article 1453 c.c.), provided that the defect in quality exceeds the *limits of tolerance* established by usage. However, as provided in Article 1495 c.c.,[145] the right to resolution is subject to forfeiture (*see* Articles 2964 c.c., 1495 section 1, c.c.) and prescription (Articles 2946 c.c. and 1495 section 3, c.c.). The defendant's arguments will generally be based on the "limit of tolerance" issue (*limite di tolleranza*).[146] For instance, in *Automega s.p.a.* v. *Pezzillo*, the first degree court of Palermo, the Court of Appeals of Palermo and finally the Court of

142. Cass. May 16, 1960, n. 1177, (*Giur. It.*, 1960, I, 1, 112). *See also* Trib. Bergamo, sez. IV, Feb. 10, 2018, n. 375; Cass. Civ., sez. II, Jul. 25, 2011, n. 16240.
143. *See* Fasano, A., "I vizi del consenso," Giappichelli, Turin, 2013, at; 76 et seq.; Trabucchi, A., "Errore, volontà ed aflidamento nel negozio giuridico," Cedam, Padova, 1990; Pietrobon, V., "Errore, volontà e affidamento," 1990, ried. *See also* Corte App. Palermo, sez. I, Jan. 13, 2016, n. 8.
144. Cass. Civ., sez. II, Nov. 27, 2018, n. 30713.
145. *See* Cass. 247/1981; Cass. 3695/1969; Cass. 2488/1967; *see also*; Bianca, M., "Diritto civile," III, "Il Contratto," 1987, at 589.
146. *See* Cass. 3550/1995 and Cass. 4923/1977.

Cassation considered the sale of a "full optioned Mercedes Benz 190" as vitiated by lack of quality for the air conditioner was not an original Mercedes optional and it had been installed in Palermo.[147]

B. *Mistake as to the Person*

171. Mistake as to the person is a ground of annulment only in contracts whereby the identity of the contracting party is essential for consent (Article 1429 n. 3, c.c.).

This is particularly the case in utmost good faith contracts where the relationship between the parties is strongly fiduciary, such as insurance, hire of professional work and skill, partnership, etc.

II. Fraud (Deceit)

172. According to Article 1439 c.c., a contract may be annulled for fraud when deception employed by one of the contracting parties was such that, without it, the other contracting party would not have entered into the contact.

When deception was employed by a third person, the contract can be annulled if the party who derived any benefit from deception was aware of such deception.

In case the deception was not such as to compel consent, the contract is binding and effective even if the outcome of the contract would have been different without the deception. However, the party acting in bad faith is liable for damages (Article 1440 c.c.).

A deception arising out of innocent misrepresentation is not fraud; equally, an exaggerated praise of one's own goods is not fraud.

173. Italian courts have had some problems at recognizing annulment of contract for nondisclosure amounting to misrepresentation.[148] However, most scholars

147. *See* Trib. Palermo, Oct. 7, 1989; App. Palermo, Jun. 7, 1991; Cass. Mar. 25, 1995, n. 3550. Before the Civil Code of 1942, Italian Courts considered the sale of a painting as an "aleatory" contract (*see* Introduction to the Law of Contracts, §3, V): "[…] one who has sold an ancient painting ignoring its artistic value, cannot, once he discovers its real value, plead to annul the sale for factual mistake." Similarly, "once an ancient painting has been sold without a warranty on its value (it was a Raffaello) […] there is no fraud by the vendor, nor any substantial mistake that could render the sale void" (*see* App. Firenze Mar. 15, 1910, in *Filangeri*, 1910, 459). The approach has not changed after the new code, although cases occur very seldom. In 1948, a court used both the former doctrine on "aleatory" contracts and the new doctrine of essential mistake on quality of the object (Art. 1429, n. 2 c.c.) in the case of a Carraccio painting sold for a ridiculous amount by a Roman antiques shop. *See* App. Roma, Nov. 23, 1948 (*Riv. dir. comm.* 1949, II, 192): The Carraccio painting had been sold as a work by an "unknown maestro." About this specific topic, *see* Campagnolo, R., "L'errore sull'identità dell'autore nella negoziazione di opere d'arte," in *Resp. civ. e prev.*, 2000, at 1093.

148. Very often do criminal courts make use of nondisclosure amounting to misrepresentation. Furthermore, the civil concept of "fraud" and the criminal concept of "deceit" are considered to be constituted by the same factual situation (*see* Cass. 7322/1986).

believe fraud perpetrated through failure to act is also a form of misrepresentation amounting to deceit. Silence in itself does not imply fraud, unless there is a fraudulent concealment of true facts or a violation of an explicit duty to speak enforced by the law.[149] In order to enforce violation of a legal duty to speak, plaintiff must convince the court that Article 1337 c.c. (duty to behave in good faith during negotiations) is really imposing a general duty to speak. The *Banca Manusardi* Decision was the only case where a court accepted such reasoning. A bank had not disclosed information concerning the economic situation of a company, whereby it was selling the company's convertible loan stocks. The bank was held liable for violation of Article 1337 c.c.[150]

III. Violence (Duress)

174. Under Article 1434 c.c. contract may be annulled for "violence" even for violence by a third party. There is no definition of "violence" in the code, although it may be said to be a constraint, physical or moral, placed on the will of a person, inducing her to consent. The nature of the violence must be such as to induce a sane, reasonable person to fear that an unjust wrong will be inferred to her own self or to her goods (Article 1435 c.c.).[151]

IV. Laesio

175. The Civil Code contains under the title Contract Rescission (*rescissione del contratto*) two totally different kinds of actions (Articles 1447 and 1448 c.c.).

Article 1447 c.c. is related to maritime salvage (*see* Article 7 L. 938 of June 14, 1925), considering the case of a contract that is being executed as a result of a situation of danger. In all such cases, a party may require contract rescission, although the court offers an equitable compensation to the "rescuer."

176. Article 1448 c.c. regulates the general action of *laesio*. In order to require rescission of contract for *laesio*, the following conditions must be met:

- one party is in a situation of "need";
- the other party takes advantage of the situation;
- the first party suffers a prejudice consisting of a loss or monetary impoverishment.

149. This statement could be found in a decision by the court of Verona (Trib. Verona, Nov. 18, 1946, in *Foro Pad.*, 1947, at 199) whereby the sale of a truck without disclosing that it was State property, was considered fraudulent and avoided.
150. App. Milan, Feb. 2, 1990 (*Giur. it.*, 1992, I, 2, 49).
151. *See* Cass. Civ., sez. I, Oct. 9, 2015, n. 20305.

According to the Court of Cassation, all such conditions, which are very difficult to prove, must be accomplished at the same time,[152] which makes it extremely difficult to use this action as a contractual remedy.

V. *Presupposizione* (Contractual Basic Assumption)

177. Another way to attempt to render a contract void is the use of the doctrine of "contractual basic assumption."[153] When parties reach an agreement on an implied basic assumption left indefinite, there is a strong possibility that the missing terms may be inferred from surrounding circumstances by a court.[154] For instance, Italian courts very often find contractual basic assumptions in contracts for the sale of land.[155]

178. Contractual basic assumptions may be considered a new form of mistake. According to the Court of Milan "contractual basic assumptions and essential mistake are two different aspects of the same factual situation."[156] If contractual basic assumptions are viewed as a new kind of mistake, the ultimate solution may soon be that contract can be annulled under such circumstances (*see* Article 1441 c.c.).

§3. Other Conditions of Validity

179. According to Article 1325 c.c., the second basic requirement of contract is *causa*. Article 1343 c.c. Civil Code states that the "*causa*" is unlawful "whenever it violates mandatory rules, rules of public policy or good morals."

---

152. *See* Cass. 2071/1978; Cass. 5040/1978; Cass. 5535/1981; Cass. 6732/1982; Cass. 7709/1987. *See also* Cass. Civ., sez. II, Mar. 6, 2007, n. 5133.
153. This doctrine has a German origin; scholars such as Windscheid considered factual situations whereby the main reasons for contract are so important and essential as to become its real *causa*. Other scholars such as Örtmann ("Die Geschäftsgrundlage. Ein neuer Rechtsbegriff," 1921) and Larenz ("Geschäftsgrundlage und Vertragserfüllung," 1963) modified the doctrine, considering the concept of "contract grounds" (*Geschäftsgrundlage*): if the "contract grounds" are substantially modified, the contract itself will not be enforceable. The English Coronation cases, such as *Krell v. Henry* (1903) 2 K.B. 740, can offer a factual example of a situation in which the *Geschäftsgrundlage* could have been invoked.
    For an extensive outlook on these principles, *see* Pontani, A., "La presupposizione nella sua evoluzione, con particolare riferimento all 'errore ed alla causa'," in *Quadrimestre*, 1991, at 833.
154. *See* Cass. Sep. 17, 1970, n. 1512 (*Foro it.*, 1971, I, 3028); Cass. Apr. 7, 1971, n. 1025 (*Foro it.*, 1971, I, 2574); Cass. Sep. 22, 1981, n. 5168, (*Foro it.*, 1982, I, 104); Cass. Oct. 31, 1989, n. 4554 (*Riv. dir. civ.*, 1990, II, 350); Cass. Aug. 11, 1990, n. 8200; Cass. Dec. 3, 1991, n. 12921 (*Giur. It.*, 1992, I, 1, 2210); *see also* Cass. 1040/1995; Cass. 8689/1995, regarding the sale of company shares under the implied term that the company owns a boat as its single estate. *See also* Cass. Civ., sez. I, Mar. 5, 2018, n. 5112; Cass. Civ., sez. un., Apr. 20, 2018, n. 9909; Cass. Civ., sez. II, Mar. 24, 1998, n. 3083.
155. *See* Cass. 6933/1983; Cass. 5512/1984. *See also* Cass. Civ., sez. II, Nov. 23, 2017, n. 27916.
156. *See* Trib. Milan, Oct. 11, 1948, (*Dir. lav.*, II, 1949 at 17), where the mistake was on the essential quality of the counterpart, but the court used the *presupposizione* doctrine instead of the essential mistake rule. *See also* Cass. Oct. 3, 1972, n. 2828.

A contractual obligation is valid and effective only if it bears a lawful *causa*. The drafters of the Civil Code adopted an objective theory on *causa* defined as "the economic and social function of contract."

The presence of a *causa* does not imply the idea of bargain. The doctrine of *causa* is not a civilian version of the common law doctrine of consideration.

I. *Causa* and Consideration

180. In common law, consideration is the price or the effort paid by the plaintiff for the defendant's promise. Consideration is described by the mutual economic efforts paid by the parties *vis-à-vis* their intention to enter the contract.

181. The canon lawyers of the thirteenth century fought against the rule *ex nudo pacto actio non oritur* and wanted the principle *pacta sunt servanda* to be accepted by courts. This principle was to provide moral foundation to the law of contract, and required scholars to seek reasonable explanations of why promisor was bound to perform a duty.[157]

182. Modern theories on *causa* include the recent "objective" theory held by the Court of Cassation,[158] defining *causa* as the "economic and social function of contract," and the traditional "subjective" theory, considering *causa* as "the common purpose of the contracting parties," as followed by some earlier decisions of the Court of Cassation.

183. According to Article 1343 c.c., *causa* is unlawful whenever it violates "mandatory rules," "public policy" and "good morals." These terms are not defined in the civil codes. Thus, such broad concepts provide courts with useful tools to define the border lines between lawful and unlawful contracts with respect to the fundamental values of the existing legal order.[159]

II. Mandatory Rules

184. The mandatory nature of a legal rule implies that the rule provides protection of interests deemed to be essential by the law. Generally speaking, case law classifies rules as "not mandatory" when no sanction exists for violation of the rule.[160]

For instance, tax regulations have no direct effect on the contractual *causa*, and are thus not held as mandatory.[161]

---

157. *See* Gorla, G., "Il Contratto," Giuffrè, Milan, 1954.
158. Cass. 3300/1975 and Galgano, F., "Diritto civile e commerciale," Padua, 1994. *See also* Cass. Civ., sez. III, Jun. 8, 2017, n. 14262.
159. *See* Cass, 1552/1972, Carusi, "Il contratto," Milan, 1947 and Cass. 4700/1988. *See also* Cass. Civ., sez. II, Sep. 18, 2013, n. 21398.
160. *See* Cass. 6601/1982.
161. Cass. 4024/1981; Cass. 5571/1981.

III. Illegality and Public Policy

185. The Constitution of 1948 is the fundamental guideline to investigate the principles and values of the Italian legal system. According to a fundamental principle, private individuals cannot violate "public policy" through their private transactions and contracts.[162] Public policy recalls the basic values of the legal system to be achieved by individuals and by the State.

186. The following are examples of public policy issues. The contract by which a worker sells to another worker his employment position has been considered contrary to the principle of public policy.[163]

Similarly, it is contrary to public policy to pay the other party to induce her to behave in a certain way in trial.[164] It is also contrary to public policy to buy political and electoral consent during the elections.[165]

"Economic and public policy" embraces a huge number of statutes, including legislation on consumer contracts, rent restrictions, insurance, labor law and many others fields.

§4. The Consequences of a Defect of Consent or a Lack of Substantive Validity

187. Italian law distinguishes between a *void* contract and an *annulled* contract. As a general rule, a contract is *void* (which implies it never was valid and effective) if it is lacking substantive validity, i.e., whenever it lacks an essential element (agreement of the parties, object, *causa*, or form). Anybody bearing an interest may require a court to declare that a contract is void (Article 1421 c.c.). The court may also declare a contract void ex officio.[166] The court's decision will have retroactive effects in that the contract will be considered as never having existed. The statute of limitations to bring action runs out after twenty years.

A contract is not void but may be *annulled* for defect of consent. Contracts may be only annulled by persons who are granted this kind of protection by the law (Article 1441 c.c.). Whenever a contract is annulled, it becomes ineffective for the future; thus, annulment has no retroactive effects. The statute of limitations to bring action runs out after five years.

I. Defect of Consent

188. The party suffering fraud, mistake or duress can annul a contract vitiated by such defects of consent.

162. *See* Cass. 4769/1989; Cass. 8/1990; Cass. 3181/1990.
163. *See* Cass. 2859/1974.
164. *See* Trib. Genova, Sep. 17, 1984 (*Nuova giur. civ.*, 1985, I, 65).
165. *See* Cass. 1574/1971.
166. *See* Cass. Civ., sez. un., Sep. 4, 2012, n. 14828; Cass. Civ., sez. un., Dec. 12, 2014, n. 26242; Cass. Civ., sez. II, Aug. 30, 2018, n. 21418.

When fraud generates an "essential" mistake, plaintiffs are better off in choosing the action of annulment for mistake instead of the one for fraud. The objective evidence of mistake is easier to reach than the psychological evidence of fraud.[167]

189. The action upon fraud (*azione di annullamento*—Articles 1441–1446 c.c.) and the action brought upon lack of quality or warranty for defects in goods (*azione redibitoria*—Articles 1490 and 1495 c.c.) are independent one from the other. These actions may eventually be concurrent in the same factual situation.[168] The real difference between them regards evidential requirements (provided that evidence of fraud is harder to seek) and statute of limitations issues. The statute of limitations runs out after five years for the action upon fraud; however, when it depends upon a defect of consent, the statute of limitations starts running from the day when the fraud or mistake was discovered.

The action upon fraud may be pleaded by the defendant within an action for performance of the contract.

II. Lack of Substantive Quality

190. Purchasers are entitled to bring action upon lack of quality or warranty for defects in goods. The right to warranty may not be exercised if the purchaser fails to notify the seller of the defects borne in the goods within eight days from discovery, unless a different time limit was set by the parties or is established by law (*see* Part II Specific Contracts, Chapter 4). Notice is not necessary if the seller has acknowledged the existence of the defects. Limitation for the action runs out after a year from delivery of the goods. However, the buyer who is being sued for performance of the contract can always plead for the warranty, provided notice of the defects was given within eight days from discovery and within one year from delivery of the goods.

191. Eventually, the plaintiff in a fraud action may claim the dissolution of contract for non-performance (*azione di risoluzione per inadempimento*) in all cases whereby the promise made by the defendant was materially and legally possible (Article 1453 c.c.). In all such cases, damages will consist of the loss sustained by the creditor and the lost profits insofar as they are a direct and immediate consequence of failure to perform.[169]

167. Bianca, M., "Il Contratto," Giuffrè, Milan, 1987, at 628.
168. *See* Cass. 1573/1968.
169. Bianca, *ult. supra*, at 628–629.

Chapter 3. The Contents of a Contract

F. Chiaves

§1. The Different Clauses

I. Ascertaining of Express Terms

192. A valid contract imposes binding obligations on the parties. Contracts are made up of a number of elements, which may or may not occur ("accidental" elements). Italian law distinguishes between conditions (Latin: *conditio*, Italian: *condizione*), deadline terms (Italian: *termine*) and compulsory behavior terms (Latin: *modus*, Italian: *modo*).

All such elements may be invoked to require breach of contract.

193. Conditions place contractual obligations under a future, uncertain event (Article 1353 c.c.), whilst terms limit the effects of contract to a certain time (Article 1184 c.c.). Compulsory behavior terms imply the duty to perform in accordance with a certain behavior, and may be only used for donations (Article 793 c.c.). For instance, a donor donating a collection of paintings may require the donee not to sell the paintings singularly.

II. Implied Terms

194. Article 1374 c.c. provides that: "Contract is binding not only in its express terms, but also in accordance with the requirements of law, usage and equity." Thus, implied terms as generally accepted in society may be invoked by parties to a contract as binding and effective. However, according to the Court of Cassation, this rule may not be invoked when the parties have failed to agree on the main contractual obligations of a given contract.[170]

III. Standard Terms and Exemption Clauses

195. Articles 1341–1342 c.c. regulate the Standard Terms and Conditions of Contract (*clausole generali di contratto*) and Standard Model Form Contracts (*contratti conclusi mediante formulari*).[171]

170. Cass. S.U., Nov. 27, 1963, n. 3044.

171. Bianca, M.,"Diritto civile," III, "Il contratto," Milan, 1984, at 340; Majo, D., "Il controllo delle condizioni generali di contratto," in *Riv. dir. comm.*, 1970, I, at 190 et seq.; Morello, "Condizioni generali di contratto," in *Digesto IV*, Turin, 1988. *See also* Addis, F., "Le clausole di forma nelle condizioni generali di contratto," Giuffrè, Milan, 2008.

196. As a general rule, Standard Terms and Conditions of Contract are effective with respect to the party who knew or should have known their content by using ordinary diligence. Thus, for example, riding a public bus without a ticket is a violation of contract provided that ticket usage is regulated in the general conditions of sale affixed in buses.

Standard Terms and Conditions of Contract must be specifically approved in writing in the following cases:

(1) clauses creating limitations on liability;
(2) clauses providing a right to rescind the contract or suspend performance;
(3) clauses setting limitations to claims;
(4) clauses implying automatic contract renewal upon expiry;
(5) clauses imposing a specific governing law and/or jurisdiction (Article 1341 c.c.).

Some courts consider the list provided for in Article 1341 c.c. as peremptory.[172] Other courts believe the list is simply illustrative and may thus be subject to broad interpretation.[173]

Should the parties add handwritten clauses to a standard contract, the handwritten clauses will prevail over the printed ones (Article 1342 c.c.).

Articles 1341 and 1342 c.c. apply to "private law" contracts between public agencies and individuals as well.[174]

197. As a general rule, under Italian law the parties to a contract may validly reduce or waive their contractual liability, but exemption clauses are generally restrictively interpreted by courts.[175]

Enactment by Parliament of the Consumer Protection Act (L. 52 of February 6, 1996) after the relevant 1994 EU Directive on Consumers, implements a strict control over exemption and limitation clauses through a new set of Civil Code Articles (1469 *bis*– 1469 *quinquies*, c.c., then repealed and encompassed in a specific section of Legislative Decree No. 206 enacted on September 6, 2005, so-called Consumers Code). According to such new rules, no liability exemption is allowed for professional sellers with respect to consumers.[176]

Furthermore, Article 1229 c.c. provides that any term excluding or limiting liability for negligence or fraud, is void. Conditions attempting to exclude liability imposed at law are equally void.[177]

---

172. Cass. S.U., Mar. 27, 1972, n. 955.
173. Cass. S.U., Nov. 11, 1974, n. 3508.
174. Corte Cost., Jan. 21, 1988, n. 61.
175. Cass. Jul. 9, 1991, n. 7603; Pret. Putignano, Apr. 2, 1990 (*Giur. merito*, 1992, 75).
176. The first case to be decided under the new rules was Trib. Torino, Aug. 14, 1996; *see also* Barela, M., "Sull'azione inibitoria in via d'urgenza ex Art. 1469 *sexies* c.c.," in *Giust. civ.*, 1997, I, 2295 et seq.; for a general introduction to Italian consumer law, *see* Alpa, G., "Consumatore (tutela del)," *Enc. Giur. Treccani,* Rome, vol. VIII, 1988.
177. Cass. S.U., Jul. 1, 1994, n. 6225: an exemption clause in a safe-box rental is void whereby the bank *must* be held liable for theft up to a certain amount; *see also* Cass. S.U., Jan. 10, 1984, n. 171.

198. Legislation limiting exemption clauses has been enacted on a number of occasions with respect to specific types of contracts. According to Article 23 of the 1935 Warsaw Convention, for instance, liability for loss or damages to goods in air-freight contracts may not be limited. Furthermore, under the Products Liability Act (D.P.R. 224 of May 24, 1988, enacted after EU Directive No. 85/374 on products liability, now repealed and encompassed in Legislative Decree n. 206 enacted on September 6, 2005, so-called Consumers Code), producers cannot exclude or limit liability towards victims of defective products except when the victim contributed to causing the said damage.

IV. Penalty Clauses

199. A penalty clause is one whereby one party, in order to ensure execution of an agreement, is bound to perform something as forfeiture in the event that party defaults.

The Italian Civil Code distinguishes in the matter of contractual penalties between *clausola penale* ("penalty clause"), *caparra confirmatoria* ("bargain money clause") and *caparra penitenziale* ("bargain money penalty clause").

200. According to Article 1382 c.c., "A *penalty clause* is one whereby one of the parties is bound to an act or to pay money in case of breach or delay in performance; payment of damages is limited to an anticipatory liquidated sum, unless further damage recovery is admitted by contract."[178]

The court can reduce liquidated damages set by the parties in contract according to her equitable reasonableness (Article 1384 c.c.).[179]

201. The *caparra confirmatoria* ("bargain money clause") is a sum of money delivered by one party to the other to confirm her intention to execute contract (Article 1385 c.c.). Should the confirming party breach the contract in any way, the other party is entitled to keep the bargaining money as penalty. However, the latter may prefer to require the contract to be performed: in such case, the normal contractual causes of action on specific performance apply.[180]

202. The *caparra penintenziale* ("bargain money penalty clause") is a clause whereby one party is granted the right to discharge the contract under payment of a sum of money (Article 1386 c.c.).[181]

178. Cass. S.U. Apr. 10, 1995, n. 4126; Cass. S.U. Aug. 29, 1990, n. 8985.
179. Cass. S.U. Dec. 5, 1977, n. 5261; Cass. Civ., sez. II, Apr. 24, 2018, n. 10046.
180. *See* Cass. Civ., sez. Un., Jan. 14, 2009, n. 553.
181. Trib. Milano, sez. V, Dec. 14, 2018, n. 12616.

V. Arbitration Clauses

203. Clauses providing for the arbitration of future controversies arising out of a contract are valid in principle. Arbitration clauses typically require special written approval by the party signing a standard form of contract.[182] The rule is enclosed in Article 1342 c.c. and in the new articles dedicated to consumer contracts encompassed in Legislative Decree 206 of September 6, 2005, so-called Consumers Code (former Articles 1469 *bis*—1469 *quinquies*, c.c.).

204. Submission of controversies to arbitration must be made in writing and signed by the parties, or may be enclosed in another binding document whereby the intention of submitting the controversy to arbitration is clearly expressed.

Terminology distinguishes between *compromesso*, which is an agreement to submit an existing controversy to arbitration, and *clausola compromissoria*, which is an arbitration clause placed within an agreement and relating to future disputes (Articles 801 et seq. c.p.c.).

205. Employer-employee agreements may not carry arbitration clauses unless a special arbitration procedure is provided by the relevant National Contract resulting from collective bargaining (Article 409 c.p.c.).[183]

§2. Contract Construction

206. In a written agreement words never fully express the intention of the parties. Furthermore, the parties making a contract may well not have thought of certain matters which later prove to be relevant. The Italian Civil Code sets a series of rules of construction which must be followed by courts in order to fully understand the true intentions of the parties to contract (Articles 1362–1371 c.c.).

207. Italian scholars have been long divided between supporters of a "subjective" interpretation of contract,[184] centered upon seeking the real understandings of the parties regardless of the literal meaning of the words, and "objective" interpretation,[185] whereby the written text was to be the only binding element regardless of what the parties believed to have agreed upon. The issue was never solved, although

182. *See* Izzo, S., "La convenzione arbitrale nel processo. Studio sui rapporti tra arbitrato e giurisdizioni statuali," Giappichelli, Turin, 2015; Fazzalari, E., "Arbitrato (teoria generale e diritto processuale civile)," in *Digesto IV*, Turin, 1987 and *Id.*, "I processi arbitrali nell'ordinamento italiano," in *Riv. dir. proc. civ.*, 1968, at 459.

183. *See* Cass. S.U. Nov. 23, 1979, n. 9179 and Barone, "Biancosegno e arbitrato irrituale nelle controversie di lavoro," in *Foro it.*, 1980, I, at 974. *See also* Vaccarella, R., "Appunti sul contenzioso del lavoro dopo la privatizzazione del pubblico impiego e sull'arbitrato in materia di lavoro," in *Arg. dir. lav.*, 1998, at 715 et seq.

184. *See* Giorgianni, M., "L'inadempimento," Milan, 1975, at 181 and 193.

185. Bigliazzi Geri, L., "Note in tema di interpretazione secondo buona fede," Milan, 1970, at 163.

the two different perspectives have now merged into one. Today, the scope of construction is to provide some kind of legal effect to unclear expressions contained in an agreement.[186]

208. The general rule (Article 1362 c.c.) requires that a contract be construed according to the common intention of the parties rather than according to the literal meaning of words.[187] The "meeting of the minds" must be discovered by evaluating the parties' behavior during formation and performance of contract.[188] Article 1363 c.c. sets a mutual standard of interpretation between the different contractual clauses, imposing to construe each clause according to the rules set forth by others, so as to define common meanings. Articles 1364 and 1369 c.c. require that general recitals contained in one clause may not involve broader issues than those contracted for, and any expression must be read according to its "natural" meaning. Article 1365 c.c. provides that rules set as an example may be extended to similar cases. Article 1366 c.c. introduces a "good faith" standard of interpretation. Article 1367 c.c. provides a subsidiary principle by setting a self-rescuing rule: the contract and the single clauses must be interpreted as to produce *some* effects.[189] Article 1368 c.c. sets a default rule providing a general standard principle referred to local or the specific business usage. Thus, if no other meaning can be given to words or expressions, the court will construe according to custom. Article 1370 c.c. contains a general rule protecting the weaker contracting party, providing that unclear, doubtful clauses contained in standard contract forms or in general conditions and terms of contract, are to be construed in favor of the weaker party.[190]

§3. Conditioned Contracts

I. Conditio

209. Conditions are elements of contract whereby effectiveness depends upon a future, uncertain event.[191] The contract may be under a Condition Subsequent (*condizione risolutiva*) or a Condition Precedent (*condizione sospensiva*).

210. Condition subsequent implies that contract is immediately enforceable until a future event occurs. Condition precedent, on the contrary, freezes contractual effectiveness until a future event occurs.[192]

211. In case of a condition subsequent, the effects of contract are retroactive as to the time when contract was executed. The parties must behave in good faith while

186. *See* Sacco-De Nova, "Il contratto," *cit.*, vol. II, at 360.
187. *See* Cass. Civ., sez. I, 13/12/2006, n. 26690.
188. Cass. S.U. Jul. 13, 1963, n. 1911.
189. *See also* Cass. S.U. Apr. 24, 1970, n. 1180.
190. Trib. Padova, May 14, 2012 (in *Resp. civ. e prev.* 2012, 5 at 1664).
191. *See* Sacco, R., "La condizione," in *Tratt. Rescigno*, Turin, 1982, 291 et seq.; Maiorca, S., "La condizione," in *Digesto IV*, Turin, 1988.
192. *See* Trimarchi, P., "Istituzioni di diritto privato," XI ed., Milan, 1997, at 271.

condition subsequent is pending, and may not attempt to endanger the other party's prospective rights. Furthermore, the principle that private individuals cannot violate public policy through their private obligations and contracts, extends to conditions.[193] Thus, according to Article 1354 c.c., a contract depending upon condition will not be effective if condition violates principles of public policy. If it is a condition precedent, the contract is void; if it is condition subsequent, the parties must act as if the condition had never been agreed upon.[194]

212. Parties can reach an agreement on an implied basic assumption left indefinite (*condizione inespressa or presupposizione*). The missing term may be inferred from surrounding circumstances by the court.[195]

II. Terms

213. Terms are limitations in time to the effects of a contract (Article 1184 c.c.). Terms may be initial (effectiveness starting from …) or final (effectiveness lasting until …). With reference to contracts containing terms, according to Article 1457 c.c. if a deadline term for performance has been agreed to be essential to a party, the latter must notify her intention to accept late performance within three days from expiration.

193. Cass. 4769/1989; Cass. 8/1990; Cass. 3181/1990.
194. Cass. May 24, 1991, n. 3185, annotated by Musy, A.M., "Condizione unilaterale di vendita immobiliare," in *Giur. it.*, 1992, I, at 908.
195. Cass. Civ., sez. I, Mar. 5, 2018, n. 5112; Cass. Sep. 17, 1970, n. 1512 (*Foro it.*, 1971, I, 3028); Cass. Apr. 7, 1971, n. 1025 (*Foro it.* 1971, I, 2574); Cass. Sep. 22, 1981, n. 5168, (*Foro it.*, 1982, I, 104); Cass. Oct. 31, 1989, n. 4554 (*Riv. dir. civ.*, 1990, II, 350); Cass. Aug. 11, 1990, n. 8200; Cass. Dec. 3, 1991, n. 12921 (*Giur. it.*, 1992, I, 1, 2210); Cass. 1040/1995; Cass. 8689/1995.

Chapter 4. Privity of Contract

M. Balestrieri

§1. The Rule of Privity of Contract

I. Third Parties and the Contract

214. Privity of contract implies that contractual rights and duties only affect the parties to a contract (*res inter alios acta neque nocere neque prodesse potest*). Under Italian law, the privity of contract rule is an implicit rule set by the Civil Code, and may also be expressed in the fundamental principle whereby contract can neither impose obligations on other people, nor confer rights upon them.

215. Examples of this rule can be found in various sections of the code. According to Article 1379 c.c., for instance, the parties may choose to be mutually barred from alienating contractual rights or interests thereof; however, such prohibition, as established by contract, is effective only between the parties. Article 1381 considers the case whereby one party promises performance by a third person: "One who has promised an obligation or an act of a third person is bound to indemnify the other contracting party if such third person refuses to be bound or fails to perform the promised act."[196] Moreover, Articles 1398–1399 c.c. require that "a person who executed a contract acting as a representative of another without having the power to do so, or acting beyond the powers conferred on him, is liable for damage to third parties," although the contract can be ratified by the principal.

II. Contracts for Persons to Be Named

216. According to Articles 1401–1402 c.c., upon execution of contract a party may reserve the power to subsequently appoint the person who is to acquire the rights and assume the obligations arising from the said contract.[197]

196. *See* Trib. Milano, Dec. 17, 2018, n. 658; Cass. Civ., sez. I, Dec. 3, 2001, n. 15235; Cass. Apr, 11, 1990, n. 3082 (*Riv. dir. comm.*, 1992, II, at 485, annotated by Colombo); Cass. Dec. 20, 1995, n. 12973 (*Danno e resp.*, 1996, at 177, annotated by Marella, M.R.; *Giur. it.*, 1997, I, 1, at 989, noted by Steidl), confirmed by Trib. Genova, Oct. 14, 1995 (*Gius*, 1996, at 1023). Few scholars have dealt with this matter: *see* Marella, M.R., "Promessa del fatto del terzo," in *Digesto IV*, XV, Turin, 1996, at 381, and Corrias, "Sulla natura e sull'estensione dell'obbligazione del promittente nella promessa del fatto del terzo," in *Giur. it.*, 1994, I, 1, at 1643.

197. *See* Cass. Civ., sez. III, Sep. 29, 2006, n. 21254; Cass. Civ., sez. II, Jan. 24, 2017, n. 1797; Cass. Civ., sez. II, Mar. 14, 2018, n. 6223; Cass. Civ., sez. III, Jun. 12, 2018, n. 15215; Cass. Mar. 17, 1995, n. 3115 (*Giur. it.*, 1995, I, 1, 2025); Cass. Dec. 12, 1995, n. 12733 (*Foro it.*, 1996, I, 2162); Trib. Salerno, Apr. 13, 1993 (*Dir. giur.*, 1993, 551 annotated by Gimmelli).

217. Appointment must be notified to the other party within three days from contract execution, unless the parties have established a different time limit.[198] Such declaration is not effective unless it includes acceptance by the person named or unless that person had previously granted power of attorney to the agent who executed the contract (Article 1403 c.c.).

218. Declaration or acceptance by the person named must be made following the same form used in making the contract, even if the law does not require such form. Thus, if the contract was made in writing, acceptance will have to be in writing as well. If the contract requires registration to produce certain effects (as is the case for mortgages), appointment requires registration as well to be effective (Article 1403 c.c.).[199]

219. When appointment was validly made, the person appointed acquires the rights and obligations arising from the contract, effective from the date when the contract was made (Article 1404 c.c.).[200]

220. If appointment is not validly made within the time set by law or by the parties, the contract is binding and effective with respect to the original contracting parties (Article 1405 c.c.).[201]

III. Contract in Favor of Third Persons

221. A stipulation in favor of a third person is valid and effective when the stipulator has an interest therein (Articles 1411–1413 c.c.).[202]

Unless otherwise agreed, the third person acquires a right with respect to the promisor as a result of such stipulation. The agreement may however be revoked or modified by the stipulator at any time until the third person declares her intention to make use of the stipulation.[203]

---

198. Radice, C., "Dichiarazione di nomina preliminare," in *Contratti*, 1994, at 261; according to Trib. Trento, Jan. 7, 1993 (*Riv. not.*, 1993, 919, annotated by Dolzani and Corso), parties may establish a different time limit as long as such limit is certain; otherwise, the legal rule will apply.
199. *See* Cass. Civ., sez. II, Sep. 21, 2011, n. 19211; Cass. Civ., sez. II, Sep. 1, 2014, n. 18490; Cass. Civ., sez. II, Mar. 2, 2015, n. 4169.
200. Cass. Civ., sez. III, May 12, 2015, n. 9595.
201. Cass. Civ., sez. III, Sep. 29, 2006, n. 21254.
202. *See* Moscarini, L., "Il contratto a favore di terzi. Artt. 1411-1413," Giuffrè, Milan, 2012; Ferranti, I., "Causa e tipo nel contratto a favore di terzo," Giuffrè, Milan, 2005; Caliceti, "Contratto e negozio nella stipulazione a favore di terzi," Padua, 1994; Regoli, "In tema di efficacia reale del contratto a favore di terzo nei suoi rapporti con il patto di opzione," in *Riv. trim. dir. proc. civ.*, 1996, at 463; Moscarini, "Il contratto a favore di terzo," in "Commentario del Codice Civile" a cura di Schlesinger, Milan, 1997.
203. Cass. Jul. 29, 1995, n. 8343 (*Giust, civ.*, 1996, I, 122), distinguishing between contract in favor of a third person, agency in favor of the agent and agency in favor of the third party.

In case of revocation of the stipulation or refusal by the third person, the duty to perform for the benefit of the stipulator remains, unless it otherwise appears from the intention of the parties or the nature of the contract.[204]

222. Examples of stipulations in favor of a third person include several different fields of law. Insurance in favor of a third party is a typical example of such stipulations.[205] Furthermore, courts have regarded mistake by the doctor during the pregnancy as a breach of contract in favor of a future child.[206] Finally, it has been considered as a contract in favor of a third party (and not as donation) to register the company shares in the name of an employee in order to compensate his work for the company.[207] Furthermore, courts are discussing about classifying suretyship as a stipulation in favor of a third party.[208]

223. If performance is to be made to the third person after the death of the stipulator, the latter can revoke the benefit, even by will, notwithstanding the fact that the third person declared her intention to make use of the stipulation (unless the stipulator waived his power of revocation).

224. Performance is made in favor of the heirs of the third person if the latter dies before the stipulator, provided that the benefit had not been previously revoked (Article 1412 c.c.).[209]

225. Claims by the promisor against the third person must always be based on the stipulation. The promisor can never base his claims on other relationships (Article 1413 c.c.).[210]

---

204. *See* Cass. Aug. 9, 1996, n. 7398; Cass. Dec. 9, 1997, n. 12447; App. Turin, Feb. 24, 1996 (*Foro it.*, 1997, I, 281).
205. *See* Trib. Vicenza, sez. I, Mar. 21, 2017, n. 946; Cass. Civ., sez. III, Nov. 10, 2003, n. 16826; Cass. civile, sez. un., Apr. 18, 2002, n. 5556; Cass. May 25, 1995, n. 5747; Cass. Mar. 1, 1994, n. 2018 (*Arch. Circolazione*, 1994, 849); Cass. Aug. 20, 1997, n. 7769; Trib. Bari Apr. 8, 1993 (*Riv. dir. civ.*, 1995, II, 95); *contra*, Cass. Nov. 15, 1994, n. 9584 (*Arch. circolazione*, 1995, 625).
206. *See* Cass. Civ., sez. III, Feb. 5, 2018, n. 2675; Trib. Reggio Emilia, sez. II, Oct. 7, 2015, n. 1298; Cass. Nov. 22, 1993, n. 11503 (*Nuova giur. civ. comm.*, 1994, I, 690 annotated by Zeno Zencovich; *Rass. dir. civ.*, 1995, 908, annotated by Venneri, "Diritto del nascituro a nascere sano, obbligo di prestazione del medico e sua responsabilità").
207. Cass. Aug. 1, 1994, n. 7160 (*Giust. civ.*, 1995, I, 761; *Società*, 1995, 54, annotated by Montesano; Trib. Alba Feb. 21, 1996 (*Società*, 1996, 1419).
208. *See* Cass. Civ., sez. un., Feb. 18, 2010, n. 3947; Cass. Mar. 18, 1997, n. 2384; Trib. Trieste, Feb. 11, 1993 (*Dir. trasporti*, 1995, 159 annotated by Quici, "L'opponibilità all'assicurato della clausola di deroga alla competenza territoriale nell'assicurazione per conto di chi spetta").
209. Cass. Civ., sez. III, Apr. 20, 2016, n. 7785.
210. Cass. Civ., sez. III, Oct. 28, 2009, n. 22809.

§2. Transfer of Contractual Rights

226. Contract assignment is regulated by the Civil Code.[211] As a general rule, each party can be substituted by a third person in the relationships arising from contract as long as performance has not yet taken place and the other party agrees for substitution (Article 1406 c.c.).[212]

The assignor is bound to guarantee the validity of the contract. If the assignor undertakes to guarantee performance of contract, he is liable for the obligations of the original contracting party (Article 1410 c.c.).

227. If the clause "to order" (*all'ordine*) or equivalent clause thereof is placed in a document containing all of the elements of contract, endorsement of the document causes the endorsee to substitute the endorser in the contract. The assignor is released from his obligations towards the other contracting party as from the time when substitution becomes effective as to the latter (Article 1407 c.c.).

228. Specific rules regard subcontracts. The law requires no particular form for subcontracts.[213] However, if the principal had expressly refused to release the contractor from his duties, he can sue the contractor if the subcontractor fails to perform.

§3. Actions: "Azione Surrogatoria" and "Azione Revocatoria Ordinaria"

I. The Oblique Action

229. By the Oblique Action (*azione surrogatoria*, Article 2900 c.c.) creditors may protect their interests by exercising any rights and/or actions of their debtor except for claims of a purely personal nature.[214] The money due to the creditor bringing the action must be certain and payable.

If the debtor is manifestly solvent or if he is already persecuting his own claims by himself, creditors may not exercise the Oblique Action provided that their interest is held to be lacking.[215]

211. *See* Cass. Jun. 21, 1996, n. 5761 (*Riv. arbitrato*, 1996, 699); Trib. Udine, Dec. 21, 1992 (*Giur. merito*, 1994, 632); Trib. Cagliari, Feb. 4, 1995 (*Riv. giur. sarda*, 1995, 663).

212. Albanese, A., "Della cessione del contratto: Art. 1406-1410," Zanichelli, Bologna, 2008; Basini, G.F., "Forma del negozio di cessione del contratto e cedibilità dei contratti ad effetti reali," in *Contratti*, 1993, at 395; Carresi, F, "La cessione del contratto," Giuffrè, Milan, 1979.

213. *See* Cass. Dec. 19, 1996, n. 11381.

214. Micheli, G.A., Azzariti, G., Scarpello, G., "Della tutela dei diritti," in "Commentario del codice civile" a cura di Scialoja e Branca, Rome-Bologna, 1977; Rosselli, F., "I mezzi di conservazione della garanzia patrimoniale," Turin, 1997. *See also* De Santis, R., "Surrogatoria (azione)," in *Enc. giur.*, XXVIII, Roma, 1991, at 128.

215. Cass. Aug. 4, 1997, n. 7187.

230. Although it is brought by the creditor in his name, any action to recover owed monies belongs to the debtor; thus, if the creditor decides to exercise the Oblique Action, he must previously notify the debtor (Article 2900 c.c.).[216]

Creditors exercising the Oblique Action do not gain any privilege on the recovered property. This property simply falls into the debtor's general estate.

The bankruptcy of the debtor bars creditors from exercising the Oblique Action, as the bankruptcy trustee only is entitled to promote any actions in favor of the estate.[217]

II. The Paulian Action

231. The Paulian Action (Italian: *azione revocatoria*, Latin: *actio pauliana*, Article 2901 c.c.) allows creditors to question deeds by the debtor made in fraud of their rights.[218] The property of a debtor is the common pledge of his creditors: thus, the purpose of the Paulian Action is to protect creditors from being affected by transactions carried out by the debtor.[219]

232. The action deals with insolvency. Under the Bankruptcy Act (R.D. 267 of March 16, 1942 and subsequent amendments), only entrepreneurs may go bankrupt. Creditors of a bankrupt entrepreneur may not exercise the Paulian Action, as such action is left to the bankruptcy trustee (Article 64 Bankruptcy Act). On the contrary, if an individual becomes insolvent, each creditor is left to protect his own interests as best as he can. Thus, each creditor may exercise the Paulian Action.

233. The Paulian Action must be exercised under several conditions:

(1) there must be a creditor, a debtor and a debt;
(2) the money owed by the debtor must derive from an obligation established before the debtor's deed which is being challenged;
(3) the debtor's deed or transaction must be causing estate detriment (*eventus damni*);[220]

216. *See* Cass. Civ., sez. III, Jun. 8, 2007, n. 13391.
217. Cass. Apr. 12, 1994, n. 3413 (*Giust. civ.*, 1994, I, 2503).
218. *See* Trib. Roma, sez. I, Aug. 29, 2018, n. 16688; Trib. Genova, sez. I, Jan. 25, 2018, n. 299.
219. Vitalone, V., Patroni Griffi, U., Riedi, R., "Le azioni revocatorie: la disciplina, il processo," UTET, Wolters Kluwer, 2014; Nicolò, R., "La tutela dei diritti," in "Commentario del codice civile" a cura di Scialoja e Branca, Rome-Bologna, 1980; Lucchini Guastalla, E., "Danno e frode nella revocatoria ordinaria," Milan, 1995.
220. *See* Cass. Civ., sez. II, Aug. 11, 2016, n. 17029; Cass. Civ., sez. un., Mar. 28, 2006, n. 7028; Cass. Civ., sez. I, Aug. 25, 2006, n. 18550; Cass. Jun. 15, 1995, n. 6777; Cass. Jul. 10, 1997, n. 6272; Cass. Mar. 18, 1994, n. 2604 (*Nuova giur. civ.*, 1995, I, 266 annotated by Giuliano, "Natura giuridica dell'atto di costituzione del fondo patrimoniale e azione revocatoria"); Cass. Apr. 9, 1996, n. 3251; Cass. Sep. 2, 1996, n. 8013; Cass. Oct. 6, 1994, n. 8188 (*Giur. it.*, 1995, I, 1, 767 annotated by Armone, "Collegamento negoziale e azione revocatoria: qualche osservazione").

(4) there must have been fraud on the part of the debtor and knowledge of fraud on part of the third party executing the transaction with the debtor (*consilium fraudis*).[221]

The sale of the debtor's property for a cheap price is a typical Paulian Action case.[222]

234. The Paulian Action, if successful, does not bring the alienated property back into the estate of the debtor. Creditors who brought the action are characterized by a privileged position whenever assignment of the debtor's property and assets for the benefit of creditors occurs: the assignee must pay the claims of such creditors before any other creditors receive any dividend.

221. App. Palermo, sez. II, Feb. 17, 2017, n. 280; Trib. Grosseto, Dec. 11, 2017, n. 1257; Cass. May 10, 1995, n. 5095; Cass. Nov. 4, 1995, n. 11518; Cass. Sep. 28, 1996, n. 8581; Cass. Nov. 20, 1996, n. 10219; Cass. Mar. 19, 1996, n. 2303; Cass. Apr. 23, 1997, n. 3541; Cass. Jan. 13, 1995, n. 383 (*Corriere giur.*, 1995, 601, annotated by Maienza, "Responsabilità dell'acquirente di malafede dell'immobile oggetto di domanda giudiziale non trascritta," in *Riv. not.*, 1995, II, at 1565).
222. *See* for instance Cass. Feb. 21, 1996, n. 1341.

Chapter 5. Termination of Contract

M. Balestrieri

§1. Dissolution for Non-performance

235. Performance of obligations or duties is expressed by the Civil Code with the word "payment" (Articles 1176–1200 c.c.). Payment or *adempimento* (performance) of the obligation does not only imply delivery of a sum of money, but also performance of any specific obligation. Performance may consist of *giving* something or *doing something*, or of *abstaining from doing* something.[223]

236. In contracts providing for mutual obligations, when one of the parties fails to perform her duties, the other party may choose to require either specific performance or termination of contract. That party will in any case be entitled to compensation for damages (Article 1453 c.c. and Article 1223 c.c.).[224]

Violations of the good faith principle do not imply contract dissolution. However, as has been previously said, such violations call for pre-contractual liability.[225]

237. Termination can be demanded even when the plaintiff has brought action demanding specific performance; however, performance can no longer be required after an Action for Termination has been brought (Article 1453 section 2 c.c.).[226]

Plaintiffs cannot change from an Action for Termination to an Action for Specific Performance (*mutatio libelli*). Change has however been considered admissible when plaintiff's interest to specific performance arose *after* the Action for Termination had been barred.[227]

238. The defaulting party can no longer perform her obligation after Action for Termination has been brought (Article 1453 c.c., III co.).[228] However, the other party can serve written notice on the defaulting party to perform her contractual

223. Mengoni, L., "Responsabilità contrattuale (diritto vigente)," in *Enc.dir.*, XXXIX, Milan, 1988, at 1072; Bessone, "Adempimento e rischio contrattuale," Milan, 1969, at 121 et seq.; Alpa, "I contratti in generale. Introduzione alla nuova giurisprudenza," Turin, 1990.

224. Monateri, P.G., "La responsabilità contrattuale e precontrattuale," Turin, 1998; De Nova, G., "Recesso e risoluzione nei contratti," Milan, 1994; Palmieri, D., "La responsabilità contrattuale," Milan, 1994; Giardina, "Responsabilità contrattuale e responsabilità extracontrattuale—Significato attuale di una distinzione tradizionale," Milan, 1993.

225. Cass. Nov. 19, 1994, n. 9802 (*Rass. locazioni*, 1995, 65, annotated by Guida).

226. *See* Cass. Mar. 2, 1996, n. 1636 (*Giust. civ.*, 1996, I, 1963); Cass. Nov. 27, 1996, n. 10506; Cass. Mar. 27, 1996, n. 2715; Cass. Apr. 17, 1996, n. 3623; Cass. Dec. 22, 1995, n. 12092; Cass. Dec. 19, 1995, n. 12943; Cass. May 24, 1993, n. 5838 (*Giur. it.*, 1994, I, 1, 1376); Cass. Mar. 27, 1996, n. 2715; Cass. Jul. 22, 1993, n. 8192; Cass. Jun. 2, 1992, n. 6701.

227. *See* Cass. Civ., sez. II, Nov. 27, 2018, n. 30713; Cass. May 11, 1996, n. 4444 (*Corriere giur.*, 1996, 898 annotated by Carnevali); Cass. Feb. 9, 1995, n. 1457 (*Giur. it.*, 1996, I, 1, 1150 annotated by Lascialfari).

228. *See* Cass. Civ., sez. II, Jan. 24, 2019, n. 2037; Cass. Feb. 14, 1994, n. 1460 (*Giur. it.*, 1995, I, 1, 1379 annotated by Vitiello); Trib. Bari, Oct. 7, 1994 (*Giur. pugliese*, 1995, 13); Cass. S.U. Apr. 10, 1995, n. 4126 (*Giust. civ.*, 1995, I, 2394; *Corriere giur.*, 1995, 557 annotated by Carbone).

duties within an appropriate time, with the warning that, unless performance takes place within such time, the contract shall be deemed dissolved (Article 1454 c.c.).[229] The deadline must be of at least fifteen days, unless the parties have otherwise agreed or unless a shorter period appears justified by the nature of the contract or by usage. If the time elapses without performance having been made, the contract is dissolved at law.[230]

239. A contract cannot be dissolved if failure to perform by one party regards duties of slight importance (Article 1455 c.c.).[231]

Moreover, contracting parties can expressly agree that the contract will be dissolved if a specific duty or obligation is not performed in a designated manner (Article 1456 c.c.).[232]

240. If the time fixed for performance is essential for the other party, the latter may require performance of the obligation notwithstanding expiration of the time limit by notifying the former within three days. In the absence of such notice, the contract is deemed dissolved by operation of law, even if dissolution was not expressly agreed upon (Article 1457 c.c.).[233]

241. Dissolution of a contract for failure to perform has a retroactive effect between the parties, except for contracts whereby performance is continued over time (such as contract for the supply of electricity), where dissolution has no effect on past performance (Article 1467 c.c.).[234] Dissolution, even if expressly agreed

229. Cass. Civ., sez. II, Jun. 11, 2018, n. 15052; Cass. Jan. 27, 1996, n. 639 (*Vita not.*, 1996, 853); Cass. Jan. 29, 1996, n. 908; Cass. Apr. 8, 1997, n. 3446.
230. Grisi, G, "Responsabilità e risoluzione del contratto," in *Europa e Dir. Priv.*, fasc.4, at 1129; Spirito, A., "Diffida ad adempiere e risoluzione del contratto," in *Corriere giur.*, 1994, at 838 commenting Cass. May 4, 1994, n. 4275.
231. Monateri, P.G., "La responsabilità contrattuale e precontrattuale," Turin, 1998; De Nova, "Recesso e risoluzione nei contratti," Milan, 1994; Sacco—De Nova, "Il contratto," *cit.*, vol. II, at 599; De Lorenzi, "Inadempimento doloso," in *Digesto IV*, vol. IX, Turin, 1993, at 360; Nova, D., "Risoluzione dei contratti di fornitura dei sistemi informatici," commenting Trib. Turin, Mar. 13, 1993 (*Contratti*, 1993, at 440).
232. Amadio, G., "La condizione d'inadempimento," Padua, 1996; Barone, Chirico, Cirillo, Di Meo, "La clausola risolutiva espressa. Rassegna di giurisprudenza 1942–1992," Padua, 1993.
233. *See* Cass. Feb. 24, 1993, n. 2263 (*Foro it.*, 1993, I, 3447); Trib. Piacenza May 2, 1994 (*Arch. civ.*, 1995, 406); App. Perugia Jan. 22, 1993 (*Rass. giur. umbra,* 1993, 257), and recently Cass. Feb. 27, 1996, n. 1537; Cass. Mar. 3, 1997, n. 1851. *See also* Sirgiovanni, B., "Termine essenziale. Spunti per uno studio sullo scioglimento del contratto," in *Europa e Dir. Priv.*, fasc. 4, 2014, at 1359; Mazzamuto, S., "Le nuove frontiere della responsabilità contrattuale," in *Europa e Dir. Priv.*, fasc. 3, 2014, at 713; Di Majo, F., "Risoluzione del contratto ed effetti restitutori: debito di valore o debito di valuta?," commenting Cass. S.U. Dec. 4, 1992, n. 12942 (*Corriere giur.*, 1993, 322); Di Majo, F., "Restituzioni e responsabilità nelle obbligazioni e nei contratti" (*Riv. crit. dir. priv.*, 1994, 291).
234. Cass. Civ., sez. II, Nov. 7, 2017, n. 26363.

upon (Article 1456 c.c.), may generally not cause prejudice to rights acquired by third persons.[235] Such rights are thus protected at law in case of contract dissolution.

242. As a general rule, failure to perform by one party in contracts whereby the parties are three or more does not cause dissolution of the contract with respect to the other parties, unless such failure is essential under the circumstances (Articles 1446, 1459 and 1466 c.c.).[236]

§2. Supervening Impossibility

243. According to Article 1463 c.c., in bilateral contracts whereby one party is released from her contractual duties for supervening impossibility to perform (Article 1256 c.c.), that party cannot demand performance by the other party, and is bound to return any monies received or restore any preexisting order between the parties in accordance with the rules concerning restitution of payments not due (Article 2033 c.c.).[237]

244. When performance by one party has become only *partially* impossible, the other party may require her own performance to be proportionally reduced, or may choose to withdraw from contract if she has no appreciable interest in partial performance (Article 1464 c.c.).[238]

245. In contracts for the transfer of ownership or other rights in rem whenever property perishes and destruction of property may not be ascribed to the transferring party, the transferee is still bound to perform his own contractual obligations (Article 1465 c.c.).[239] The same provision applies if transfer of interest is deferred until expiration of a time limit. Whenever the object of the transfer is specified only as to kind (Article 1178 c.c.), and the transferor has made delivery or the object of

235. Cass. Feb. 24, 1995, n. 2135 (*Giur. it.*, 1995, I, 1, 1632); Cass. Feb. 16, 1994, n. 2456 (*Giur. it*, 1994, I, 1, 680); Trib. Potenza Jun. 20, 1991 (*Giur. merito*, 1993, 364); Trib. Cagliari Apr. 29, 1991 (*Riv. giur. sarda*, 1993, 29); App. Milan Mar. 4, 1994 (*Società e dir.*, 1994, 508); Cass. Civ., sez. II, Jan. 29, 1983, n. 817.

236. *See* App. Roma Jul. 15, 1997, n. 2413; Pret. Forlì May 31, 1993 (*Giust. civ.*, 1994, I, 815 annotated by Calì).

237. On supervening impossibility, *see* Inzitari, B., "Inesigibilità della prestazione, impossibilità della prestazione per l'embargo contro l'Iraq," in *Nuova giur. civ.*, 1995, II, at 48; Stella, "Impossibilità della prestazione per fatto imputabile al creditore," Milan 1995, at 352 et seq.; *see also* Cass. Nov. 9, 1994, n. 9304; Cass. Jan. 28, 1995, n. 1037; Cass. Aug. 28, 1993, n. 9125 (*Foro it.*, 1995, I, 1601 annotated by Cosentino); Cass. Feb. 14, 1996, n. 1104; Trib. Napoli, Feb. 25, 1993 (*Riv. dir. comm.*, 1994, II, 545 annotated by De Michel); Cass. Jul. 13, 1996, n. 6354; App. Roma Jun. 10, 1997, n. 2007; Cass. Apr. 10, 1995, n. 4119; Cass. Mar. 20, 1997, n. 2487.

238. Cass.civ., sez. lav., Aug. 3, 2018, n. 20497; Cass. Apr. 29, 1993, n. 5066 (*Nuova giur. civ.*, 1994, I, 489 annotated by De Poli); Cass. Feb. 12, 1993, n. 1782; Cass. Mar. 14, 1997, n. 2274.

239. *See* Cass. Civ., sez. II, Mar. 10, 2011, n. 5734; Lopez De Gonzalo, "Consegna e trasferimento del rischio nella vendita marittima," in *Dir. maritt.*, 1994, at 105; Cass. Nov. 15, 1995, n. 11834 (*Società*, 1996, 771).

transfer is identified (Article 1378 c.c.), the transferee must perform his own contractual obligations.[240] In all such cases the transferee is released from his duty to perform if the transfer was subject to condition precedent and impossibility occurred before fulfillment of the condition (Article 1465 section 3, c.c.).

246. In agreements whereby there are more than two contracting parties, impossibility of performance by one of the parties does not cause dissolution of the contract with regard to the others, unless performance not made must, under the circumstances, be considered essential (Article 1466 c.c.).[241]

§3. Excessively Burdensome Performance

247. According to Article 1467 c.c., in contracts where performance is continued or deferred, if extraordinary and unforeseeable events make performance for one of the parties excessively burdensome, that party may require dissolution of the contract.[242] In contracts where performance is continued, the effect of dissolution does not extend to performance already made.[243]

The other party may avoid dissolution by offering to modify conditions of contract in a reasonable and equitable way.[244] In contracts whereby only one party has duties and obligations, excessively burdensome performance entitles that party to require his performance to be reduced or modified (Article 1468 c.c.).[245]

248. Dissolution cannot be demanded if burdensome performance is part of the normal risk of contract, such as for insurance coverage against fire or earthquake (Article 1469 c.c.).[246]

---

240. *See* Trib. Cagliari Mar. 15, 1993 (*Banca, borsa*, 1994, II, 442).
241. *See* for instance App. Roma Jul. 15, 1997, n. 2413.
242. Cass. Civ., sez. II, Aug. 8, 2003, n. 11947; Cass. civile, sez. III, May 25, 2007, n. 12235.
243. On excessively burdensome performance, *see* Gabrielli, E., "L'eccessiva onerosità sopravvenuta," Giappichelli, Turin, 2012; Terranova, "L'eccessiva onerosità sopravvenuta nei contratti," Milan, 1996; Breccia, "Le obbligazioni," Milan, 1991, at 743.
244. *See* Cass. Jun. 13, 1997, n. 5349; Cass. Jan. 30, 1995, n. 1090; Cass. Jan. 5, 1995, n. 191 (*Foro pad.*, 1995, fasc. 2, I, 11); Cass. Feb. 13, 1995, n. 1559 (*Foro it.*, 1995, I, 2897); Cass. Jan. 28, 1995, n. 1027 (*Foro it.*, 1995, I, 2898).
245. Cass. Civ., sez. II, 25 marzo 2009, n. 7225; Cass. Jan. 13, 1995, n. 369; App. Milan Mar. 4, 1994 (*Dir. ind.*, 1995, 33, annotated by Leone).
246. Cass. Civ. sez. VI, Oct. 2, 2018, n. 23912; Trib. Potenza, Sep. 1, 2007; Cass. Feb. 19, 1997, n. 1516; Cass. Jan. 26, 1993, n. 948 (*Contratti*, 1993, 532); Trib. Turin Oct. 15, 1996 (*Giust. civ.*, 1997, I, 1409 annotated by Cervini, "Risoluzione per ecces-siva onerosità sopravvenuta nei mutui di valuta"); *Id.*, "Mutui di valuta e rischi di cambio per realità e presupposizione" (*Giust. civ.* 1996, II, 327).

Chapter 6. Remedies

P.G. Monateri

§1. Specific Performance, Restitution, Termination

249. If one party to a contract fails to perform her obligation to deliver a specified movable or immovable thing (Article 1218 c.c.), the party entitled to performance may obtain forced delivery in accordance with the provisions of the Code of Civil Procedure (Article 2930 c.c.). In the case of failure to perform an obligation *to do something*, the party entitled thereto can require specific performance at the expense of the party who failed to perform, according to the formalities set out in the Code of Civil Procedure (Article 2931 c.c.).[247]

250. It is also possible to require specific performance of the obligation *to make a contract*. Whenever the party being contractually bound to such duty fails to perform, the other party may require a court judgement producing the same effects as the contract which was not executed (Article 2932 c.c.).[248]

251. In the case of contracts for the transfer of ownership or contracts establishing or transferring rights (Article 1376 c.c.), no action can be granted if the party bringing the action fails to perform her own obligations or does not offer to do so according to the formalities prescribed by the law (Articles 1208 et seq., c.c.), unless, under the circumstances, the other party cannot yet require such performance.[249]

252. In the case of failure by one party to perform an obligation to *refrain from doing* something, the other party may require her counterpart to destroy, at her expense, that which was done in violation of such obligation (Article 2933 c.c.).[250] This rule often applies to buildings constructed on premises without the owner's consent. If destruction may cause prejudice to "national economy," such destruction cannot be ordered and the person entitled to require it can only recover damages.[251]

---

247. *See* Cass. Civ., sez. II, Oct. 4, 2018, n. 24239; Cass. Mar. 1, 1995, n. 2346; Cass. Dec. 11, 1995, n. 12653.
248. *See* for instance Cass. Civ., sez. II, Nov. 23, 2018, n. 30469; Cass. Mar. 8, 1995, n. 2697; Cass. May 30, 1995, n. 6071 (*Foro it.*, 1995, I, 2819); Cass. Jan. 24, 1997, n. 752; Cass. Jul. 15, 1997, n. 6471; Cass. Mar. 26, 1997, n. 2692; Cass. Oct, 23, 1995, n. 11001 (*Dir. giur. agraria*, 1996, II, 313).
249. Guarnieri, P., "Contratto preliminare, contratto definitivo e '*mutatio libelli*'," in *Arch. civ.*, 1996, at 1134 and 1331; Visalli, "L'esecuzione in forma specifica dell'obbligo di concludere un contratto," Padova, 1995, at 11et seq.; La Rocca, "L'esercizio in via surrogatoria del diritto nascente dal preliminare: profili problematici," in *Foro it.*, 1996, I, at 882; Regine, "Questioni in tema di contratto preliminare e di comunione legale," in *Nuova giur. comm.*, 1995, I, at 889; Fabrizio, "Esecuzione del preliminare di società," in *Società*, 1996, at 1179.
250. Trib. Verbania, Feb. 8, 2018, n. 600.
251. *See* Cass. May 24, 1997, n. 4770; Cass. Dec. 17, 1997, n. 12735.

§2. Exceptio Non Adimpleti Contractus

253. The Civil Code provides several examples of situations where one party to a contract may refrain from performing on the basis of the other party's failure to perform (*exceptio non adimpleti contractus*).

254. In bilateral contracts, for example, each party can refuse to perform her obligation if the other party does not perform or offer to perform her own at the same time. The rule clearly does not apply if different times for performance were established by the parties or appear from the nature of the contract.[252] Furthermore, performance cannot be refused if, considering the circumstances, such refusal is contrary to "good faith" (Article 1460 c.c.).[253]

By another example, each party to contract can withhold performance if the other party's state of insolvency is such as to obviously endanger fulfillment of her performance. The rule does not apply if the insolvent party provides adequate security (Article 1461 c.c.).[254]

255. A contractual clause providing that one of the parties cannot set up defenses for the purpose of avoiding or delaying contractual performance, has no effect with respect to claims for nullity (Article 1418 c.c.), subsequent annulment (Article 1425 c.c.) and rescission (Article 1447 c.c.) of contract. In cases whereby the clause is effective courts may withhold sentence requiring the other party to provide security (Article 1462 c.c.).

§3. Damages

256. The measure of damages arising from delay in performance or failure to perform contractual obligations comprises of the *loss* sustained by the creditor and the *lost profit* s, insofar as they are a direct and immediate consequence of the delay or failure to perform (Article 1223 c.c.).[255]

---

252. *See* Sacco—De Nova, "Il contratto," *cit.*, vol. II, at 243; Breccia, "Le obbligazioni," *cit.*, at 563; Zampetti, E., "Eccezione di inadempimento e onere della prova," in *Foro it.*, 1995, I, at 2615; Giombini, "Inapplicabilità della tutela ex Art.1460 c.c. alla vendita forzata," in *Corriere giur.*, 1996, at 437.

253. Cass. Civ., sez. II, Oct. 31, 2018, n. 27994; Cass. Jan. 10, 1994, n. 162 (*Giur. It.*, 1994, I, 1, 982); Cass. Jun. 19, 1995, n. 6940 (*Corriere giur.*, 1996, 437); Cass. Aug. 11, 1997, n. 7480; Cass. Jun. 13, 1997, n. 5351; Pret. Turin Feb. 20, 1995 (*Foro it.*, 1995, I, 2615); Pret. Rome Jan. 10, 1995 and Pret. Rome Jul. 20, 1994 (*Dir.e giur.*, 1995, 190).

254. *See* Cass. Civ., sez. I, Oct. 31, 2018, n. 27932; Cass. Dec. 3, 1993, n. 12011 (*Dir. Ed econ. Assicuraz.*, 1994, 301); Cass. Apr. 19, 1996, n. 3713 (*Foro it.*, 1996, I, 2389); Cass. Sep. 28, 1996, n. 8567; Cass. Jan. 28, 1995, n. 1032; Cass. Jun. 22, 1994, n. 5979.

255. Monateri, P.G., "La responsabilità civile," Utet, Turin, 1997, at 101 et seq.; Bianca, "Diritto civile. La responsabilità," V, Giuffrè, Milan, 1994, at 109 et seq.; Visintini, "Trattato breve della responsabilità civile," Padua, Cedam, 1996, at 509 et seq.; Carbone, "Il rapporto di causalità," in "Responsabilità civile" a cura di Alpa e Bessone, 1988–1996, I, Turin, 1997, at 51 et seq.; Alpa, Bessone, Zeno Zencovich, "I fatti illeciti," in "Trattato Rescigno," XIV, Turin 1995, at 464 et seq.; Franzoni, "Fatti illeciti," in "Commentario del codice civile" a cura di Scialoja e Branca, Zanichelli, Bologna-Rome, 1993, at 795 et seq.

When damages cannot be proved in their exact amount, they are equitably liquidated by the court (Articles 2056 c.c. and 1226 c.c.).[256]

257. With reference to obligations regarding sums of money (Articles 1217 et seq., c.c.), legal interest is due from the day of default even if it was not previously due and even if the creditor fails to prove that he has suffered any damage (Article 1284 c.c.). If interest was due at a rate higher than the legal rate before default, interest after default shall be due at the same rate.[257] The creditor who proves having suffered greater damages is entitled to recover additional compensation, unless interest to be paid after default had been previously agreed upon by the contracting parties (Article 1224 section 2, c.c.).[258]

258. If delay or failure to perform is not caused by the debtor's fraud or malice, compensation is limited to the damages that could have reasonably been foreseen at the time when the obligation was established (Article 1225 c.c.).[259]

If the debtor employed any third persons for performance of the obligation, he is also liable for their malicious, fraudulent or negligent deeds, unless otherwise agreed by the parties (Article 1229 c.c.).[260]

If the creditor's negligence has contributed to causing the damage, damage compensation is reduced accordingly.[261]

Moreover, compensation is not due for damages that the creditor could have avoided by using ordinary diligence (Article 1227 c.c.).[262]

256. *See* Cass. Dec. 27, 1996, n. 11535 (*Gius*, 1997, 6, 743); Cass. Nov. 11, 1996, n. 9835 (*Gius*, 1997, 3, 318); Cass. Jul. 13, 1996, n. 6366 (*Not. Giur. Lav.*, 1996, 847); Cass. Mar. 6, 1995, n. 2605 (*Giust. Civ.*, 1995, I, 1462). *See also* recently Comm. Trib. Reg. Potenza, sez. II, Mar. 2, 2018, n. 146; Cass. Civ., sez. II, Feb. 22, 2018, n. 4310; Cass. Civ., sez. III, May 18, 2017, n. 12470; Cass. Civ., sez. III, Oct. 17, 2016, n. 20889; Cass. Civ., sez. III, Jan. 8, 2016, n. 127; Cass. Civ., sez. II, Sep. 8, 2015, n. 17752; Trib. Roma, sez. XII, May 28, 2014, n. 11883.

257. *See* Cass. Oct. 19, 1994, n. 8533 (*Gius*, 1995, 6, 522); Cass. Mar. 29, 1994, n. 3078; Cass. Nov. 18, 1996, n. 10069 (*Gius* 1997, 4, 469); Cass. Jun. 27, 1997, n. 5772 (*Fallimento*, 1998, 47).

258. *See* Cass. S.U. Apr. 5, 1986, n. 2368 (*Foro it.*, 1986, I, 1265 annotated by Pardolesi and Amatucci; *Foro it.*, 1986, I, 1540, annotated by Valcavi and *Foro it.*, 1986, I, 3034 annotated by Quadri; *Giur. It.*, 1986, I, 1, 1160, annotated by Inzitari, *Giur. It.*, 1986, I, 1, 1389, annotated by Eroli).

259. Pinori, A., "Prevedibilità del danno," in *Riv. dir. civ.*, 1994, II, at 139; *see also* Cass. Mar. 6, 1995, n. 2605 (*Giur. it.*, 1995, I, 1462).

260. *See* Cass. Jul. 28, 1997, n. 7061; Cass. Jul. 10, 1996, n. 6298 (*Gius*, 1996, 21, 3185); Cass. Dec. 6, 1994, n. 10457 (*Foro it.*, 1995, I, 3258 annotated by Simone).

261. *See* Cons. Stato, sez. V, Dec. 22, 2014, n. 6253; Cass. Civ., sez. III, Oct. 23, 2014, n. 22514; Cass. Civ., sez. III, Feb. 10, 2005, n. 2704; T.A.R. Napoli, sez. V, Jul. 4, 2002, n. 3927; Monateri, P.G., Gianti, D., Balestrieri, M., "Causazione e giustificazione del danno," Giappichelli, Turin, 2006; Bianca, M., "Dell'inadempimento delle obbligazioni," in "Commentario del codice civile" a cura di Scialoja e Branca, II ed., Bologna-Rome, 1979, at 403; Traverso, M.C., "Causalità e colpevolezza nel concorso di colpa del danneggiato," in *Nuova giur. Civ.* 1994, II, at 235 et seq.; Bochicchio, M., "Il concorso colposo del danneggiato. Responsabilità e correttezza," in *Riv. crit. dir. priv.*, 1992, at 23.

262. *See* Cass. Civ., sez. III, Oct. 5, 2018, n. 24522; Cass. Civ., sez. III, Jan. 21, 2010, n. 1002; Cass. Mar. 28, 1997, n. 2763 (*Gius*, 1997, 12, 1518); Cass. Sep. 6, 1995, n. 9359 (*Fallimento*, 1996, 349); Cass. Mar. 6, 1995, n. 2605 (*Giust. civ.*, 1995, I, 1462).

259. According to the Civil Code, any agreement whereby liability of the debtor for fraud, malice or gross negligence is excluded or limited in advance, is void. Any agreement tending to exonerate from liability or limit liability in advance in cases whereby the act of the debtor or his staff (Article 1228 c.c.) constitutes a violation of a duty arising from rules of public policy, is also void.[263]

§4. Limitation of Actions

260. Limitation of actions fixes the time within which parties must take judicial action to enforce rights or else be thereafter barred from enforcing them. All rights are subject to limitation of actions (Article 2946 c.c.),[264] except for non-disposable rights and other rights specified by the law. Limitation of actions begins to run whenever a right is enforceable (Article 2935 c.c.). Any agreement intended to modify the legal rules on limitation of actions is void (Article 1418 c.c.).[265]

The right to enforce limitation of actions may be waived. A person who cannot validly dispose of a right, cannot waive the right to enforce limitation of actions (Article 2937 c.c.).[266] Furthermore, such right cannot be waived when the statute of limitations has run out.[267] Any act which is incompatible with the intention to take advantage of limitation of actions implies automatic renunciation thereof.[268]

261. When limitation of actions is not pleaded as a defense, the court cannot take notice of it ex officio (Article 2938 c.c.).[269] Limitation of actions can be claimed by creditors and by anyone having an interest thereof, even upon renunciation by the party entitled thereto (Article 2900 c.c., Article 2939 c.c.).[270]

As a general rule, the law provides no recovery of what has been spontaneously paid for in fulfillment of a debt whereby the statute of limitations has run out (Article 2940 c.c.).[271]

---

263. Trib. Torino, sez. VIII, Jan. 9, 2018, n. 24; Cass. Civ., sez. III, May 17, 2001, n. 6756; Cass. Feb. 20, 1996, n. 1321 (*Gius*, 1996, 11, 1358); Cass. Aug. 11, 1995, n. 8820 (*Banca, borsa*, 1997, II, 139).
264. Caponi, R., "Gli impedimenti all'esercizio dei diritti nella disciplina della prescrizione," in *Riv. dir. civ.*, 1996, I.
265. *See* Cass. Nov. 22, 1996, n. 10306; Cass. Mar. 14, 1994, n. 7618; Cass. Jun. 21, 1996, n. 5739; Cass. Jul. 26, 1996, n. 6750 (*Not. giur. lav.*, 1996, 957); Cass. Feb. 14, 1997, n. 1380; Cass. Mar. 10, 1997, n. 2111.
266. *See* Cass. Civ., sez. II, 04 giugno 2018, n. 14289.
267. *See* Cass. Aug. 9, 1996, n. 7318; Cass. Jan. 12, 1996, n. 178 (*Giust. civ.*, 1997, I, 215 annotated by Balzano).
268. *See* Cass. Jan. 7, 1994, n. 94 (*Giur. it.*, 1994, I, 1, 1160).
269. *See* App. Bari, sez. II, Dec. 22, 2017, n. 2194; Cass. Civ., sez. lav., Jan. 30, 2006, n. 2035; Cass. Oct. 28, 1994, n. 8913; Cons. Stato, Ad. plen., Jun. 27, 1996, n. 10 (*Giur. it.*, 1996, III, 1, 648); Cass. Feb. 7, 1996, n. 963; Cass. Mar. 2, 1995, n. 2412.
270. *See* Cass. May 1, 1995, n. 2328 (*Giur. it.*, 1997, I, 1, 276).
271. *See* Cass. Civ. sez. I, Dec. 14, 2018, n. 32524; Trib. Gela, Nov. 3, 2018, n. 585; Cass. Apr. 17, 1996, n. 3636; Cass. Civ., sez. I, Aug. 8, 1978, n. 3856.

262. Limitation of actions can be suspended at law due to special relationships between parties.[272] Such is the case between spouses, between parents, between guardian and infant or guardian and person of unsound mind subject to guardianship. Limitation of actions is suspended between a corporate entity and its administrators holding office with respect to actions for liability. It is also suspended between the debtor who has fraudulently concealed the existence of a debt and his creditor, until fraud has been discovered (Article 2941 c.c.).[273]

Suspension of limitation of actions also occurs with respect to certain persons under certain conditions,[274] such as non-emancipated minors and mentally insane persons whenever they do not have a guardian and for six months following his appointment. In time of war, limitation of actions is suspended with respect to any members of the Italian Army, whether regular or temporary, and with respect to those who, by reason of their office, are in any way attached to armed forces (Article 2942 c.c.).

263. Limitation of actions is interrupted by serving of process through delivery of a pleading, notice, or other paper in a suit (Articles 2905 and 2910 c.c.).[275] Limitation of actions is interrupted by the acknowledgement of the relevant right (Article 2944 c.c.).[276] It is also interrupted by actions brought in the course of judicial proceedings (Article 2945 c.c.),[277] and by any other act placing the debtor in default (Article 2943 c.c.).[278]

Interruption is effective even if the court hearing a matter lacks jurisdiction.

A new limitation of actions period begins as a result of interruption (Article 2945 c.c.).[279]

When a right must be exercised within a given time under penalty of forfeiture, the rules relating to interruption of limitation of actions do not apply (Article 2943 c.c.). The rules relating to suspension of limitation of actions are likewise inapplicable, unless otherwise provided (Article 2965 c.c.).[280]

264. Under the statute of limitations, ordinary limitation of actions runs out after ten years. With respect to the right to compensation for damages arising from torts, the statute of limitations runs out after five years from the date when damages

272. *See* Corte Cost. Jun. 27, 1997, n. 207; Cass. Mar. 21, 1997, n. 2515; Cass. Oct. 4, 1996, n. 8716.
273. On the point, *see* Notargiacomo, G., "Sospensione della prescrizione per doloso occultamento del debito da parte del debitore," in *Giur. It.*, 1996, I, at 2037.
274. *See* Cass. Jun. 2, 1993, n. 2169 (*Vita not.*, 1994, I, 240; *Giur. It.*, 1994, I, 1, 1214).
275. *See* Cass. Sep. 7, 1994, n. 7688; Cass. Jul. 1, 1994, n. 6232; Cass. Sep. 15, 1997, n. 9177; Cass. Feb. 22, 1994, n. 1727; Cass. Aug. 7, 1996, n. 7247.
276. *See* Cass. May 9, 1997, n. 4060; Cass. Jul. 2, 1997, n. 5948; Cass. Jun. 26, 1995, n. 7216 (*Giust. Civ.*, 1996, I, 1061).
277. Pisani, P., "Appunti sulla tutela c.d. costitutiva," in *Riv. dir. Proc. Civ.*, 1991, at 60.
278. *See* Cass. Jan. 19, 1995, n. 561; Cass. Dec. 3, 1994, n. 10384; Cass. Mar. 25, 1995, n. 3572; Cass. Apr. 18, 1997, n. 338.
279. *See* Cass. Civ., sez. III, Jul. 17, 2014, n. 16408; Cass. Nov. 6, 1995, n. 11556; Cass. May 22, 1995, n. 5603; Cass. Sep. 20, 1996, n. 8367; *see also* L. 96 of Apr. 7, 1997 (Art. 3, s. 1); D.L. 30 of Mar. 4, 1976 and Cass. Sep. 6, 1994, n. 7683.
280. Rosselli, F., "Decadenza," in *Enc. giur.*, X, Rome, 1988; Caponi, R., "Gli impedimenti all'esercizio dei poteri giuridici nella disciplina della decadenza," in *Riv. dir. civ.*, 1997, I, at 46.

occurred.[281] With respect to the right to compensation for damages arising from the circulation of vehicles of any kind, the statute of limitations runs out after two years (Articles 2054 c.c. and 2946 c.c.).[282] In any case, if the act is considered a criminal offense by the law and a longer limitation of actions term is established by criminal law provisions of the offense, such longer term applies to the civil action as well.[283] In all such cases, limitation of actions occurs upon expiration of the last day of the term set out by the law (Article 2962 c.c.).[284] Time is counted in accordance with the ordinary calendar and if the last day of the time limit falls on a holiday, it is postponed to the following working day by operation of law. Article 2963 c.c. provides specific rules whenever limitation of actions is measured on a monthly basis.

281. *See* Cass. Jul. 16, 1997, n. 6515; Cass. Sep. 23, 1997, n. 9368.
282. *See* Cass. Oct. 17, 1997, n. 10176; Cass. S.U., Nov. 11, 1991, n. 12014.
283. *See* Cass. Feb. 18, 1997, n. 1479 (*Foro it.*, 1997, I, 1868).
284. *See* Art. 3 Lease Act (L. 392/ 1978); *see also* Cass. Oct. 6, 1997, n. 9701.

Part II. Specific Contracts

Chapter 1. Agency

M. Balestrieri

§1. MANDATE, "DIRECT" AND "INDIRECT" AGENCY

265. Agency is a relationship between two persons, by agreement or otherwise, where one (the agent) may act on behalf of the other (the principal) and bind the principal by words and actions.[285] Agency may be created by express or implied contract, or by law. The contract whereby one party delegates the transaction of some lawful business to another is called a "mandate" and is governed by Articles 1703–1730 c.c.[286] Agency by operation of law regards situations where agency is imposed by statute or by court orders, such as parents and tutors acting on behalf of minors and insane persons (*see* Articles 320, 357 and 424 c.c.), or trustees in bankruptcy acting for the creditors and for bankruptcy estate (Article 31 Bankruptcy Act, R.D. 267 of March 16, 1942). As a general rule, nobody may act on behalf of another without that person's consent, except in certain situations where the other person is absent or may not otherwise deal with her business (*negotiorum gestio*, *see* below, Chapter 13).

266. A first distinction may be made between "direct" and "indirect" agency.[287] A direct agent acts in place of his principal with the power to do the things which the principal may do, and the affair is transacted on account of the principal (Article 1704 c.c.). Thus, the agent may negotiate and enter into an agreement which is binding for the principal only. An "indirect" agent acts under his own name although on behalf of his principal (Article 1705 c.c.): thus, if by mandate an agent is entrusted

285. *See* Bertolino, L., "Il contratto di agenzia," Giappichelli, Turin, 2016; Magri, M., "La rappresentanza del contratto," CEDAM—Wolters Kluwer, 2007; De Lorenzi, V., "Rappresentanza diretta volontaria nella conclusione dei contratti e analisi economica del diritto Valeria De Lorenzi," Giuffrè, Milan, 2002; Galgano, F., Visintini, G., "Degli effetti del contratto della rappresentanza," in "Commentario del codice civile" diretto da Scialoja—Branca, a cura di Galgano, F., Libro IV, Zanichelli-Foro Italiano, Bologna-Rome, 1993, at XXXi-388 et seq.

286. *See* Di Rosa, G., "Il mandato," Giuffrè, Milan, 2012; Lupoi, M., et al., "Fiducia, *trust*, mandato ed *agency*," Giuffrè, Milan, 1991, at 362 et seq.

287. *See* Cuffaro, V., "Il mandato. Disciplina e prassi," Zanichelli, Bologna, 2011; Chinè, G., "Mandato senza rappresentanza e *pactum fiduciae* a confronto," in *Giur.it.*, 1994, I, 1, 581.

to procure certain property for a principal and that agent buys the property, the conveyance is binding for the agent only, who becomes the owner of that property. It is the agent's duty according to the mandate agreement, to convey the property to his principal (Article 1706, section 2, c.c.).

267. Another distinction regards "special" and "universal" agency. In a "special" agency, the agent is authorized to conduct a single transaction or a series of transactions not involving continuity of service, whilst a "universal" agency is one in which the agent is empowered to conduct any transaction lawfully delegable by principal to agent.

268. Scholars also distinguish between an agent and a *nuncius*. A *nuncius*[288] is like a herald or an ambassador, who simply "brings the news" about another person's intention without cooperating in any way to the formation of that intention. For instance, when A goes to B and declares: "C has entrusted me to tell you that he accepts your proposal," he simply refers somebody else's statement. On the contrary, an agent acting for and on behalf of another person may bring about, modify, affect, accept performance of, terminate or manage certain affairs or business of his principal.

§2. Proxies

269. The power to act for and on behalf of another person is generally granted by procuracy. The instrument containing the appointment of a person as agent representing and acting for principal is called a power of attorney, or proxy (*procura*). A proxy differs from a mandate contract in that the former is a unilateral act granting representative powers to the agent, while the latter is a bilateral agreement whereby one person agrees to transact for another person and in his name one or several affairs in exchange for remuneration for the services rendered (Article 1703 c.c.). Although mandates generally require remuneration, the parties may agree that the agent's services be gratuitous (Article 1709 c.c.).[289] If the agent's interests are in conflict with those of the principal with respect to a mandate agreement, the latter may be made void (Article 1394 c.c.).

270. Proxies usually contain detailed instructions on how to transact some business or manage some affair of the principal, and often limit the agent's powers. Any transaction carried out by the agent which goes beyond such limitations is considered to be conducted personally by the agent, unless the principal ratifies the agent's

288. *See* Cossu, C., "*Nuncius*," in *Digesto IV*, Turin, 1995, vol. XII, at 329.
289. Cass. Civ., sez. II, Oct. 19, 2018, n. 26522.

conduct ("apparent" agency, *see* Article 1711 section 1, and Article 1399, c.c.). Failure to ratify implies that no valid transaction has occurred, and the agent is thus liable for any damages deriving from his behavior.[290]

An agent may appoint a third person to substitute him in his duties only if he is authorized to do so by the principal. Otherwise, the agent is personally responsible for any business conducted by his substitute on behalf of the principal (Article 1717 c.c.).[291]

271. Proxies may be granted informally or may be implicitly recognized by the principal: for instance, a cashier or a clerk in a retail shop is implicitly granted the power to sell the goods on behalf of the owner of the shop.[292] However, proxies *must* be granted in a special form whenever the business transaction which the agent is entrusted to conduct requires that form. Thus, for instance, a proxy authorizing an agent to sell his principal's house requires notarization.

Proxies may be granted to two or more agents who may be authorized to act jointly: in such case, if the proxy is contained in a mandate, the contract will not be operative unless each of the agents has accepted to act jointly with the others (Article 1716 c.c.).[293]

272. Proxies may be revoked by the principal at any time and do not require specific forms. Implied revocation occurs whenever the principal appoints another agent as a substitute of the original one (Article 1724 c.c.).[294] Proxies may be granted irrevocably: if such is the case, the principal may only revoke the proxy if he is supported by specific reasons, such as for unlawful conduct or unfaithful behavior by the agent (Articles 1723 section 2 and 1726 c.c.). Otherwise, unjustified revocation by the principal holds him liable for any damages caused to the agent.

It is the agent's duty to inform his counterparts of his powers and of any changes in the contents of his proxy or revocations thereof: thus, for instance, an agreement

---

290. For instance, third parties who were negotiating in good faith with the powerless agent may have relied on his position sustaining costs for negotiations, or may have given up other business opportunities. *See* Cass. Civ., sez. II, Jan. 24, 2018, n. 1751; Cass. Civ., sez. II, Dec. 27, 2017, n. 30938; Trib. Trani, sez. lav., Mar. 1, 2018, n. 462; Cass. Civ., sez. III, Jul. 9, 2001, n. 9289; Cass. Jul. 9, 1994, n. 6493, (*Riv. giur. edilizia*, 1995, I, 114); Cass. Jan. 24, 1995, n. 835; Cass. May 14, 1997, n. 4258 (*Foro it.*, 1997, I, 1748); Cass. Mar. 11, 1997, n. 2174 (*Giur. it.*, 1997, I, 1, 1300 annotated by Tassinari). For further comments, *see* Orlandi, "*Falsus nuncius e falsus procurator*," in *Riv. dir. civ.*, 1995, I, at 347; Gregorio, D., "La rappresentanza apparente," Padova, 1996. On ratification by the principal, *see* Cass. Mar. 9, 1995, n. 2730 (*Giust. civ.*, 1995, I, 2078); Cass. Mar. 20, 1995, n. 3225 (*Foro it.*, 1996, I, 203); *see also* Salanitro, U., "Contratto concluso con il falso rappresentante e tecniche di tutela del terzo contraente," in *Riv. dir. civ.*, 1997, I, at 469.
291. *See* Cass. Civ., sez. III, Jan. 23, 2018, n. 1580.
292. *See* Arts. 2210 and 2213 c.c.
293. *See* Cass. Civ., sez. II, Mar. 31, 2017, n. 8525; Cass. Civ., sez. II, May 23, 2012, n. 8164; Cass. Civ., sez. II, Mar. 8, 2006, n. 4921.
294. Cass. Civ., sez. II, Jun. 9, 1994, n. 5608; Cass. Civ., sez. II, Jun. 9, 1994, n. 5608.

entered into by third parties in good faith with the agent whose proxy had been previously revoked, is binding for the former agent only, not for the principal (Articles 1396 section 1 and 2207, c.c.).[295]

§3. Termination of Agency

273. Mandate agreements automatically terminate whenever the agent successfully achieves his task, or whenever the time limits to successfully achieve it have elapsed (Article 1722 c.c.).[296] Also, the death of the agent or principal implies early termination of a mandate agreement (Article 1722 c.c.). In case of death of the agent, his heirs must promptly inform the principal and may have to take further necessary steps according to the circumstances (Article 1728 c.c.).

274. Agency may cover any kind of business transaction: with very limited exceptions,[297] an agent may be authorized to execute any kind of contract on behalf of his principal. Agency is widely used in all major fields of business: corporate agents, soliciting agents, managing agents, mercantile agents, real estate agents are just some examples of how much agency relationship is used in modern society.

§4. Commission Merchants, Contracts to Procure Business and Shipment

275. Commission merchants execute mandates whereby they undertake to purchase or sell certain goods for and on behalf of another in exchange for a fee or commission. Commission merchants take no business risk provided that they are employed by the person on behalf of whom they are acting (Articles 1731 et seq., c.c.).[298]

276. Contracts to procure business are agreements whereby one party undertakes, in exchange for a fee or commission, to procure entry into arrangements on behalf of the other with reference to a particular market or area and with respect to a certain business (Article 1742 c.c.). The agent is *not* an employee of the principal:

295. Corporate law imposes stricter rules for proxies granted to the board of directors of a company: the company is directly responsible for any transactions executed in good faith by third parties with powerless directors even if the revocation of powers was recorded at the Public Registry of Corporations. In order to avoid the binding effect of the transaction, the company must prove the third party knew the directors were powerless and nevertheless conducted the transaction in bad faith (*see* Arts. 2383, 2384 and 2384 *bis*, c.c.).
296. Cass. Civ., sez. III, Aug. 11, 2000, n. 10739.
297. A donor may neither grant an agent the power to define the object of donation or to appoint the donee (Art. 777 c.c.), nor may parents or tutors acting for a minor or an insane person execute a donation for their principal (Art. 778 c.c.).
298. *See* Robles, M., "Il contratto di commissione. Artt. 1731-1736," Giuffrè, Milan, 2017.

he is a professional taking business risk, who is hired to take purchase orders or prepare drafts of agreements for the principal.[299] The agent may also be authorized to execute final agreements on behalf of the principal (Article 1752 c.c.). Contracts to procure business usually grant to agent an exclusive right to operate within a particular market or area: if the parties provide nothing of the sort, exclusivity is presumed to be operating (Article 1743 c.c.). The parties may agree for the contract to have limited or unlimited duration.

277. Contracts to procure business are frequently executed between property owners and real estate brokers, whereby the owner promises to pay a fee or commission to broker if his real property is sold during the listing period, regardless of whether the broker is responsible for the sale. Under L. 204 of May 3, 1985, real estate brokers must register under special rolls and listings kept by the Chambers of Commerce. Contracts to procure business with brokers who are not registered are in strict violation with legislative provisions and thus considered void.[300]

278. Contracts to procure business are to be distinguished from "mediation agreements," whereby a neutral person helps parties to get in contact and/or to reach an agreement (Article 1754 c.c.). If the parties actually reach an agreement and they had in any way requested the mediator's services, the mediator is entitled to remuneration even if the parties had not acknowledged any remuneration whatsoever (Article 1755 c.c. and Article 6 section 2, L. 39 of February 3, 1989). Under L. 39 of February 3, 1989, mediators must register under special listings kept by governmental agencies, and mediation agreements regarding mediators who are not registered are void.

279. Shipment is another form of agency. The seller or producer of goods puts the goods in the hands of a shipper, who tenders the goods to a carrier for transportation (Article 1737 c.c.). The shipper usually bears the risk of loss until the goods are tendered to the carrier.

299. *See* Cass. civ. Mar. 18, 1989, n. 1388; Cass. civ. Jan. 10, 1984, n. 182; Cass. civ. Dec. 10, 1982, n. 6770; Cass. civ. Nov. 10, 1977, n. 4845; Cass. civ. Apr. 22, 1974, n. 1131.
300. *See* Cass. civ. S.U. Apr. 3, 1989, n. 1613.

Chapter 2. Bailment

M. Balestrieri

§1. Ordinary Bailment

280. Bailment[301] is a delivery of movable assets by one person (the bailor) to another (bailee) upon a contract, express or implied, for the bailor to keep custody of the movable assets and redeliver them to the bailor (Article 1766 c.c.). Bailment only regards movable assets: custody with respect to immovable assets such as land or buildings may be the object of other kinds of contracts, such as surveillance or hire of work and skill. The bailor need not necessarily be the owner of the bailed goods. Bailments require delivery of the bailed goods for the contract to be binding (Article 1766 c.c.).

281. The parties to a bailment may contemplate some price or compensation for the bailee in return for the bailee's duties of custody and care. However, if remuneration is not expressly provided for, the contract is presumed to be gratuitous (Article 1767 c.c., what in American law is referred to as *depositum* or "naked bailment").[302]

282. The bailee is responsible for exercising due care towards the goods and for their custody (Article 1768 c.c.). He may neither dispose of the goods (Article 1770 c.c.), nor may he sub-bail them to another bailee without the bailor's consent.

283. As a general rule, the bailee must return the goods to the bailor upon the bailor's request, unless specific terms are provided by contract (Article 1771 c.c.). The bailee must also return any profits of the property (Article 1775 c.c.). The bailee may himself require that the bailor take the bailed goods back at any time (Article 1771, section 2 c.c.). If a third party claims to be the owner of the bailed goods and requires the bailee to return them, the bailee must wait until the controversy between the bailor and the claimant is settled in court before taking any possible step (Article 1777 c.c.).

§2. Bank Deposit Contracts

284. Bank deposit contracts are agreements between a payor bank and a customer governing rights and duties of the parties with respect to funds deposited by

301. On bailments, *see* Scalisi, A., "Il contratto di deposito. Artt. 1766-1797: Del deposito in generale, del deposito in albergo, del deposito nei magazzini generali," Giuffrè, Milan, 2011; Gardella Tedeschi, B., "Deposito—Comodato—Mutuo," in *Riv. dir. civ.*, 1995, II, 633; Martellino, G., "Il deposito: un contratto in bilico tra gratuità ed onerosità," in *Nuova giur. civ.*, 1993, I, 884.
302. App. Roma, sez. III, Mar. 15, 2011, n. 1077; Cass. Civ., sez. II, Nov. 17, 2010, n. 23211; Cass. Civ., sez. III, Jan. 13, 1993, n. 359.

the customer in an account maintained at the bank.[303] Bank deposit contracts are considered special kinds of bails, whereby the bailed goods consist of money or other consumables and the bank must return an equal amount of money upon specific request by the customer (Article 1782 c.c.). Bank deposit contracts are generally governed by the rules provided for by loans, except that bank customers may require their money to be returned at any time, while this does not apply to lender-debtor relations. Bank deposit contracts differ from current accounts, which are open, running accounts between two parties (Article 1823 c.c.).

§3. Special Bailments

285. For some bailments, by law a bailee is given greater duties and liabilities than those imposed on an ordinary bailee. Innkeepers and common carrier bailees are examples,[304] whereas they are liable under the strict liability theory for any destruction or theft of things kept in custody.[305] Innkeepers may be held liable for an amount equal to one hundred times the price of an average hotel room for one night (Article 1783 c.c.). Unlimited liability occurs when theft or destruction were due to the innkeeper's faulty or reckless behavior (Article 1785 *bis*, c.c.), and any agreement to reduce such liability is void (Article 1785 *quater*, c.c.). The same rules apply to theatres, cinemas, pensions, restaurants,[306] taxis, trains, etc. (Article 1786 c.c.).

Other special bails include "conventional" seizures, which occur whenever two parties to a dispute over the ownership of certain property agree to deliver that property to a bailee until their controversy is settled. In all such cases, the rules on ordinary bails apply (Article 1798 c.c.). However, the bailee is entitled to remuneration for the services rendered except where otherwise required (Article 1802 c.c.).

303. *See* Capobianco, E., "I contratti bancari," UTET—Wolters Kluwer, 2016.

304. *See* Salomoni, A., "La responsabilità del custode per la perdita della detenzione del bene ricevuto," in *Resp. civ. e prev.*, 2014, *at* 1435B; Di Bella, D., "Deposito, custodia e responsabilità delle officine di autoriparazione," in *Nuova giur. civ.*, 1997, I, 42; Natale, A., "In tema di deposito per la conservazione di merce deperibile," in Contratti, 1997, 141; Petricone, F., "Cassette bancarie di custodia e deposito in albergo," in *Nuova giur. civ.*, 1996, II, 185; Bonofiglio, A., "Il contratto di albergo ed il contratto di deposito alberghiero," in *Giust. civ.*, 1995, I, 2222; Tassoni, G., "Contratto di campeggio ed obblighi del gestore," in *Giur. it.*, 1994, I, 1, 1827.

305. Innkeepers are not liable for thefts or destruction due to irresponsible or reckless behavior by their guests, or due to force majeure (Art. 1785 c.c. as amended by L. 316 of Jun. 10, 1978). *See also* Caligiuri, S., "Furto della cosa depositata e responsabilità del custode," in *Giur. merito*, 1996, 68; Balzano, A., "Perdita della cosa depositata ed obbligo di denuncia," in *Giur. it.*, 1993, I, 1, 463. In case of theft involving the use of threat or violence against the bailee, courts tend to exclude liability: *see* Cass. Civ., sez. III, Mar. 7, 1981, n. 1288.

306. *See* App. Firenze, sez. II, Dec. 10, 2018, n. 2862; Trib. Milano, sez. VII, Apr. 13, 2012, n. 4342; Cass. Civ., sez. III, Oct. 4, 1991, n. 10393. *See also* Chinè, G., "Furto di indumenti e responsabilità del ristoratore (nota a Cass. sez. III, 4 ottobre 1991, n. 10393, Monteverda v. Di Primio)," in *Giur. it.*, 1992, I, 1, 1326.

Chapter 3. Gaming and Wagering

F. Chiaves

286. Wagers are agreements whereby two or more parties agree that a certain sum of money shall be paid or delivered to one of them or that they shall gain or lose on the happening of an uncertain event or upon the ascertainment of a fact in dispute.[307] Gaming differs from suretyship in that by gambling or betting, the parties have no interest in the event except that arising from the possibility of such gain or loss, whilst an insured chooses to be insured to prevent the property insured from a preexisting danger or hazard of a loss, injury or destruction.

287. In Italy, gaming is a monopoly of the State. Betting in horse races (Snai) or soccer matches (Sisal) are businesses organized by the State, and the same rule applies to lotteries and games such as bingo or lotto. Gambling is allowed in authorized casinos only. There are five authorized casinos in the country: entry requires an ID card and implies registration, and access to local residents is forbidden.

288. Gaming is subject to restrictions in both civil and criminal law.[308] An agreement aimed at organizing and conducting a gaming house is a crime and is considered against good morals and thus void. Similarly, loans which enable them to further gamble are against good morals. These agreements are void even if they are made within an authorized gaming house, although criminal sanctions may not be applicable.[309]

289. The winner of a game or bet may not file a petition in court claiming his money from the loser: no protection is granted to gaming and betting as there is not public interest in such activities. However, if the loser spontaneously pays his debt, he may not require the winner to return the money (Article 1933 c.c.). The winner of a game or bet may however file an application claiming his money from the State with respect to State lotteries, contests, competitions or other events organized under State monopoly (Articles 1934 and 1935 c.c.).

---

307. Paradiso, M., "I contratti di gioco e scommessa," Giuffrè, Milan, 2003; D'Acquino, F., "Il rischio-scudetto: assicurazione o scommessa?," in Riv. dir. sport., 1995, 745; Pollari, N., Senatore, S., "Le scommesse sulle corse dei cavalli," in Impresa, 1996, 1564; Migliorelli, G., "Bookmakers stranieri: un tentativo di invasione fallito?," in *Riv. giur. polizia locale*, 1996, 571; Tusset, A., "Sulla causa e prova della scommessa," in *Giur. it.*, 1995, I, 1, 73; Simone, S., "Totocalcio: conclusione del contratto e clausole vessatorie," in *Giur. pugliese*, 1995, 50; Roberto, Z., "Sulla illiceità delle scommesse con allibratori stranieri," in *Riv. dir. sport.*, 1994, 464; Merone, A., "L'esercizio abusivo di attività di giuoco e di scommessa," in *Rass. trib.*, 1991, fasc. 3 at 13.
308. *See* Mann, M.A., "Giochi, scommesse e responsabilità penale," Giuffrè, Milan, 2008.
309. *See* Cons. Stato, sez. IV, Aug. 20, 2013, n. 4199; Cass. Civ., sez. III, Oct. 7, 2011, n. 20622; Cass. Pen., sez. III, Nov. 10, 2009, n. 2993; Cass. civ. Oct. 14, 1958, n. 3255 (*Giust. civ.* 1959, I, 71) and Cass. civ. Jul. 9, 1953, n. 2205 (*Giust. civ.* 1953, 2434).

Chapter 4. Sale of Goods

P.G. Monateri

290. A sales agreement is a contract whereby the ownership of goods or other rights is transferred from a seller (or vendor) to a buyer (or purchaser) for a fixed price paid by the buyer (Article 1470 c.c.).[310] Any transferable right may be the object of a sales agreement: movable and immovable assets, property and other rights in rem, intangible assets such as a trademark, etc. The contract does not usually require a specific form except for the sale of land, buildings and other immovable assets (Article 1350 c.c.).

291. As a general rule, according to Article 1376 c.c. title and possession are transferred upon the meeting of the minds: thus, whenever the parties have agreed on the basic elements of the transaction (object and price) the transfer has immediate effect as long as the object of sale is determined, the seller disposes of it (and may thus deliver it) and the parties mutually consent that the contract has immediate effect to the "world at large" (*executed sale*). Otherwise, parties' assent to the same proposition only implies that both parties are bound by obligations arising out of the contract, but the transfer will take place in the future, provided that the sale has been definitively agreed upon as to terms and conditions, but has not been carried into full effect in respect to some of its terms or details (*executory sale*). Examples of executory sales include:

- *sale of unascertained goods*: in the case of sale of existing goods not specifically identified but referred to by description, transfer will take place upon identification (Article 1378 c.c.). Example: A agrees to sell a ton of steel to B, whereby A does not dispose of the goods for they are still to be purchased (or produced);
- *alternative sale*: the purchaser must choose between two or more goods, (Article 1285 c.c.) and transfer will take place upon his choice only;
- *sale of goods currently owned by another*: transfer will not occur until the vendor procures ownership of the goods (Article 1478 c.c.); if the purchaser ignored the goods that were not owned by the vendor, he may treat the contract as repudiated, unless the vendor has procured ownership of the goods in the meantime (Article 1479 c.c.);

310. On sale of goods contracts, *see* Frignani, A., "Il contratto di franchising. Orientamenti giurisprudenziali prima e dopo la legge 129 del 2004," Giuffrè, Milan, 2012; Valentino, D., "I contratti di vendita," UTET—Wolters Kluwer, 2007; Bianchi, G., "Il contratto di vendita. Fattispecie e profili applicativi," UTET—Wolters Kluwer, 2009; Ferrari, F., "Princìpi generali inseriti nelle convenzioni internazionali di diritto uniforme: l'esempio della vendita, del *factoring* e del *leasing* internazionali," in *Riv. trim. dir. e proc. civ.*, 1997, 629; Cartella, M., "Concessione di vendita –*Franchising* [voce aggiornata 1997]," in *Enc. dir.*, 1997, Giuffrè, Milan, 1997, I, 327; De Tilla, M., "I contratti immobiliari nella prassi giudiziaria," tomo I, "Vendita—appalto—permuta," Giuffrè, Milan, 1992.

- *sale of future goods*: the goods are still to be manufactured or acquired, thus the object of sale is not yet existing and the transfer will take place upon existence of the good. Example: the sale of a grape-harvest, or of a newborn pony, or of a future invention;
- *conditional sale*: transfer of title is made to depend on the performance of a condition or upon particular terms.

292. The obligations of the parties in a sales contract basically consist of the buyer's duty to pay the price and any expenses incurred for the sales (Articles 1498 and 1475 c.c.), and the seller's duty to deliver the goods to the buyer and to procure title of ownership to the buyer. If the seller fails to deliver the goods or delivers goods differing from those agreed upon, the buyer may choose to require specific performance of the contract or treat the contract as repudiated. If the seller fails to procure ownership of the goods from the buyer, or third parties have any liens, encumbrances, rights or claims about the goods sold, the seller must hold harmless and indemnify the buyer. If the buyer ignored the seller who did not have full title to the goods, he may require immediate termination of the contract; if the goods are only partially owned by another, the buyer may only require price reduction if it may reasonably be presumed that he would have equally purchased the goods had he been previously informed of the existing liens (Articles 1479, 1480, 1482 and 1489 c.c.). If the buyer was informed of existing liens on the goods when he purchased them, he has no action against the seller, for the law presumes he accepted to purchase the goods with liens (Article 1489). If, however, the liens on the goods are such as to fully prevent the buyer from acquiring title to the goods (example: the goods are made the object of seizure or pledge), the buyer who was initially conscious of the liens upon purchasing the goods, may treat the contract as repudiated or require price reduction if the goods are actually claimed by those entitled to the seizure or pledge (Articles 1483 and 1484 c.c.).

293. The seller must guarantee quality fitness of the goods as well. Thus, the seller will be responsible for lack of promised qualities in the goods or if the goods are unfit for purpose (Articles 1490 and 1497 c.c.). However, no warranty applies if, upon purchase of the goods, the buyer was informed of any defect in the goods or existing defects were clearly apparent to buyer by reasonable observation (Article 1491 c.c.). As a general rule, the purchaser must give formal notice to the seller that the goods are defective within eight days from discovery of the defects. The purpose of this rule is to push purchasers to control the quality of the goods bought. The buyer may thus treat the contract as repudiated and require restitution of the paid price, or ask for a price reduction (Article 1492 c.c.). The statute of limitation to file such claims before a court runs out after a year from delivery of the goods to the buyer (Articles 1495 and 1497 section 2, c.c.).

294. Generally speaking, if the parties have not otherwise agreed, in the sale of movable assets goods are to be delivered by the seller to the buyer's domicile or where the goods were originally placed when the sale was agreed (Articles 1510 et seq., c.c.). Other delivery conditions implying carriage of the goods include:

- *Sale by shipment*: the seller performs his duty of delivery by handing the goods to the shipper; thus, the seller may not be held liable if the goods perish during shipment or final delivery is delayed (Article 1510, section 2, c.c.).[311] The parties may otherwise agree that formal delivery (and the risk of property) take place upon arrival of the shipped goods (Article 1228 c.c.).
- *Cif contracts*: the seller undertakes to ship the goods at his own expense to the port of the destination and to insure them during the voyage; title to the goods is transferred to the buyer when the shipping documents are tendered to him by the seller; the risk of property passes when the goods cross the ship's rail.
- *Fob contracts*: carriage and insurance of the goods are arranged by the buyer, whilst the seller's duty is limited to the delivery of the goods to the ship; the risk of property passes when the goods cross the ship's rail.
- *Bills of lading, warehouse receipts*: when ownership of goods is represented by written documents such as bills of lading or warehouse receipts, transfer of ownership of the goods occurs when the documents are tendered to the buyer (Article 1527 c.c.).

295. Other forms of sales include:

- *Conditional sale whereby the seller reserves title as security for payment of the purchase price*: usually, a sale in which the buyer makes periodic payments in installments, and title transfer is reserved by seller until full payment is made. The sold goods are usually delivered to the buyer in advance, and the risk of property passes to the buyer upon delivery (Article 1523 c.c.). However, the buyer cannot sell the goods as he holds possession but not ownership, and thus would commit the crime of embezzlement (Article 646 Criminal Code).
- *Installment sale*: the law provides that failure to pay a single installment does not imply automatic termination of contract, unless the installment exceeds one-eighth of the total purchase price (Article 1525 c.c.); early termination of contract implies restitution of paid installments by the seller to the buyer.
- *Pre-emption*: the buyer is accorded the privilege to be preferred to other buyers in case the seller decides to sell the goods; this agreement is of course binding only between the parties, not the world at large.
- *Sale or return*: the seller delivers goods to the buyer on the understanding that he may ask restitution of the goods upon restitution of the price (Article 1500 c.c.). If the buyer sells the goods to a third party, the original seller may equally claim the goods unless the third party acquired title in good faith (Articles 1504, 1505 and 1153 c.c.).
- *Sale and return*: the seller delivers a quantity of goods to the buyer on the understanding that if the latter should desire to retain or resell any portion of such goods, he will consider such part as having been sold to him, and will pay their price (Articles 1556 c.c.). Sale and return contracts are typically agreed between retail stores and suppliers or distributors.

311. *See* Cass. civ. May 28, 1952, n. 1506.

Chapter 5. Building Contracts, Hire of Work and Skills

M. Balestrieri

§1. Hire of Work and Skills and Building Contracts

296. Work and services provided by independent workers or professionals in a principal-contractor relationship are characterized by the fact that the contractor is totally independent from the principal, and fully taking the risk of business in providing professional intellectual or manual work or services in exchange for remuneration (Article 1655 c.c.). The contractor may be an entrepreneur (Article 2083 c.c.), a professional (Article 2238 c.c.) or a skilled worker or an artisan (Article 2222 c.c.).

297. Examples of principal-contractor relationships include carriage agreements and construction contracts.

Carriage agreements contracts are agreements whereby a carrier undertakes to transfer persons or things from one place to another (Article 1678 c.c.)

Construction contracts, whereby a principal or owner commissions a contractor to construct a building on certain premises (Article 1656 c.c.). The principal is entitled to control construction phases and to make variations to initial plans (Articles 1661 and 1662 c.c.). Subcontracting is conditioned to approval by the principal (Article 1656 c.c.). Price adjustments for the finished work may be due to supervened construction problems on site or to changes in the costs of materials. When work is terminated, contractor is entitled to deliver the finished work only after approval by the principal (Article 1665 c.c.). Principal may reject the work and hold contractor liable for damages if the finished work is in any way defective (Article 1668 c.c.). Public procurements are regulated by Legislative Decree No. 50 enacted April 18, 2016, so-called Code for Public procurement (repealing former statutory legislation from 2006).

§2. Employer-Employee Relationships

298. Work made for hire must be distinguished from services rendered by an independent contractor, an agent or a professional. Performing work under an employer-employee relationship implies providing intellectual or manual work, where the employer has the right to control or direct the employee in the material details of how the work is to be performed (Articles 2094 and 2239 c.c.). A professional or an artisan, on the contrary, may provide services to different clients without being controlled or directed by anybody but himself, and takes the business risk. Employer-employee relationships arise out of contracts which are deeply covered by protective legislation, mainly consisting of the Employment Act of 1970 (L. 300 of May 20, 1970) and collective bargaining, which is a constitutional right in

Italy.[312] Employees may be classified as directors and managers, clerks and workers (Article 2095 c.c.), with further distinctions existing within these categories (*see* R.D. 1825 of November 13, 1924). The contract usually describes the duties and tasks of the employee, his salary and working hours. An employee may be moved to a different position or task and is entitled to a proportionate salary (Article 2103 c.c.). He may not be discriminated in any way (Article 15 Employment Act) and is free to manifest their political opinions and religious beliefs (Article 1 Employment Act). Employers and employees must not work more than a limited amount of hours per week (usually, no more than forty-eight ordinary working hours and eight overtime working hours: *see* R.D. 692 of March 15, 1923). Employees have the right to a day's rest every week (Article 2109 c.c.) and on national holidays (as provided for by L. 90 of March 31, 1954), as well as holidays with pay (Article 2109 c.c.). Employers are responsible for the employee's safety and security at work: specific legislation provides detailed rules on security measures for offices, factories, construction sites, etc. (Security Measures Acts, D.P.R. 754 of April 27, 1955 and D.P.R. 303 March 19, 1956, and other statutory provisions). Employees are entitled to keep their job and be absent from work for illness or pregnancy or if they are elected for a public duty (Article 2110 c.c.). Article 36 of the Constitution states that workers are entitled to a fair salary; salaries (Article 2099 c.c.) are generally regulated by collective bargaining between employers' unions and employees. Employer-employee relationships may be limited or unlimited in time. An employee may terminate his unlimited working relationship at any time by previously giving notice to his employer. An employer is generally entitled to dismiss an employee from his position for cause, which implies reasons which law and public policy do not regard as capricious or arbitrary but for some cause rendering it unfit for the employee to longer occupy his position (such as unlawful behavior or gross failure by the employee to perform his duties, or radical changes in the strategy and purposes of the employer, etc. (*see* Article 18 Employment Act). In any case, the employer must previously give notice of his intention to terminate the relationship and must provide severance compensation (Article 2120 c.c.). Significant framework rules governing employment-employee relationships were introduced by the so-called Jobs Act (Legislative Decrees 22 and 23 enacted March 4, 2015).

312. On collective bargaining and employer-employee relationships, *see* Magnani, M., Pandolfo, A., Vares, P.A., "I contratti di lavoro: Commentario al d.lgs. 15 giugno 2015, n. 81, recante la disciplina organica dei contratti di lavoro e revisione della normativa in tema di mansioni, a norma dell'articolo 1, comma 7, della legge 10 dicembre 2014, n. 183," Giappichelli, Turin, 2016; Del Punta, R., "Diritto del lavoro," Giuffrè, Milan, 2010; Carinci, F., De Luca Tamajo, R., Tosi, P., Treu, T., "Diritto del lavoro," I, Utet, Turin, 1994, at 247 et seq.

Chapter 6. Lease

F. Chiaves

299. Lease is a contract wherein one person (the lessor) lets to another a certain space, property or building for specified unit of time in exchange for a fee (Article 1571 c.c.).[313] The object of the lease may be both immovable (land, building) and movable assets (automobile, welding machine). The contract need not be drafted in any particular form, except for leases lasting more than nine years, which require to be executed in writing (Article 1350 n. 8, c.c.). Leases may be terminated by giving notice in advance (Articles 1596, 1597 and 1574 c.c.).

300. The lessor's duties include delivery of the leased thing, and to ensure full enjoyment of the thing by the lessee during the lease period (Article 1575 c.c.). The duties of the lessee basically consist of keeping good custody of the leased thing, using it properly and taking care of maintenance and paying the lease fee (Article 1587 c.c.). The lessee may file a petition in court in case he is deprived of his possession of the leased thing by any third parties (Articles 1168 et seq., c.c.). If any third party claims proprietary rights on the leased thing, the lessee may require the lessor intervene. If the lessor sells the leased thing, the purchaser must abide by the existing lease contract (Article 1599 c.c.).

301. Leases are generally regulated by the civil code (Articles 1571 et seq., c.c.). Leases for residential purposes of urban dwellings are governed by the Rents Act of 1978 (L. 392 of July 27, 1978) and further regulated by L. 431 of December 9, 1998 on urban housing leases and evictions. These rules impose minimum and maximum rent fees, providing a detailed list of duties expenses referable to the owner and to the lessee (Article 8 Rents Act). Leases must last for at least four years, and the contract may be renewed for another four-year term (Articles 1 and 3 Rents Act). The lessee may terminate the contract by giving notice to the lessor six months in advance (Article 4 Rents Act), whilst the lessor may not anticipate termination before natural expiry of the contract, except if the lessee fails to pay the lease fee (Articles 5 and 55 Rent Act). If the lessee dies, his cohabiting heirs[314] are entitled to substitute him as lessees (Article 6 Rent Act).

302. Leases of space for business or other non-residential purposes apply similar rules; however, minimum contract duration is six years, and the law imposes no

313. On leases, *see* Grasselli, G., Masoni, R., "Le locazioni," CEDAM, Padua, 2013; Carrato, A., Scarpa, A., "Le locazioni nella pratica del contratto e del processo," Giuffrè, Milan, 2010; Lazzaro, F., Preden, R., "Codice delle locazioni. Annotato con la giurisprudenza," Giuffrè, Milan, 2008; De Tilla, M., "Le locazioni," in "Il diritto immobiliare—Trattato sistematico di giurisprudenza ragionata per casi.," vol. VIII, V ed., Giuffrè, Milan, 1997, at 1194 et seq.; Patti, S., et al., "Il contratto di locazione," in "Giurisprudenza sistematica di diritto civile e commerciale" fondata da Walter Bigiavi, Utet, Turin, 1996, at XII-534 et seq.; Cuffaro, V., "Regole e deroghe nella disciplina del contratto di locazoione," in *Giur. it.*, 1996, I, 473.

314. Including non-married companions of the lessee: *see* Corte Cost., Apr. 7, 1968, n. 404.

limitations on lease fees (Article 32 Rent Act). Financial leases (referred to as *leasing* in Italy) are regulated by the general rules on lease enclosed in the Civil Code in Articles 1571 et seq. Most of the rules on financial leasing, which did not exist when the code was enacted in 1942, were defined by case law.[315]

303. Leases of agricultural land and other productive things (mines, hotels, factories) are regulated by the Civil Code (Articles 1615 et seq., c.c.). The lessor must deliver the leased thing in a condition to be fully productive (Article 1617 c.c.), and the lessee may take any profitable business initiative regarding the leased thing, as long as it is in the interest of production (Articles 1615 and 1620 c.c.).

---

315. On financial leasing, *see* De Martinis, P., "L'atipicità dei nuovi leasing. Obbligo al subentro, patto di riacquisto ed altre garanzie," Giappichelli, Turin, 2018; Buoncuore, V., "La locazione finanziaria," Giuffrè, Milan, 2008; Bellini, F., "Alcune notazioni sul negozio di locazione finanziaria di beni detto *leasing*," in *Riv. dir. trib.*, 1997, I, at 179; Clarizia, R., "La locazione finanziaria," Giappichelli, Turin, 1996; Vassallo Paleologo, F., "I contratti di locazione finanziaria," Cedam, Padova, 1994; Clarizia, R., "La convenzionc Unidroit sulla loocazione finanziaria: analogie e differenze rispetto al modello italiano," in *Riv. dir. impresa*, 1994, at 27; Palisi, F., "Note sulla locazione finanziaria," in *Riv. it. leasing*, 1991, 11; Carbone, P., "Locazione finanziaria. Natura, locazione finanziaria con scopo traslativo," in *Nuova giur. civ.*, 199, I, at 90; Bonfante, G., "Nuovi orientamenti della Cassazione in tema di locazione finanziaria," in *Giur. it.*, 1990, I, 1, at 379.

Chapter 7. Compromise and Settlement Agreements

P.G. Monateri

304. Compromise and settlement agreements (*transazioni*)[316] are arrangements between conflicting parties to settle a disputed claim by mutual concession to avoid a lawsuit or to amicably terminate a pending controversy (Article 1965 c.c.). The parties may reach an amicable agreement either in court or out of court. Compromise and settlement agreements must be proved in writing, and written form is required for amicable agreements regarding land and other immovable assets (Articles 1967 and 1350 n. 12, c.c.).

305. Compromise and settlement contracts imply the parties reach an agreement upon what they believe are equitable terms, regardless of the soundness of their initial claims. Thus, no party who executed such an agreement may subsequently return to her initial claims asserting their soundness. However, an amicable agreement may be avoided by proving one of the parties was perfectly conscious of the rashness and foolhardiness of her initial claims (Article 1971 c.c.). Finally, parties may claim having been induced to execute the agreement by mistake only under very limited circumstances (*see* Articles 1969–1975 c.c.).

306. Compromise and settlement contracts require mutual concessions by the parties, which imply that both parties must give up some of their initial claims. The object of the agreement may include duties and obligations in no way related to the initial dispute: thus, for instance, in a dispute arisen out of the price for the sale of a parcel of land, the buyer and seller may reach a compromise and settlement agreement providing the sale of another parcel of land for the same price.

A compromise and settlement agreement in a dispute regarding an unlawful contract is in itself unlawful and thus void (Article 1972 c.c.). Also, rights which may not be disposed of (such as marriage, legal capacity, personal status) may not form the object of such agreements (Article 1966 c.c.).

---

316. *See* Cicero, C., "Trattato di diritto civile—I singoli Contratti. Vol. IX: La transazione," UTET—Wolters Kluwer, 2014; Franzoni, M., "La transazione," CEDAM, Padua, 2001; Panuccio Dattola, F., "La transazione novativa," Giuffrè, Milan, 1996, at 90 et seq.; Recchioni, F., "Nota sul contratto di transazione, sulla definizione transattiva del danno e sull'atto di quietanza," in *Arch. civ.*, 1996, 1345; Moscarini, L.V. e Corbo, N., "Transazione (diritto civile)," in *Enc. giur. Treccani*, Rome, 1994, vol. XXI; Bozzola, G., "Presupposti ed effetti preclusivi della transazione," in *Contratti*, 1994, 176; Rotondi, E., "La transazione nella giurisprudenza," Giuffrè, Milan, 1993, at VIII-274; Del Prato, E., "La transazione," Giuffrè, Milan, 1992, at VI-138; *see also* Delfini, F., "Obbligazione solidale e transazione (nota a Cass. sez. III, 3 marzo 1997, n. 1873, valente v. Tosi)," in *Contratti*, 1997, 485; Cerdonio Chiaromonte, G., "La transazione nelle obbligazioni solidali," in *Studium iuris*, 1997, 798; Moretti, M., "Contratto di transazione e rapporti di diritto familiare," in *Contratti*, 1996, 523; Fiumara, O., "Decisione giudiziaria e transazione giudiziaria nella convenzione di Bruxelles del 27 settembre 1968," in *Rass. Avv. Stato*, 1994, I, 275.

Chapter 8. Insurance and Suretyship

F. Chiaves

307. Insurance and suretyship are typical "aleatory" contracts in that obligations by the parties imply assumption of a risk. In the case of insurance, obligations depend upon the occurrence of a future, uncertain event; in the case of sureties one person engages to be answerable upon failure to perform, default or miscarriage of another.

§1. Insurance

308. Insurance is a contract whereby one party (the insurer or underwriter) undertakes in return for premium payments to compensate the other (the insured or assured) for loss, damage or liability arising from an unknown or contingent event that may occur in the future (Article 1882 c.c.). If the risk of occurrence of the event ceases to exist or never existed, the contract is void as it lacks a valid *causa*[317] (Article 1895 c.c.). If the risk increases or diminishes,[318] both parties may require the premium to be revised (Articles 1987–1988 c.c.). Insurance contracts must be proved in writing before courts (Article 1888 c.c.), and the insurer must deliver a copy of the insurance policy to the insured.

As coverage depends upon periodical premium payment, failure to pay implies interruption of coverage (Article 1901 c.c.). Insurance agreements covering accidents caused voluntarily by the insured are unlawful (Articles 1900 and 1917 c.c.). Insurance companies are regulated by the law and controlled by government agencies (Articles 1883 and 1884 c.c.; *Insurance Act*, D.P.R. 449 of February 13, 1959).

309. Insurance contracts are classified according to the type of coverage they provide. For instance, *accident insurance* regards insurance to indemnify the assured against expense, loss of time and suffering resulting from accidents causing him physical injury. Restoration may never go beyond the actual loss incurred (*see* Articles 1904–1916 c.c.). *Life insurance* contracts are agreements whereby the underwriter agrees to pay a specified sum to the designated beneficiary upon the death of the insured (Articles 1920 et seq., c.c.). Other kinds of agreements include *health insurance* covering bodily injury and sickness, and *liability insurance* covering suits against the assured driver of an automobile or other vehicle for such damages as injury or death to other drivers, or passengers, or property. Liability insurance is compulsory in Italy for any person involved in the operation of a motor vehicle.

---

317. *See above*, Introduction to the Law of Contracts, §1, II, B.
318. If the increase or diminution of risk is due to temporary circumstances, no fee revision will occur: *see* Cass. civ. Apr. 7, 1982, n. 2142; Cass. civ. May 4, 1977, n. 1678; Cass. civ., Sep. 8, 1970, n. 1352.

§2. SURETYSHIP

310. Suretyship contracts are agreements whereby one party, upon request by another and for the purpose of securing him a benefit, becomes responsible for the performance by the latter of some act in favor of a third person (Articles 1936 et seq., c.c.). Basically, the surety is primarily liable for payment of debt or performance of obligation of another. Sureties are usually the business of companies who assume the responsibility of a surety on the bonds of client companies for a fee proportioned to the amount of the security required.

Chapter 9. Pledge and Mortgage

M. Balestrieri

311. Mortgage and pledge are basically deposits of property as security for a debt. Mortgage regards immovable assets such as land or buildings, whilst pledge regards movable things such as jewelry, furniture, objects as well as certified credits and negotiable instruments. Pledges and mortgages are characterized by being rights in rem, in that security is attached to the thing regardless of its owner: for instance, if an owner having a mortgage on his land sells that land, he also transfers the mortgage (unless he pays his debt and cancels the mortgage). Furthermore, creditors entitled to mortgages and pledges are characterized by a privileged position whenever assignment of the debtor's property and assets for the benefit of creditors occurs: if the assignee must prefer a specified creditor or class of creditors, he must always pay the claims of creditors entitled to mortgages and pledges in full before any other preferred creditors receive any dividend.

§1. Pledge

312. A pledge is a lien or contract that calls for the transfer of personal, movable property only as security (Articles 2784 et seq., c.c.).

313. In order for the contract to be binding and effective, pledges usually require delivery of the pawned things to the creditor or to a bailee (Article 2786 c.c.), or at least that the debtor be deprived of full possession of the pawned thing (joint possession by the debtor and creditor being sufficient). Negotiable instruments and any document certifying money or assets may be pawned as well by means of delivery of the document to the creditor. Notice of the pledge must be given to the debtor who is bound by the document (Article 2800 c.c.).

314. If pledge is made as security for a debt amounting to more than the equivalent of USD 3.00, the contract is required to be in writing in order for the creditor to acquire a privileged position in case of assignment of the debtor's property and assets for the benefit of creditors (Article 2787 c.c.). Thus, practically any pledge must be made in writing.

§2. Mortgage

315. Mortgage (Articles 2808 et seq., c.c.) is a conveyance or conditional fee of land or other immovable assets by a debtor to his creditor intended as a security for the repayment of a loan or performance of a duty. Mortgages require title and registration to be binding (Article 2808 c.c.). Title may derive from a written contract (i.e., the owner of a parcel of land granting a mortgage to his creditor as security for a debt, Article 2821 c.c.), or from a court order as security for the performance of a duty or payment of a debt (Article 2818 c.c.). In order for a mortgage to be valid and binding, title must be registered in the relevant public record (Vehicle Record for automobiles and other vehicles, Public Registry for land, buildings, houses, apartments, etc.). Since registration is limited to notarized documents, title must be generally procured in a notarized form. Registration lasts twenty years and automatically expires, but may be renewed. Expiry implies cancellation of the mortgage. Mortgage cancellation also occurs in case of loss or peril of the mortgaged property, or if the creditor's claims are satisfied in full, or if the creditor expresses his intention to abandon his claims by renunciation (Article 2878 c.c.). Mortgage cancellation is also registered in the relevant public records (Article 2882 c.c.).

316. If a debtor fails to pay money owed to a creditor having title to a mortgage, the creditor may apply for attachment to the debtor's property. Seizure of the debtor's mortgaged property in accordance with a writ or judicial order results in the sale of the property by public sale to the highest bidder. Monies gained from the auction are then assigned for the benefit of creditors. In all such cases, mortgage creditors form a separate class of privileged creditors. Furthermore, mortgage creditors are satisfied according to the time of registration of their mortgages: thus, in case of assignment for benefit of creditors, within a class of two mortgage creditors the assignee must prefer the creditor who registered his mortgage title before, by paying his claims in full before the second creditor.

Chapter 10. Loans

P.G. Monateri

317. Loans are contracts whereby one party (the lender) delivers to the other a sum of money or a certain quantity of goods upon agreement to return an equal amount of money or goods, with or without interest (Article 1813 c.c.).[319] Loans imply transfer of ownership of the original money or goods from the lender to the grantee and were originally sought to be "real" contracts (*see above*, Introduction to the Law of Contracts, §3, VII). Loans are presumed to be granted in exchange for remuneration, which generally consists of interest (Article 1815 c.c.). If the grantee fails to pay for the interest, the lender may terminate the agreement and require the original money or goods to be immediately returned to him (Article 1820 c.c.). The parties may agree for an interest rate superseding the legal interest rate; however, this agreement is binding only if it is executed in writing (*see* Article 1284 c.c.). Clauses providing exorbitant interest rates imposed by lenders taking advantage of a person's dire poverty or urgent need for money, beyond resulting in a crime, are void.[320]

318. Bailments, "conventional" seizures and bank deposit contracts are peculiar forms of loans which are dealt with in specific sections of Chapter 2, above.

319. Loans differ from commodate agreements whereby goods are borrowed gratuitously for the sole benefit, use and accommodation of the borrower. The borrower does not become owner of the goods, and must return the same, specific, borrowed goods to the owner (Article 1803 c.c.). If the parties agreed for a limited duration of contract, the borrower may be asked to return the borrowed thing only if the owner urgently needs it. If no contractual time limits were defined, the owner may require the borrower to return the borrowed thing at any time (Articles 1809–1810 c.c.).

---

319. On loans, *see* Graziano, N., "Il mutuo bancario," Cedam, Padua, 2013; Natali, A.I., "Il contratto di mutuo. Guida pratico-operativa," Giuffrè, Milan, 2012; Cafaro, R., Pagliaro, P., "Il contratto di mutuo," Giuffrè, Milan, 2012; Frattarolo, V., Iorio, E., "Il mutuo nella giurisprudenza," Giuffrè, Milan, 2009; Cristofari, R., "Mutuo e risoluzione del contratto," Giuffrè, Milan, 2002; Ferroni, L., "La nuova disciplina civilistica del contratto di mutuo," Esi, Naples, 1997; Gardella Tedeschi, B., "Deposito—Comodato—Mutuo," in *Riv. dir. civ.*, 1995, II, 633; De Tilla, M., "Mutuo," in "Il diritto immobiliare. trattato sistematico di giurisprudenza ragionata per casi.," vol. VII, Giuffrè, Milan, 1995, at 814 et seq.; Gazzara, M., "Crediti speciali, prestito a consegna differita e consensualità del mutuo," in *Banca, borsa*, 1995, I, 335; Gallo, P., "Mutuo in diritto comparato," in *Digesto IV*, Turin, 1994, vol. XI, at 580; Giomaro, A.M., Morosini, P.G., "Mutuo nel diritto romano, medioevale e moderno," in *Digesto IV*, Turin, 1994, vol. XI, at 584; Carbone, V., "Mutuo: *traditio rei e* strumenti alternativi alla consegna," in *Corriere giur.*, 1992, 1329.

320. Trib. Roma, sez. XVII, Sep. 27, 2018, n. 18278; Trib. Milano, sez. VI, Sep. 18, 2018, n. 9154; Cass. Civ., sez. un., Oct. 19, 2017, n. 24675; Corte Cost., Feb. 25, 2002, n. 29; Cass. civ., Nov. 11, 1974, n. 3517; Cass. civ., Aug. 9, 1973, n. 2330 (*Banca, Borsa*, 1974, II, 169); Cass. civ., Oct. 29, 1971, n. 3047.

Chapter 11. Contracts with Government Agencies and Other Public Administrations

P.G. Monateri

320. In order to achieve their purposes, governmental agencies, administrative agencies and all other State or local government bodies execute contracts with other public agencies and with private individuals or legal entities. Agreements with private persons differ from governmental or administrative "acts." Administrative "acts" are an exercise of constitutional, legislative, administrative or judicial power conferred on general or local government for the benefit of the public. They consist of regulations or orders issued by an administrative agency having force of law. Administrative "acts" are generally unilateral and are a result of the sovereign functions of a public body, thus are usually governed by administrative law, which generally assigns a privileged position to the public authority with respect to the private individuals involved.

321. Agreements with public bodies, on the contrary, are governed by private law,[321] which implies the public agency and the private individual have equal rights and liabilities. Public Agencies execute private law contracts in a large number of situations. Public agencies may also be held liable for any wrongful damage caused to any third person under tort law. Thus, public agencies may be subject to both contractual and noncontractual liability.

Examples of contracts executed by public agencies with individuals or private companies include agreements to carry persons or things from one place to another (mail, parcels and passengers by train), electricity, heating and water supply, leases of spaces for government offices, hire of work and skills (civil servants and, in general, any State employees), building contracts, etc.[322]

322. Private law contracts were traditionally distinguished from administrative contracts, which were governed by administrative law and were basically limited to hire of work and skills for State employees and bids for construction contracts with State, government or local agencies. Such a distinction appears outdated today provided that construction contracts are regulated by the civil code (except for the bidding procedure), whilst State employees now enjoy the same position as any private worker with regards to welfare, salary and other benefits.

---

321. *See* General Introduction, §5.

322. Postage and telecommunications are regulated by D.P.R. 156 of Mar. 29, 1973, later amended by several other statutory provisions; transport by train is defined under D.P.R. 197 of May 30, 1961 and in international law by the Bern Conventions of Oct. 25, 1952 and Feb. 25, 1961, ratified by Italy with L. 916/1955 and L. 806/1963, whereas ticketing, fees and general conditions of transport are regulated by L. 911/1935 and amendments.

323. As a general rule, public agencies entering into contracts with individuals or private companies have no privileged position with respect to their counterparts.[323] Regarding form, all contracts with public bodies must be executed in writing in order to be effective and binding according to Article 95 of the State Finances Act (R.D. 827 of May 23, 1924).[324] Interpretation of the terms and conditions of contract is governed by the ordinary rules of the civil code (Articles 1362–1371 c.c.) and fall under the jurisdiction of ordinary civil courts, not administrative courts:[325] interpretation of the public body's contractual intentions will strictly refer to the clauses contained in the agreement, regardless of any internal resolutions by boards or officers of the agency.

324. Other typical contract law rules apply to contracts involving public agencies in the field of contractual liability. The burden of proof rule applies,[326] in that contract law requires the debtor (and not the injured party) to prove that failure to perform was not due to his fault (Article 1218 c.c.). Furthermore, damage recovery is limited, provided that under contract law an injured party may only seek to recover damages which could have reasonably been predicted when the parties agreed upon performance (Article 1225 c.c.). All other rules provided by the civil code with respect to contractual liability (Articles 1218–1229 c.c.) are equally applicable to contracts executed by public agencies.[327] Similarly, rules on enrichment without *causa* apply (Article 2041 c.c., *see* Chapter 13 below).

325. Offers to perform contracts for work, or to supply materials, services or goods are frequently awarded on basis of submitted, competitive bids. Bidding procedures may vary; however, before finalizing an agreement with private entities, public agencies and governmental bodies must generally follow several procedural steps. A government agency generally issues a bid after a resolution. Bids are usually submitted as the result of public notice and advertising. To assure independence of bidding, bids are commonly submitted under seal not to be opened until a specified time at which all bids are opened and compared. The winner is the bidder with the best bid, which is not necessarily the lowest, but rather the one fitting the

---

323. Courts have long stated this rule: Cass. Civ., sez. I, Oct. 12, 2018, n. 25553; Cass. Civ., sez. lav., May 24, 2005, n. 10904; Cass. civ. Jul. 29, 1987, n. 6547; TAR Lazio, I, Nov. 29, 1988, n. 1613 (*Foro amm.*, 1989, 2471); Cass. Aug. 9, 1977 (*Mass. Foro it.*, 1977, n. 3647). Scholars confirm the rule: Garri, F., "La responsabilità civile della pubblica amminsitrazione," in "Giurisprudenza sistematica civile e commerciale diretta da Walter Bigiavi," Turin, 1994, at 146–147; Santoro, P., "I controlli sull'attività contrattuale della pubblica amministrazione," Milan, 1992, at 227; Sandulli, A., "Diritto amministrativo," Iovene, Naples 1989, at 1167; Bortolotti, D., "Contratti dell'amministrazione pubblica," in *Digesto IV*, Turin, 1989, at 37; Meloncelli, A., "L'informazione amministrativa," Rimini, 1983, at 283. The entire subject matter is now included in the new Code for Public Procurement (Legislative Decree Apr. 12, 2006, n. 163). *See* Caranta, R., "I contratti pubblici," Giappichelli, Turin, 2012; Corradino, M., et al., "I contratti pubblici," Wolters Kluwer, 2017, at 55; Mastragostino, F., "Diritto dei contratti pubblici," Turin, Giappichelli, 2019.

324. Contracts renewal must also be in writing.

325. Cass. Civ., sez. un., Feb. 10, 2010, n. 2906; Corte Cost., May 11, 2006, n. 191; Corte Cost., Jul. 6, 2004, n. 204; TAR Lazio, sez. III, Oct. 1, 1987, n. 1624 (*Riv. trim. app.*, 1989, 525).

326. Cass. Civ., sez. II, Apr. 29, 1998, n. 4350; Cass. civ. Mar. 28, 1987, n. 3027 (*Corr. giur.*, 1987, 733).

327. Garri, *supra*, at 180; Buscema, A., "Trattato di diritto amministrativo," Padua, 1994, at 574.

best interests of the issuer, taking into consideration the solvency of the bidder, the quality of his work, his reputation, etc. When the bidder who made the best bid is proclaimed the winner of the bid, the contract, however formalized, is not yet binding for the agency until the competent controlling body gives its final approval.

326. European Union legislation provides for several common procedures and principles in the field of public bids. Italy enacted L. 142 of February 19, 1992 and especially D. Lgs. 48 of January 15, 1992 (in accordance with EEC Directive n. 88/295/CEE) providing common European rules for public bids in general. Liability rules are a result of EEC Directives Nos. 77/62/CEE, 80/767/CEE and 88/295/CEE, enacted in Italy with D. Lgs. n. 358 July 24, 1992, and recently EU Directive 24/2014, enacted in Italy with Legislative Decree No. 501 of April 8, 2016.[328]

328. De Nictolis, R., "I nuovi appalti pubblici. Appalti e concessioni dopo il d.lgs. 56/2017," Zanichelli, Bologna, 2017.

Chapter 12. Partnerships

P.G. Monateri

327. Partnerships are agreements whereby two or more persons place their money, effects, labor and skill in lawful commerce or business with the understanding that there shall be a proportional sharing of the profits between them (Article 2247 c.c.).

The money or assets placed by partners in the partnership are detached from the original owner and become a separate "patrimony": thus, a partnership is distinct from the individuals who comprise it (partners or shareholders).

§1. Companies

328. Companies[329] are partnerships characterized by a *lucrative purpose*, generally consisting of the production of goods or the provision of services. Partnerships which are established by two or more partners for the sole purpose of managing and enjoying a certain estate or assets, are regulated by the rules on community property (Articles 2248 c.c. and 1100 et seq., c.c.). Furthermore, if the partners have established an organization for the purpose of providing services and profits to its members and not for corporate profit, one has a cooperative (Articles 2511 et seq., c.c.).

329. Partnership members, or shareholders, proportionally share the profits and enjoy several rights, including the right to vote (Articles 2257 and 2351 c.c.) in the shareholders' meetings (which basically function on a majority basis), the right to question resolutions by the board of directors (Article 2377 c.c.), and the right to exercise control over the directors' decisions, to consult documents relating to the company's conduct of business and management, to obtain statements of account, reports and minutes of meetings (Articles 2261 and 2320 c.c.) and to report complaints to the board of audit or file claims before a court (Articles 2408–2409 c.c.). Any agreement to fully deprive one or more parties from sharing the profits or losses of the partnership is unlawful and void (Article 2265 c.c.).[330]

Partnerships generally survive the death of their investors and the shares can usually be transferred.

329. On partnerships, *see* Cottino, G., "Lineamenti di diritto commerciale," Zanichelli, Bologna, 2018; Buoncore, V., "Manuale di diritto commerciale," Giappichelli, Turin, 2016; Abriani, N., "Diritto commerciale," Giuffrè, Milan, 2011; Galgano, F., "Diritto commerciale—II. Le società. Contratto di società. Società di persone, società per azioni, altre società di capitali. Società cooperative," rist. aggiornata Zanichelli, Bologna, 1991, at 486 et seq.; Marasà, G., Spada, P., Cottino, G., Covelli, M.R., "Contratto di società," in *Enc. giur. Treccani*, Rome, 1993, XXIX; Galgano, F., "Contratto e persona giuridica nelle società di capitali," in *Contratto e impresa*, 1991, 1.

330. *See* Spezia, F., "Il divieto del patto leonino nel contrarto di società," in *Arch. civ.*, 1991, 993.

330. Partnerships are regulated in Title V of the Fifth Book of the Civil Code (Articles 2247–2642 c.c.). Partnerships have been classified along functional lines as follows:

- *Limited liability partnerships and unlimited liability partnerships*, according to whether partners are liable to losses and expenses of the partnership to the amount furnished and no more, or partners' liability is limitless.
- *De jure and de facto partnerships.* De jure partnerships exist by reason of full compliance with the requirements of the law. De facto companies are associations of men claiming to be a legally incorporated company but without actual lawful authority to do so. De facto companies are not registered companies, thus are imposed a fine (Article 2626 c.c.). All partners are fully liable to losses and expenses of the partnership (Article 2297 c.c.).
- *"Personal" partnerships and "capital" partnerships.* "Personal" partnerships are characterized by major ties between the founding partners, and generally assign more importance to individual members than to the group.[331] "Capital" partnerships, on the contrary, are impersonal and the board of directors and majority stockholders hold a prominent position whereas most partners basically own minority shares for the purposes of investment. "Personal" partnerships usually identify smaller business with a limited number of partners who are personally involved with the partnership. "Capital" partnerships deal with broader businesses in the trade or industry field, and are often present in the stock market. "Personal" partnerships are usually directly managed by partners (Articles 2257–2258 c.c.), and all members have direct control over the company's conduct of business. At least a portion of the partners are liable to losses and expenses of the partnership, while in "capital" partnerships no shareholder is ever directly liable to company losses and expenses. A member of "personal" partnership may not perform a business being in direct competition with that of the partnership (Article 2301 c.c.), and if he goes bankrupt, he must withdraw from the partnership (Article 2288 c.c.). On the contrary, events regarding single shareholders generally have no influence on "capital" partnerships.

331. There are three kinds of "personal" partnerships and three kinds of "capital" partnerships:

"Personal" partnerships	1. *società semplice* (s.s)
	2. *società in nome collettivo* (s.n.c.)
	3. *società in accomandita semplice* (s.a.s)

331. On "personal" partnerships, *see* Conforti, C., "Le società di persone. Amministrazione e controlli," Giuffrè, Milan, 2009; Bellagamba, G., Cariti, G., "Le società di persone—Le società di fatto—Le società cooperative," Giuffrè, Milan, 1997; Casadei, D., "Le società di persone," Giuffrè, Milan, 1997.

"Capital" partnerships	1. *società in accomandita per azioni* (s.a.p.a.) 2. *società per azioni* (s.p.a.) 3. *società a responsabilità limitata* (s.r.l.)

332. The *società semplice* corporate model is the simplest kind of company (Article 2251 c.c.). No company registration is required and no written instrument is necessary to establish the company, unless the assets placed by partners in the partnership require a certain form (such as real estate or bonds). The company must have a lucrative purpose but may not exercise trade. All partners are managers of the company who may operate jointly or independently, although separate management is the rule unless otherwise agreed. Conflicts are settled on the basis of the majority rule. All partners are equally entitled to represent the company, unless otherwise required. Finally, all partners are jointly and fully liable to losses and expenses of the partnership even beyond the amount furnished. Creditors of individual partners may require their debtors to liquidate their interest in the partnership. Unless otherwise provided, these kinds of partnerships do not survive the death of their investors.

333. The *società in nome collettivo* corporate model must have a lucrative purpose but may exercise trade (Articles 2291 et seq., c.c.). The Articles of Partnership embodying the terms and conditions of partnership must be in writing and must be registered at the Company Registry together with the names and signatures of the managers and liquidators of the company and the partnership's assets and offices (Articles 2296, 2298, 2299, 2300, 2309 and 2312 c.c.). Bookkeeping is required (Article 2302 c.c.). Appointment and dismissal of managers and directors, and any other event affecting management of the company must be entered into the registry in order to inform business partners and third parties. Creditors of individual partners may not require their debtors to liquidate their interest in the partnership except in case the debtor has gone bankrupt (Articles 2305, 2288 and 2293 c.c.). Finally, all partners are jointly and fully liable to losses and expenses of the partnership even beyond the amount furnished, but creditors must first try to collect their debt from the company and may only require individual partners to pay if the company is insolvent (Articles 2291 and 2304 c.c.).

334. The *società in accomandita semplice* corporate model (Articles 2313 et seq., c.c.) is very similar to the *società in nome collettivo* except that there exist two kinds of partners: some partners (*accomandatari*) are granted representative powers at law and act as directors, and are jointly and fully liable to losses and expenses of the partnership even beyond the amount furnished (Articles 2314 and 2318 c.c.). Other partners (*accomandanti*) simply enjoy profit and have no managing powers, and are liable to losses and expenses of the partnership to the amount furnished and no more (Article 2313 c.c.).

335. The *società per azioni* corporate model[332] is the most commonly used "capital" partnership model (Articles 2325 et seq., c.c.). This model requires an initial capital stock of the equivalent of at least USD 120,000. The partners' interest in the company is represented by shares, and shareholders are not directly liable to losses and expenses of the partnership. Shareholders have very indirect relations with the company: they do not manage the company, and have limited access to documents related to the company's conduct of business (Article 2424 c.c.). The Articles of Partnership embodying the terms and conditions of partnership must be executed in writing and notarized and must bear the name, registered offices, duration and purposes of the company, as well as the names and signatures of its founding members, the capital stock of the company and its distribution amongst shareholders, the number of directors and their powers. Founder members must also approve the bylaws of the company, which integrate the Articles of Partnership (Article 2328 c.c.). Before registration, the Articles of Partnership must meet approval by the local court of justice. Record of all such documents must be kept at the Company Registry. Registration implies the birth of the company as a separate legal entity; thus, before registration, founder members are fully liable to losses and expenses of the partnership. (Article 2331 c.c.). Shareholders share the profits and enjoy several rights, including the right to vote in the shareholders' meetings (Article 2351 c.c.), the right to put and call and to question resolutions by the board of directors (Article 2377 c.c.), and the right to exercise control over the directors' decisions, to consult documents relating to the company (Article 2320 c.c.) and to report complaints to the board of audit or file claims before a court (Articles 2408–2409 c.c.). The shareholders' meeting appoints and dismisses the directors and auditors, decides about their conduct, approves the balance sheet at the end of every fiscal year, approves resolutions on fundamental issues or modifications of the Articles of Partnership (Articles 2364–2365 c.c.). Any decisions are taken on a majority of the votes basis. A sole director or a board of directors may be in charge of administration and management of the company; directors may appoint an executive committee for day-by-day business (Articles 2380–2381 c.c.). The board's powers are defined by the Articles of Partnership. Directors may not attend board meetings regarding matters of conflicting with their personal interests, and may not take part in any business in direct competition with that of the company (Articles

---

332. On *società per azioni* corporations, *see* Montalenti, P., "La società per azioni quotata," Zanichelli, Bologna, 2010; Montalenti, P., "Società per azioni, corporate governance e mercati finanziari," Giuffrè, Milan, 2011; Cottino, G., "Società per azioni. Costituzione e finanziamento," UTET—Wolters Kluwer, 2013; Weigmann, R., "Società per azioni," in *Digesto IV*, Commercial Law Section, Utet, Turin, 1997, at 338 et seq.; Menghi, I., "Il bilancio di esercizio della società per azioni," Cedam, Padua, 1997; D'Antino, M., "Delega di poteri e responsabilità degli amministratori delle società per azioni," in *Arch. Civ.*, 1997, at 353; Various Authors, "Trattato delle società per azioni," Utet, Turin, 1996; Easterbrook, F.H., Fischel, D.R., "L'economia delle società per azioni," Giuffrè, Milan, 1996; Cavalli, G., Marulli, M. et al., "Le società per azioni. Gli organi e il controllo giudiziario," Utet, Turin, 1996; Salanitro, N., "Società per azioni e mercati finanziari," Giuffrè, Milan, 1996; Battista Bisogni, G., "La struttura amministrativa della società per azioni tra diritto comunitario e disciplina della *public company*," in *Giur. comm.*, 1996, I, at 954 et seq.; Baudino, A., Frascinelli, R., "Gli amministratori delle società per azioni e a responsabilità limitata," Giuffrè, Milan, 1996.

2390, 2391 and 2631 c.c.). Directors are responsible for their conduct towards the company, towards single shareholders and towards injured third parties (Articles 2392 and 2395 c.c.).

The balance sheet must be prepared according to detailed rules enlisted in the civil code (Articles 2423 et seq., c.c.) and is controlled by the Board of Audit. The Board of Audit also controls the bookkeeping and general conduct of business of the company. Auditors are originally appointed in the Articles of Partnership, and subsequently designated by the shareholders meeting (Article 2400 c.c.).

Special rules are provided for corporate auditing by third-party independent auditors (Article 2409 *bis* c.c. as amended in 2010).

Moreover, new corporate management and surveillance principles were introduced in 2010 prescribing that companies may choose to opt for a dualistic system whereby under the company bylaws corporate management and control be exercised by a management board (*consiglio di gestione*) and a supervisory board (*consiglio di sorveglianza*) respectively, or to opt for a monistic system where corporate management and control be exercised by a board of directors and a committee therein (Article 2409 *octies* to Article 2409 *noviesdecies* c.c.).

336. The *società in accomandita per azioni* corporate model[333] is basically organized like the previous model, but provides for two kinds of shareholders: some partners (*accomandatari*) are granted representative powers at law and act as directors, and are jointly and fully liable to losses and expenses of the partnership, while other shareholders (*accomandanti*) simply enjoy profit and have no managing powers (Article 2462 c.c.).

337. The *società a responsabilità limitata* corporate model[334] differs from the *società per azioni* in that partners' interest in the company is represented by subscription fees instead of shares (Article 2472 c.c.) and foundation requires an initial minimum capital stock of the equivalent of USD 12,000 only (Article 2474 c.c.). Shareholders are not directly liable to losses and expenses of the company. In accordance with the XIIth EEC Directive on Unipersonal Corporate Models, from 1993 *società a responsabilità limitata* corporate models may be established by a single member holding 100% of the corporate interest. This model is generally used for

---

333. *See* Barcellona, E., "Società in accomandita per azioni," Zanichelli, Bologna, 2005; Corsi, F., "Società in accomandita per azioni," in *Digesto IV*, Commercial Law Section, Utet, Turin, 1997, at 234 et seq.

334. On *società a responsabilità limitata* corporations, *see* Fortunato, S., "La società a responsabilità limitata. Lezioni sul modello societario più diffuso," Giappichelli, Turin, 2017; Zanarone, G., "Della società a responsabilità limitata," Giuffrè, Milan, 2010; Stassano, G., "Società a responsabilità limitata," Giuffrè, Milan, 1997; Zamperetti, G.M., "La società unipersonale a responsabilità limitata," Giuffrè, Milan, 1997; Cagnasso, O., Irrera, M., "Società a responsabilità limitata," in *Digesto IV*, Turin, 1997, at 183 et seq.; Racugno, G., "Società a responsabilità limitata," in *Giur. comm.*, 1996, I, at 157 and 352; di Belmonte di Tarsia, F., "La società a responsabilità limitata con unico socio," in *Riv. not.*, 1996, at 793; Ibba, C., "La società a responsabilità limitata con unico socio," Giappichelli, Turin, 1995; Cimei, F., "Società a responsabilità limitata," in *Gius*, 1995, at 1137; Bovesi, M., "La dodicesima Direttiva CEE sulle società unipersonali a responsabilità limitata ed il suo recepimento da parte dell'Italia," in *Dir. scambi internaz.*, 1994, at 477.

medium-sized companies composed of a limited number of members wishing to interfere in the management of the company without being directly liable for losses and expenses.

338. Companies may change from one corporate model to another by modifying the Articles of Partnership (Articles 2498–2500 c.c.). Company merging is also regulated in detail by the Civil Code (Articles 2501 et seq., c.c.).

§2. Cooperatives

339. Cooperatives[335] are organized for the purposes of rendering economic services, without gain to itself, for shareholders or members who own and control them (Articles 2511 et seq., c.c.). Cooperatives may be classified according to their basic function: *consumer cooperatives* (including housing cooperatives, health cooperatives) purchase goods directly from producers and assign them to their members at a price below the market price. *Financial cooperatives* (mutual savings banks, production credit associations) are established for the purposes of granting loans to their members at very good conditions. *Insurance cooperatives* are sureties whereby the policy holders are the sole owners, and are exposed to the same type of risk; members place money in a fund and the cooperative restores any casualty suffered by one of the members. *Workers' productive cooperatives* are agreements whereby members work for the cooperative and profits are divided among them.

340. Cooperatives may have a lucrative purpose, as long as that purpose does not prevail over the mutual one. Thus, the law provides that each partner has one and only one vote, regardless of the share interest he holds in the cooperative (Article 2532 c.c.).

Cooperatives may be established as limited or unlimited liability companies (Articles 2513, 2514 and 2541 c.c.).

335. On cooperatives, *see* Macrì, L., et al., "Società cooperative e consorzi," Wolters Kluwer, 2018; Paolucci, L., "Le società cooperative," UTET—Wolters Kluwer, 2012; Bellagamba, G., Cariti, G., "Le società di persone—Le società di fatto—Le società cooperative," Giuffrè, Milan, 1997.

Chapter 13. Quasi-Contracts

F. Chiaves

341. Quasi-Contracts include *negotiorum gestio*, payment of undue amounts and enrichment without *causa*.[336]

§1. Negotiorum Gestio

342. *Negotiorum gestio* occurs when a person conducts another person's business without having been explicitly entrusted to do so or however without being bound to do so.[337] Typical examples of *negotiorum gestio* include urgent repairs by a neighbor of a leak in the roof of the house on adjoining premises whereby the owner is away and cannot be traced (Article 2028 c.c.). Any costs and expenses sustained for the conduct of the business must be paid by the principal (Article 2031 c.c.).

§2. Payment of Undue Amounts and Enrichment Without Causa

343. Payment of undue amounts and enrichment without *causa* occur every time a person pays monies to another person without there being an agreement to do so or a duty imposed by the law.[338] Examples include payment by mistake, or consuming goods of another which are believed to be one's own. As a general rule, in all such cases the law prescribes the impoverished person to be fairly indemnified (Articles 2033 and 2041 c.c.).

344. The Civil Code grants a special action to enforce recovery from unjust enrichment (Articles 2033 et seq. c.c.).

---

336. On Quasi-Contracts, *see* Breccia, U., "La ripetizione dell'indebito," Milan, 1974; Moscati, E., "Indebito soggettivo ed attuazione del rapporto obbligatorio," in *Riv. dir. civ.*, 1974, 72 et seq. *See also* De Bonis, D., "Indebito oggettivo—errore—aricchimento senza causa—rimedi altermnativi e non concorrenti" (nota a Giudice di Pace Roma, 13 maggio 1997, *Sai Assicurazioni v. Terzi*), in *Riv. giur. circolaz. e trasp.*, 1997, 639; Annunziata, M., "Pubblica amministrazione e arricchimento senza causa (Nota a Cass. S.U., 10 febbraio 1996, n. 1025, *Prov. Atrezzo* v. *Comunità montana Zona H Alto Tevere Val Tiberina*)," in *Foro amm.*, 1996, 2579; Donatelli, R., "Vecchie e nuove 'categorie' comprese nel 'genere' dell'arricchimento senza causa" (nota a Pret. Salerno—Eboli, 2 marzo 1993, *Trinca v. Trinca*), in *Giur. merito*, 1995, 541; Alberti, A.M., "Il riconoscimento di debito," in *Rass. dir. tecnica doganale*, 1995, 95; Spitali, E., "L'arricchimento mediante intermediario e l'Art. 2038 c.c. (nota a Cass. sez. II, 10 febbraio 1993, n. 1686, *Castagni* v. *ENEL*)," in *Giur. it.*, 1994, I, 1, 1861; Gallo, P., "Arricchimento senza causa (sintesi di informazione)," in *Riv. dir. civ.*, 1993, II, 677.
337. *See* Geraci, I., "La gestione d'affari altrui. Artt. 2028-2032," Giuffrè, Milan, 2018.
338. *See* Bargelli, E., "Ripetizione d'indebito," Wolters Kluwer, 2014; Abatangelo, C., "Intermediazione nel pagamento e ripetizione dell'indebito," CEDAM, Padova, 2010; Gallo, P., "Arricchimento senza causa," Giuffrè, Milan, 2003.

Thus, the person who unjustifiably receives certain goods or a given amount of money, must return the same goods or an equivalent amount of money. If the goods were sold in good faith to a third party in the meantime, or if they were consumable goods (such as wine or firewood) and they were used, the enriched party shall return an amount of money equivalent to the value of such goods. The rule also applies to unjustified performance of any other obligation, forcing the enriched person to return a monetary equivalent of that performance.

Selected Bibliography

Overviews of Case Law

Alpa, G., Bessone, Zeno Zencovich, V., *I fatti illeciti,* in *Trattato Rescigno*, XIV, Turin 1995.

Bartolini, F., *Il codice civile commentato esclusivamente con la giurisprudenza, massimario a cura di P. Dubolino ed F. Bartolini*, La Tribuna, Piacenza, 1998.

Bianca, M., *Dell'inadempimento delle obbligazioni,* in *Commentario del codice civile a cura di Scialoja e Branca*, II ed., Bologna Rome, 1979.

Carpi, F., Colesanti, V., Taruffo, M., *Commentario breve al codice di procedura civile—complemento giurisprudenziale, Breviaria Iuris a cura di G. Cian ed A. Trabucchi*, Cedam, Padua, 1996.

Carpi, F., Colesanti, V., Taruffo, M., *Commentario breve al codice di procedura civile—complemento giurisprudenziale appendice 1996–98, Breviaria Iuris a cura di G. Cian ed A. Trabucchi*, Cedam, Padua, 1998.

Cendon, P., Com*mentario al codice civile. Artt. 1343-1469 bis. Contratto in generale, Volume 1*, Giuffrè, Milan, 2010.

Cian, G., Trabucchi, A., *Commentario breve al codice civile—complemento giurisprudenziale, Breviaria Iuris a cura di G. Cian ed A. Trabucchi*, Cedam, Padua, 1996.

Cian, G., Trabucchi, A., *Commentario breve al codice civile—complemento giurisprudenziale appendice 1996–98, Breviaria Iuris a cura di G. Cian ed A. Trabucchi*, Cedam, Padua, 1998.

De Tilla, M., *Mutuo*, in *Il diritto immobiliare. Trattato sistematico di giurisprudenza ragionata per casi*, vol. VII, Giuffrè, Milan, 1995.

Dubolino, P., *Il codice delle leggi civili complementari commentate con la giurisprudenza*, La Tribuna, Piacenza, 1998.

Franzoni, M., *Fatti illeciti*, in *Commentario del codice civile a cura di Scialoja e Branca*, Bologna-Rome, 1993.

Gabrielli, E. (a cura di), *I contratti in generale*, in *Tratt. Rescigno-Gabrielli*, 2a ed., Turin, 2006.

Galgano, F., Visintini, G., *Degli effetti del contratto della rappresentanza, in Commentario del codice civile diretto da Scialoja e Branca, a cura di Galgano, F.*, Libro IV, Zanichelli-Foro Italiano, Bologna-Rome, 1993.

Gallo, P., *Arricchimento senza causa e quasi contratti (i rimedi restitutori)*, in *Trattato di diritto civile diretto da R. Sacco*, Utet, Turin, 1996.

Selected Bibliography

Garri, G., *La responsabilità civile della pubblica amministrazione*, in *Giurisprudenza sistematica civile e commerciale diretta da Walter Bigiavi*, Turin, 1994.***
Micheli, G.A, Azzariti, G., Scarpello, G., *Della tutela dei diritti*, in *Commentario del codice civile a cura di Scialoja e Branca*, Rome-Bologna, 1977.
Moscarini, L.V., *Il contratto a favore di terzo,* in *Commentario del Codice Civile' a cura di Schlesinger*, Milan, 1997.
Navarretta, E., et al., *Commentario al Codice civile. Dei contratti in generale, Volume 1–3*, UTET, Turin, 2011.
Nicolò, R., *La tutela dei diritti*, in *Commentario del codice civile a cura di Scialoja e Branca*, Rome-Bologna, 1980.
Patti, S., et al., *Il contratto di locazione*, in *Giurisprudenza sistematica di diritto civile e commerciale fondata da Walter Bigiavi*, Utet, Turin, 1996.

Books

Private and Constitutional Law

Bin, R., Pitruzzella, G., *Diritto Costituzionale*, Turin, Giappichelli, 2016.
Caretti, U., De Siervo, F., *Diritto Costituzionale e Pubblico*, Turin, Giappichelli, 2018.
De Vergottini, G., *Diritto Costituzionale*, Padua, Cedam, 2017.
Garri, F., *La responsabilità civile della pubblica amministrazione*, 1996.
Giannini, M.S., *Istituzioni di diritto amministrativo*, Milan, 1981, at 403;
Martines, T., *Diritto costituzionale*, Giuffrè, Milan, 1990.
Meloncelli, A., *L'informazione amministrativa*, Rimini, 1983.
Pugliatti, S., *Gli istituti del diritto civile*, Milan, 1943, at 24.
Roppo, V., *Diritto privato*, Giappichelli, Turin, 2018.
Sandulli, A., *Manuale di diritto amministrativo*, Naples, 1989.
Stanzione, P., *Manuale di Diritto Privato*, Giappichelli, Turin, 2017.
Torrente, A., Schlesinger, P., *Manuale di diritto privato*, Milan, Giuffrè, 1978 and further revised editions
Trimarchi, P., *Istituzioni di diritto privato*, Milan, Giuffrè, 2018.

Contracts

Bianca, M., *Il Contratto*, Milan, 1987.
Carusi, D., *Il Contratto*, Milan, 1947.
Cataudella, A., *I contratti. Parte generale*, 2a ed., Turin, 2000.
Galgano, F., *Diritto civile e commerciale*, Padua, 1994.
Galgano, F., *Trattato di diritto civile, II, Le obbligazioni in generale. Il contratto in generale. I singoli contratti. Gli atti unilaterali e i titoli di credito. I fatti illeciti e gli altri fatti fonte di obbligazioni. La tutela del credito*, Padua, 2009, 129–577.
Gorla, G., *Il Contratto*, 1954.
Oberto, G., *Le cause in materia di obbligazioni*, Giuffrè, Milan, 1994.
Sacco, R., De Nova, F., *Il Contratto*, UTET–Wolters Kluwer, 2016.
Sicchero, G., *Il contratto con causa mista*, Cedam, Padua, 1995.

Torts

Alpa, G., Bessone, M., *Atipicità dell'illecito*, Milan, 1977.

Alpa, G., Bessone, M., *La responsabilità civile*, Milan, 1976.
Cendon, P., *Responsabilità civile*, UTET–Wolters Kluwer, 2017.
Fava, P., *La responsabilità civile*, Milan, Giuffrè, 2018.
Monateri, P.G., Bona, M., *Il danno alla persona*, Cedam, Padua, 1998.
Trimarchi, P., *La responsabilità civile: atti illeciti, rischio, danno*, Giuffrè, Milano, 2017.

Contractual Liability

Cendon, P., *Inadempimento contrattuale e risarcimento del danno*. Vol. 1, Turin, UTET, 2006.
Comporti, M., *Esposizione al pericolo e responsabilità civile*, Naples, 1965.
Costanza, M., *Il danno contrattuale*, Bologna, Zanichelli, 2014.
Di Prisco, N., *Concorso di colpa e responsabilità civile*, Naples, 1973.
Monateri, P.G., *La responsabilità contrattuale e precontrattuale*, Utet, Turin, 1998.
Moro, P., *La resposabilità contrattuale. Atti giudiziali commentati*, Giuffrè, Milan, 2011.
Ottolenghi, M., *Prescrizione dell'azione per danni*, Milan, 1975.
Realmonte, F., *Il problema del rapporto di cousalità nel risarcimento del danno*, Milan, 1967.
Trimarchi, P., *Causalità e danno*, Milan, 1967.
Trimarchi, P., *Rischio e responsabilità oggettiva*, Milan, 1961.

Quasi Contracts

Barbiera, L., *L'arricchimento senza causa*, Naples, 1964.
Breccia, U., *La ripetizione dell'indebito*, Milan, 1974.
Gallo, P., *L'arricchimento senza causa, la responsabilità civile*, Turin, Giappichelli, 2018.
Sacco, R., *L'arricchimento ottenuto mediante fatto ingiusto*, Turin, 1959.
Trimarchi, P., *L'arricchimento senza causa*, Milan, 1962.

Law of Property

Bessone, M., *Casi e questioni di diritto privato*, vol. IV: *Proprietà e diritti reali*, a cura di Alpa, G., Comporti, M., Di Prisco, N., Francario, L., Gambaro, A., Guarneri, A., Mazzoni, C.M., VII ed., Giuffrè, Milan, 1993.
Clarizia, R., *Proprietà e diritti reali*, Turin, UTET, 2016.
De Tilla, M., *Il diritto immobiliare. Trattato sintetico di giurisprudenza ragionata per casi. Vol. II*, Giuffrè, Milan, 1996.
Gambaro, A., *La proprietà. Beni, proprietà, possesso*, Giuffrè, Milano, 2017.
Gasparrelli, V., *La proprietà immobiliare. Diritti, limitazioni, servitù prediali*, Maggioli, Rimini, 1992.
Grossi, P., *Il dominio e le cose. Percezioni medievali e moderne nei diritti reali*, Giuffrè, Milan, 1992.
Lepri, A., *La compravendita immobiliare*, Giuffrè, Turin, 1993.
Mattei, U., *La proprietà immobiliare*, III ed., Giappichelli, Turin, 2015.
Rossi, G., *Duplex est usufructus: ricerche sulla natura dell'usufrutto nel diritto comune*, Cedam, Padua, 1996.

Tamborrino, F., *La compravendita di appartamenti, uffici e negozi*, II ed., Giuffrè, Milan, 1995.

Trusts

Bassetti, R., *Il trust: criticità, correzioni, sviluppi*, Turin, Giappichelli, 2017.
Graziadei, M., D*iritti nell'interesse altrui. Undisclosed agency e trust nell'esperienza giuridica inglese*, Università degli Studi di Trento, 1995.
Lupoi, M., *Introduzione ai trusts. Diritto inglese, Convenzione dell'Aia, diritto italiano*, Milan, Giuffrè, 1994.
Lupoi, M., *Trusts*, Giuffrè, Milan, 1997.
Santoro, L., *Il trust in Italia*, Giuffrè, Milano, 2009.

Good Faith and Construction of Contract

Bigliazzi Geri, L., Note in tema di interpretazione secondo buona fede, Milan, 1970.
Falco, G., La buona fede e l'abuso del diritto. Principi, fattispecie e casistica, Milan, Giuffrè, 2010.
Gallo, P., Contratto e buona fede. Buona fede in senso oggettivo e trasformazioni del contratto, Turin, Utet, 2014.
Irti, N., Testo e contesto. Una lettura dell'Art. 1362 c.c., Cedam, Padua, 1996.
Sacco, R., De Nova, G., *Il Contratto*, vol. II, Utet, Turin, 1993.
Villanacci, G., La buona fede oggettiva, ESI, Naples, 2013.

Solemn Contracts and Notaries

Chianale, G., L'atto pubblico. Contributo allo studio dei costi transattivi, Giappichelli, Turin, 1992.
Costamagna, G., Alle origini del notariato italiano, Consiglio Nazionale del Notariato, Rome, 1975.
Delfini, F., Aa. Vv., L'atto Pubblico Informatico. Commentario Ai D.Lgs. 110/2010 E 235/2010, Turin, UTET, 2011.
Di Fabio, M., Manuale di notariato, Giuffrè, Milan, 1981.
Ferrari, E., L'atto notarile, Giuffrè, Milan, 1977.
Salito, G., Del notaio e dell'atto notarile, Naples, ESI, 2018.

Precontractual Liability

Bellomia, V., La responsabilità precontrattuale tra contrattazione civile, del consumatore e di impresa, Giuffrè, Milan, 2018.
Benatti, F., La responsabilità precontrattuale, Milan, 1963.
Caruso, D., La culpa in contrahendo. L'esperienza statunitense e quella italiana, Milan, 1993.
Grisi, G., L'obbligo precontrattuale di informazione, Naples, 1990.
Loi, M., Tessitore, F., Buona fede e responsabilità precontrattuale, Milan, 1975.
Nanni, L., La buona fede contrattuale, Padua, 1988.
Sacco, R., De Nova, G., Il Contratto, vol. I, Trattato di Diritto Civile direttoda R. Sacco, Turin, 1993.
Sapone, N., La responsabilità precontrattuale, Giuffrè, Milan, 2008.
Visintini, G., La reticenza nella formazione dei contratti, Padua, 1972.

Contract Validity

Bianca, M., *Il Contratto*, Milan, 1987.
Bianchi, G., *Vizi del contratto e simulazione*, Padua, Cedam, 2008.
Carusi, D., *Il Contratto*, Milan, 1947.
Galgano, F., *Diritto civile e commerciale*, Padua, 1994.
Gorla, G., *Il Contratto*, 1954.
Larenz, K., *Geshäftsgrundlage und Vertragserfüllung*, 1963.
Örtmann, P., *Die Geshäftsgrundlage. Ein neuer Rechtsbegriff*, 1921.
Pietrobon, V., *Errore, volontà e affidamento*, 1990.
Zweigert, K., Kötz, H., *Introduction to Comparative Law*, Second Part, Oxford, 1990.

General Terms and Conditions of Contract

Alcaro, F., La condizione nel contratto. Tra "atto" e "attività," CEDAM, Padua, 2008.
Bianca, M., Diritto civile, III, Il contratto, Milan, 1984.
Trimarchi, P., Istituzioni di diritto privato, XI ed., Milan, 1997.

Contracts In Favor of Third Parties

Caliceti, P., Contratto e negozio nella stipulazione a favore di terzi, Padua, 1994.
Ferranti, I., Causa e tipo nel contratto a favore di terzo, Milan, Giuffrè, 2005.
Moscarini, L., Il contratto a favore di terzi. Artt. 1411–1413, Milan, Giuffrè, 2012.

Contract Assignment

Carresi, P., La cessione del contratto, Milan, 1979.
Clarizia, R., La cessione del contratto. Artt. 1406–1410, Milan, Giuffrè, 2005.

Actions to Protect Contractual Rights

Lucchini Guastalla, E., Danno e frode nella revocatoria ordinaria, Milan, 1995.
Rosselli, F., I mezzi di conservazione della garanzia patrimoniale, Turin, 1997.

Termination of Contract

Alpa, G., I contratti in generale. Introduzione alla nuova giurisprudenza, Turin, 1990.
Amadio, G., La condizione d'inadempimento, Padua, 1996.
Barone, O., Chirico, P., Cirillo, G., Di Meo, M., La clausola risolutiva espressa. Rassegna di giurisprudenza 1942–1992, Padua, 1993.
Bessone, M., Adempimento e rischio contrattuale, Milan, 1969.
Breccia, U., Le obbligazioni, Milan, 1991.
De Nova, G., Recesso e risoluzione nei contratti, Milan, 1994.
De Nova, G., Recesso e risoluzione nei contratti, Milan, 1994.
Giardina, F., Responsabilità contrattuale e responsabilità estracontrattuale—Significato attuale di una distinzione tradizionale, Milan, 1993.
Monateri, P.G., La responsabilità contrattuale e precontrattuale, Turin, 1998.
Mongillo, R., Inadempimento e risoluzione di diritto, ESI, Naples, 2012.

Paladini, M., L'atto unilaterale di risoluzione per inadempimento (Studi di diritto privato), Turin, Giappichelli, 2013.
Palmieri, A., La responsabilità contrattuale, Milan, 1994.
Rossetti, M., La risoluzione per inadempimento, Milan, Giuffrè, 2012.
Sacco, R., De Nova, G., Il contratto, vol. II, Turin, 1993.
Stella, G., Impossibilità della prestazione per fatto imputabile al creditore, Milan, 1995.
Terranova, C.G., L'eccessiva onerosità sopravvenuta nei contratti, Milan, 1996.

Specific Performance

Bianca, M., Diritto civile. La responsabilità, V, Milan, 1994.
Carbone, V., Il rapporto di causalità, in Responsabilità civile a cura di Alpa e Bessone, 1988–1996, I, Turin, 1997.
Carrato, A., L'esecuzione in forma specifica. Per consegna e rilascio degli obblighi di fare e di non fare, Giuffrè, Milan, 2005.
Monateri, P.GM., La responsabilità civile, Turin, 1997.
Visalli, N., L'esecuzione in forma specifica dell'obbligo di concludere un contratto, Padua, 1995.
Visintini, G., Trattato breve della responsabilità civile, Padua, 1996.

Specific Contracts: Agency

Di Gregorio, V., La rappresentanza apparente, Padua, 1996.
Lupoi, M., et al., Fiducia, trust, mandato ed agency, Giuffrè, Milan, 1991.

Specific Contracts: Construction Contracts, Hire of Work and Skills

Carinci, F., De Luca Tamajo, R., Tosi, P., Treu, T., *Diritto del lavoro*, I, Utet, Turin, 1994.
De Tilla, M., *I contratti immobiliari nella prassi giudiziaria*, tomo I, *Vendita—appalto—permuta*, Giuffrè, Milan, 1992.

Specific Contracts: Lease

Calvo, R., *La locazione*, Giappichelli, Turin, 2016.
Clarizia, R., *La locazione finanziaria*, Giappichelli, Turin, 1996.
De Tilla, M., *Le locazioni*, in *Il diritto immobiliare—Trattato sistematico di giurisprudenza ragionata per casi*, vol. VIII, V ed., Giuffrè, Milan, 1997.
Trimarchi, M., *La locazione*, ESI, Naples, 2013.
Vassallo Paleologo, F., *I contratti di locazione finanziaria*, Cedam, Padua, 1994.

Specific Contracts: Settlement Agreements

Colangeli, D., *La transazione*, Giuffrè, Milan, 2012.
Del Prato, E., *La transazione*, Giuffrè, Milan, 1992.
Panuccio Dattola, F., *La transazione novativa*, Giuffrè, Milan, 1996.
Rotondi, E., *La transazione nella giurisprudenza*, Giuffrè, Milan, 1993.

Specific Contracts: Loans

Ferroni, L., La nuova disciplina civilistica del contratto di mutuo, Esi, Naples, 1997.

Graziano, N., Il Mutuo Bancario, Cedam, Padua, 2013.

Specific Contracts: Government Contracts

Buscema, S., Trattato di diritto amministrativo, Padua, 1994.
Mele, E., I contratti delle Pubbliche Amministrazioni, Giuffrè, Milano, 2011.
Meloncelli, A., L'informazione amministrativa, Rimini, 1983.
Sandulli, A., Diritto amministrativo, Iovene, Naples, 1989.
Santoro, P., I controlli sull'attività contrattuale della pubblica amministrazione, Milano, 1992.

Specific Contracts: Partnerships and Companies

Baudino, A., Frascinelli, R., Gli amministratori delle società per azioni e a responsabilità limitata, Giuffrè, Milan, 1996.
Bellagamba, G., Cariti, G., Le società di persone—Le società di fatto—Le società cooperative, Giuffrè, Milan, 1997.
Bellagamba, G., Cariti, G., Le società di persone—Le società di fatto—Le società cooperative, Giuffrè, Milan, 1997.
Casadei, D., Le società di persone, Giuffrè, Milan, 1997.
Cassese, G., Economia dei mercati finanziari, Roma, Carocci, 2017.
Cavalli, G., Marulli, M. et al., Le società per azioni. Gli organi e il controllo giudiziario, Utet, Turin, 1996.
Cottino, G., Diritto societario, Padua, Cedam, 2011.
Easterbrook, F.H., Fischel, D.R., L'economia delle società per azioni, Giuffrè, Milan, 1996.
Galcano, F., Diritto commerciale—II. Le società. Contratto di società. Società di persone, società per azioni, altre società di capitali. Società cooperative, rist. aggiornata Zanichelli, Bologna, 1991.
Garesio, G., La società in generale. Le società di persone. Le società tra professionisti, UTET, Turin, 2014.
Ibba, C., La società a responsabilità limitata con unico socio, Giappichelli, Turin, 1995.
Menghi, I., Il bilancio di esercizio della società per azioni, Cedam, Padua, 1997.
Palumbo, A., Le società in generale e le società di persone, Giuffrè, Milan, 2008.
Salanitro, N., Società per azioni e mercati finanziari, Giuffrè, Milan, 1996.
Stassano, G., Società a responsabilità limitata, Giuffrè, Milan, 1997.
Zamperetti, G.M., La società unipersonale a responsabilità limitata, Giuffrè, Milan, 1997.

Articles and Notes

Private and Public Law

Bortolotti, F., Contratti della amministrazione pubblica, in: Digesto IV, Utet, Turin, 1989.
Giorgianni, M., Il diritto privato e i suoi attuali confini, in Riv. Trim, dir. e proc. civ., 1961.
Pugliatti, S., Diritto pubblico e diritto privato, in Enc. Dir., XII, 1964.

Romano Tassone, A., A proposito del potere, pubblico e privato, e della sua legittimazione, in Dir. Amm., 2013, at 559, fasc. 04.
Scognamiglio, R., Responsabilità contrattuale ed extracontratuale, in NssDI, XV.

General Principles of the Law of Contract

Achille, D., La funzione ermeneutica della causa concreta del contratto, in Riv. Trim. di Dir. e Proc. Civ., 2017, at 37, fasc. 01.
Alpa, G., Causa e tipo, in Vita not., 1997.
Alpa, G., L'uso giurisprudenziale della causa nel contratto, in Nuova giur. civ., 1995, II, 1.
Battaglia, C., Contratti innominati e causa atipica (nota a Cass. sez. I, 20 novembre 1992, n. 12401, Soc. immob. turistica H.M. c. Ministero dei Trasporti), in Giust. civ., 1993, I, 2761.
Marinelli, F., La causa e l'oggetto del contratto nella dottrina civilistica italiana, in Giust. civ., 1995, II, 327, Rep. Foro it., 1995, contratto in genere, n. 131.
Nervi, A., Il contratto come strumento di conformazione dell'assetto di mercato, in Europa e Diritto Privato, fasc.1, 2018, at 95.
Pirruccio, P., La nullità del contratto tra causa illecita e motivo illecito comune, in Giur. merito, fasc.1, 2005, at 203.
Ragusa Maggiore, G., La scomparsa degli idola fori: la causa del contratto, in Dir. fallim., 1995, I, 553.
Sicchero, G., Appunti sulla causa del contratto (nota a Cass. sez. II 15 luglio 1993, n 7844, Torresin c. Torresin)', in Giur. it., 1995, I, 1, 733.

Contractual Liability

Antonini, A., Responsabilità contrattuale ed extracontrattuale: il diritto dei trasporti, banco di prova di una adeguata evoluzione del regime del concorso, in Resp. civ. e prev., fasc.2, 2010, at 253.
Anzani, G., Il concorso di responsabilità contrattuale ed extracontrattuale, in Resp. Civ. e Prev., fasc.1, 2018, at 278.
De Martini, D., Responsabilità per danni da attività pericolosa e responsabilità per danni nell'esercizio di attività pericolosa, in Giur. it., 1973, I, 2, 963.
Scognamiglio, R., Responsabilità contrattuale ed extracontrattuale, in NSSDI, XV, 1968, 670.

Quasi Contracts

Albanese, A., Fatto illecito, fatto ingiusto e restituzione dell'arricchimento in assenza di danno, in Resp. civ. e prev., fasc.2, 2004, at 538.
Alberti, A.M., Il riconoscimento di debito, in Rass. dir. tecnica doganale, 1995, 95.
Annunziata, M., Pubblica amministrazione e arricchimento senza causa (Nota a Cass. S.U., 10 febbraio 1996, n. 1025, Prov. Arezzo c. Comunità montana Zona H Alto Tevere Val Tiberina), in Foro amm., 1996, 2579.
De Bonis, D., Indebito oggettivo—errore—aricchimento senza causa—rimedi altermnativi e non concorrenti (nota a Giudice di Pace roma, 13 maggio 1997, Sai Assicurazioni c. Terzi), in Riv. giur. circolza. e trasp., 1997, 639.
Dell' Aquila, e., L'arricchimento senza causa come correttivo dell'autonomia contrattuale, in Riv. giur. sarda, 1994, 849.

Donatelli, R., Vecchie e nuove "categorie" comprese nel "genere" dell'arricchimento senza causa (nota a Pret. Salerno—Eboli, 2 marzo 1993, Trinca c. Trinca), in Giur. merito, 1995, 541.
Gallo, P., Arricchimento senza causa (sintesi di informazione), in Riv. dir. civ., 1993, II, 677.
Moscati, E., Indebito soggettivo ed attuazione del rapporto obbligatorio, in Riv. dir. civ., 1974, 72 et seq.
Romanato, N., Danno, arricchimento ingiustificato, arricchimento ingiusto nell'art. 125 c.p.i., in Riv. dir. ind., fasc.1, 2013, at 23.
Spitali, E., L'arricchimento mediante intermediario e l'Art. 2038 c.c. (nota a Cass. Sez II, 10 febbraio 1993, n. 1686, Castagni c. ENEL), in Giur. it., 1994, I, 1, 1861.

Law o Property, Usufructs, Easements and other rights In Rem

Bellini, L, Il contratto preliminare di compravendita immobiliare, in Corriere trib., 1997, 11.
Bessone, M., Di Paolo, M., Superficie (diritto civile), in Enc. giur. Treccani, Roma, 1993, vol. XXX.
Bigliazzi Geri, L., Usufrutto, uso e abitazione, in Enc. giur. Treccani, "Diritto civile," Roma, 1994, vol. XXXII.
Caterini, E., Enfiteusi tra lavoro e proprietà (nota a Corte Costit. 9 dicembre 1991, n 441, Battaglia c. Denaro), in Giur. costit., 1991, 3698.
Catti, S., Costituzione del diritto di superficie, donazione e riserva d'usufrutto in Vita not., 1997, 1040.
Chianale, A., Il diritto di superficie: epitomi giudiziarie ed occasioni perdute (nota a Cass. sex. II, 13 febbraio 1993 n. 1844, Sgroia c. Gaudieri), in Giur. it., 1994, I, 1, 1851.
Chiodi, A., Situazioni prodromiche in common law e in diritto italiano: uno sguardo comparativo su reversion, nuda proprietà e aspettativa reale, in Quadrimestre, 1992, 109; Rep. Foro it., 1992, diritto comparato, 148.
Colletti, R., Le servitù e la cessione di cubatura, in Nuova rass., 1996, 68.
Palazzolo, S., Servitù coattive, in Enc. giur. Treccani, Rome, 1992, vol. XXVIII.
De Cuppis, A., Usufrutto (diritto vigente), in Enc. dir., vol. XLV, Giuffrè, Milan, 1992, 1111.
De Tilia, M., Sui rapporti tra affitto, locazione ed usufrutto (nota a Cass. sez. III, 28 gennaio 1995, n. 1051, Laudani c. Carciola), in Rass. locazioni, 1996, 287.
Guarneri, A., Superficie (sintesi d'informazione), in Riv. dir. civ., 1996, II, 507.
Lipari, M., Il capitale di affrancazione dell'enfiteusi: si accentua il contrasto tra proprietà ed impresa agricola (nota a Corte Costit. 23 maggio 1997, n. 143, Calenda c. Parrocchia Brignano), in Dir. e giur. agr. ambiente, 1997, 392.
Ludovici, R., I canoni di natura enfiteutica previsti dalla vigente normativa in materia di usi civici, loro revisione ed affrancazione, in P. Q. M., 1996, 2, 104.
Mogorovich, S., L'usufrutto di azienda, in Impresa, 1992, 2825.
Morsillo, G., In tema di affrancazione di fondo enfiteutico (nota a Trib. Roma 25 maggio 1995, Bartolazzi c. Bartolazzi), in Dir. e giur. agr. ambiente, 1997, 139.
Musolino, G., Usufrutto e proprietà, in Riv. del Not., 2011, at 1321, fasc. 06.

Musolino, G., Il diritto di superficie ovvero la proprietà in atto e in potenza, in Riv. del Not., fasc.4, 2017, at 865.
Musolino, G., Il diritto di superficie ovvero la proprietà in atto e in potenza—Seconda parte, in Riv. del Not., 2017, at 1041.
Riaro Sforza, M., L'inammissibilità della tutela possessoria nelle servitù non apparenti. Spunti per una riflessione critica, in Giur. merito, fasc. 5, 2013, at 1212AB.
Salis, L., Proprietà superficiaria e proprietà separata (nota a Cass. sez. II, 13 febbraio 1993, n. 1844, Sgroia c. Gaudieri), in Riv. giur. edilizia, 1993, I, 1026.
Tosi, E., Il sistema delle garanzie nel contratto di compravendita, in Società e dir., 1994, 714.

Trust

Capaldo R., Atto pubblico di trust, in Notariato, 1997, 176.
F Albisinni, R. Gambino, The Italian Civil Law System and the Hague Convention on Trusts, in 2 Journal of International Planning (1993) 73, 86.
Laroma Jezzi, P., La fiscalità dei trust aspettando il "Trust di diritto italiano," in Riv. dir. trib., fasc.6, 2012, at 587.
Lenzi, R., Operatività del trust in Italia, in Riv. not., 1995, 1379.
Lupoi, M., Il trust nell'ordinamento giuridico italiano dopo la Convenzione de L'Aia del 10 luglio 1985, in Vita not., 1992, 966.
Lupoi, M., Si fa presto a dire "trust," in Riv. Trim. di Dir. e Proc. Civ., fasc.2, 2017, at 669.
Palermo, G., Il principio di mutual trust: ultimo baluardo della comunitarizzazione dell'arbitrato commerciale?, in Riv. dell'Arbitr., fasc. 4, 2015, at 645.
Piccoli, P., Possibilità operative del trust nell'ordinamento italiano. L'operatività del trustee dopo la convenzione de L'Aia (dal Convegno di Treviso del 18–19 novembre 1994 sul tema "Esercizio di poteri gestori nel contesto internazionale. Profili delle varie forme di rappresentanza e intermediazione"), in Riv. not., 1995, 37.
Ponzanelli, Gli enti non profit in Italia. Associazioni, fondazioni, volontariato, trust, fondi pensione, in Rep. Foro it., 1994, diritto civile, 54.

Construction of Contract

Costanzo, P., Il principio in claris non fit interpretatio nel sistema delle norme relative alla interpretazione del contratto, in Giust. civ., fasc.3, 1997, at 151.
Fonsi, G., L'interpretazione del contratto in giurisprudenza e in dottrina (Art. 1362 e 1363 c.c.), in Vita not., 1993, 1624.
Irti, N., Princìpi e problemi di interpretazione contrattuale, in Riv. trim. dir. proc. civ., fasc.4, 1999, 1139.
Morace Pinelli, A., In claris non fit interpretatio: un brocardo che non trova asilo nel nostro ordinamento giuridico (nota a Cass. sez. II. 23 dicembre 1993, n 12759, Marino c. Soc. coop. iliade), in Giur. it., 1994, I, 1, 1163.
Petruso, R., L'interpretazione del contratto secondo le corti superiori del Regno Unito, in Europa e Diritto Privato, fasc.1, 2016, 95.

Solemn Contracts and Notaries

Barone, R., Campo d'azione del notaio. Limiti, differenze, analogie, prospettive, in Riv. not., XLVI, Giuffrè, Milan, 1992.
Boero, P., Autenticazione, in Digesto IV, vol. I, Utet, Turin, 1995.
Carnelutti, F., La figura giuridica del notaro, in Riv. dir. proc. civ., Cedam, Padua, 1950.
Crisci, G., Atto pubblico (diritto civile), in Enc. dir., IV, Giuffrè, Milan, 1959.
Brugi, B., Atti pubblici, in NSSDI, I, sez. II, Utet, Turin, 1958.
Guasti, F., I notariati francese e italiano di fronte all'Europa: problemi e scelte, in Riv. not., XLV, Giuffrè, Milan, 1981.
Marmocchi, E., Atto pubblico tra clausole vessatorie e clausole abusive, in Riv. notariato, fasc.1–2, 1997, 55.
Mazzola, M., Notaio e notariato, in Digesto IV, vol. XII, Utet, Turin, 1993.
Tommaseo, F., L'atto pubblico nel sistema delle prove documentali, in Riv. notariato, fasc.4, 1998, 593.

Rules of Evidence

Andrioli, *Prova (diritto processuale civile)*, in *NSSDI*, XIV, Utet, Turin, 1967.
Carnelutti, F., *Documento (teoria moderna)*, in *NSSDI*, VI, Utet, Turin, 1956.
Carnelutti, F., *Documento e negozio giuridico*, in *Riv. dir. proc. civ.*, Padua, 1926.
Poli, R., *La prova scientifica e il suo controllo in Cassazione*, in *Riv. Trim. di Dir. e Proc. Civ.*, fasc.4, 2017, at 1222.
Taruffo, M., *Verità e prova nel processo*, in *Riv. Trim. di Dir. e Proc. Civ.*, fasc.4, 2018, 1305.
Verde, G., *Prova (diritto processuale civile)*, in *Enc. dir.*, XXXVII, Giuffrè, Milan, 1988.

Precontractual Liability

Alpa, G., Italian Report to The XIIIth Congress International Academy of Comparative Law, in Precontractual Liability, Kluwer, 1991, 165.
Benatti, F., Culpa in contrahendo, in Contratto e impresa, 1987, 287.
Bessone, M., Rapporto precontrattuale e doveri di correttezza, in Riv. trim. dir. proc. civ., 1955, I, 360.
Carnicelli, C., Risarcimento del danno da responsabilità precontrattuale: qualificazione e quantificazione, in Giust. civ., fasc.6, 2011, 293.
Cuffaro, V., Responsabilità precontrattuale, in Enc. dir., XXXIX, Milan, 1988, 1265.
Ferrarini, G., Investment banking, prospetti falsi e culpa in contrahendo, in Giur. comm., 1988, II, 585.
Franzina, P., La responsabilità precontrattuale nello spazio giudiziario europeo, in Riv. dir. internaz., fasc.3, 2003, 714.
Fusaro, A., Fondamenti e limiti della responsabilità precontrattuale, in Giur. it., 1984, I, 1, 1199.
Ilacqua, A., La responsabilità precontrattuale della pubblica amministrazione. Evoluzioni giurisprudenziali, in Foro amm. CDS, fasc.9, 2008, 2571.
Rasi, S.A., La responsabilità precontrrattuale, in Riv. dir. civ., 1974, 496.
Mengoni, L., La responsabilità precontrattuale, in Riv. dir. comm., 1956, II, 365.

Contract Validity

Selected Bibliography

Abas, P., Errore di previsione e sopravvenienza contrattuale: un'indagine comparatistica, in Riv. trim. dir. proc. civ., fasc.3, 2011, 787.

Pontani, A., La presupposizione nella sua evoluzione, con particolare riferimento all'errore ed alla causa, in Quadrimestre, 1991, 833.

General Conditions and Terms of Contract

Alpa, G., Consumatore (tutela del), Enc. giur. Treccani, Rome, vol. VIII, 1988.

Astone, M., Diritti dei consumatori e obblighi di informazione tra direttiva 25-10-2011 n. 83 e d.lgs. 21-2-2014 n. 24. Ambito applicativo: i contratti standard di servizi di assistenza legale, in Europa e Diritto Privato, fasc.3, 2015, 671.

Barela, M., Sull'azione inibitoria in via d'urgenza ex Art. 1469 sexies c.c., in Giust. civ., 1997, I, 2295.

Barone, C.M., Biancosegno e arbitrato irrituale nelle controversie di lavoro, in Foro it., 1980, I, 974.

Di Majo, F., Il controllo delle condizioni generali di contratto, in Riv. dir. comm., 1970, I, 190.

Fazzalari, Arbitrato (teoria generale e diritto processuale civile), in Digesto IV, Turin, 1987.

Fazzalari, I processi arbitrali nell'ordinamento italiano, in Riv. dir. proc. civ., 1968, 459.

Maiorca, S., La condizione, in Digesto IV, Turin, 1988.

Mancuso, C., La clausola compromissoria nei contratti dei consumatori tra vessatorietà e consenso, in Riv. Trim. di Dir. e Proc. Civ., fasc.3, 2018, 1213.

Morello, Condizioni generali di contratto, in Digesto IV, Turin, 1988.

Sacco, R., La condizione, in Tratt. Rescigno, Turin, 1982, 291.

Privity of Contract

Corrias, P.E., Sulla natura e sull'estensione dell'obbligazione del promittente nella promessa del fatto del terzo, in Giur. it., 1994, I, 1, 1643.

Marella, M.R., Promessa del fatto del terzo, in Digesto IV, XV, Turin, 1996, at 381.

Navarretta, E., L'adempimento dell'obbligazione del fatto altrui e la responsabilità del medico, in Resp. civ. e prev., fasc.7–8, 2011, 1453B.

Radice, P., Dichiarazione di nomina preliminare, in Contratti, 1994, 261.

Contracts in Favor of Third Parties

Dogliotti, M, Morello di Giovanni, D., *Contratto a favore di terzo*, in *Giur. merito*, fasc.2, 2001, 513.

Regoli, G., In tema di efficacia reale del contratto a favore di terzo nei suoi rapporti con il patto di opzione, in *Riv. trim. dir. proc. civ.*, 1996, 463.

Assignment of Contract

Basini, G.F., Forma del negozio di cessione del contratto e cedibilità dei contratti ad effetti reali, in Contratti, 1993.

Pescatore, V., Cessione del contratto ed interpretazione, in Riv. trim. dir. proc. civ., fasc.2, 1999, 583.

Termination of Contract

Cervini, A., Mutui di valuta e rischi di cambio per realità e presupposizione, in Giust. civ. 1996, II, 327

Cervini, A., Risoluzione per eccessiva onerosità sopravvenuta nei mutui di valuta, in Giust. civ., 1997, I, 1409.

De Lorenzi, V., Inadempimento doloso, in Digesto IV, vol. IX, Turin, 1993, 360.

De Nova, G., Risoluzione dei contratti di fornitura dei sistemi informatici, (nota a Trib. Torino, 13.03.1993), in Contratti, 1993, 440.

Di Majo, A., Restituzioni e responsabilità nelle obbligazioni e nei contratti, in Riv. crit. dir. priv., 1994, 291

Di Majo, A., Risoluzione del contratto ed effetti restitutori: debito di valore o debito di valuta? (nota a Cass. S.U. 04.12.1992 n. 12942), in Corriere giur., 1993, 322.

Inzitari, B., Inesigibilità della prestazione, impossibilità della prestazione per l'embargo contro l'Iraq, in Nuova giur. civ., 1995, II, 48.

Lopez De Gonzalo, M., Consegna e trasferimento del rischio nella vendita marittima, in Dir. maritt., 1994, 105.

Mengoni, L., Responsabilità contrattuale (diritto vigente), in Enc. dir., XXXIX, Milan, 1988, 1072.

Montanari, A., Risoluzione del contratto e risarcimento dell'interesse negativo, in Europa e dir. priv., fasc.3, 2010, 785.

Spirito, Diffida ad adempiere e risoluzione del contratto (nota a Cass. 04.05.1994 n 4275), in Corriere giur., 1994, 838.

Tranquillo, C., Risoluzione per inadempimento e funzione delle restituzioni, in Europa e Dir. Priv., fasc.4, 2015, 813.

Specific Performance

Bochicchio, G., Il concorso colposo del danneggiato. Responsabilità e correttezza, in Riv. crit. dir. priv., 1992, 23.

Fabrizio, B., Esecuzione del preliminare di società, in Società, 1996, 1179.

Formiggini, A., Rivoluzione nella revocatoria, evoluzione nei contratti preliminari?, in Riv. trim. dir. proc. civ., fasc.4, 2001, 1163.

Giombini, F., Inapplicabilità della tutela ex Art. 1460 c.c. alla vendita forzata, in Corriere giur., 1996, 437.

Guarnieri, A. Contratto preliminare, contratto definitivo e "mutatio libelli," in Arch. civ., 1996, 1134, 1331.

La Rocca, G., L'esercizio in via surrogatoria del diritto nascente dal preliminare: profili problematici, in Foro it., 1996, I, 882.

Montesano, L., Contenuti e sanzioni delle obbligazioni da contratto preliminare, in Riv. trim. dir. proc. civ., fasc.1, 2001, 33.

Pinori, A., Prevedibilità del danno, in Riv. dir. civ., 1994, II, 139.

Regine, F., Questioni in tema di contratto preliminare e di comunione legale, in Nuova giur. comm., 1995, I, 889.

Traverso, M.C., Causalità e colpevolezza nel concorso di colpa del danneggiato, in Nuova giur. civ. 1994, II, 235

Zampetti, M.S., Eccezione di inadempimento e onere della prova, in Foro it., 1995, I, 2615.

Limitation of Actions

Selected Bibliography

Caponi, R., Gli impedimenti all'esercizio dei diritti nella disciplina della prescrizione, in Riv. dir. civ., 1996, I.

Caponi, R., Gli impedimenti all'esercizio dei poteri giuridici nella disciplina della decadenza, in Riv. dir. civ., 1997, I, 46.

Chindemi, D., Prescrizione e decadenza in caso di proroga dei termini, in Resp. civ. e prev., fasc.1, 2008, pag. 0234B.

Granieri, M., La prescrizione, in AIDA, fasc.1, 2015, 80.

Notargiacomo, A., Sospensione della prescrizione per doloso occultamento del debito da parte del debitore, in Giur. it., 1996, I, 2037.

Proto Pisani, A., Appunti sulla tutela c.d. costitutiva, in Riv. dir. proc. civ., 1991, 60.

Rosselli, F., Decadenza, in Enc. giur., X, Rome, 1988.

Specific Contracts: Agency

Chinè, G., Mandato senza rappresentanza e pactum fiduciae a confronto, in Giur. it., 1994, I, 1, 581.

Cossu, C., Nuncius, in Digesto IV, Turin, 1995, vol. XII, 329.

Di Rosa, G., Per una regolamentazione comune della rappresentanza, in Europa e Dir. Priv., fasc.1, 1 2018, 1.

Orlandi, "Falsus nuncius e falsus procurator," in Riv. dir. civ., 1995, I, at 347.

Palma, S., La Cassazione ritorna sulla forma del mandato ad acquistare: un vero "revirement?," in Riv. Trim. di Dir. e Proc. Civ., fasc.2, 2015, pag. 675.

Salanitro, Contratto concluso con il falso rappresentante e tecniche di tutela del terzo contraente, in Riv. dir. civ., 1997, I, 469.

Specific Contracts: Bailments

Balzano, A., Perdita della cosa depositata ed obbligo di denuncia, in Giur. it., 1993, I, 1, 463.

Bonofiglio, A., Il contratto di albergo ed il contratto di deposito alberghiero, in Giust. civ., 1995, I, 2222.

Caligiuri, S., Furto della cosa depositata e responsabilità del custode, in Giur. merito, 1996, 68.

Chineè, G., Furto di indumenti e responsabilità del ristoratore (nota a Cass. sez. III, 4 ottobre 1991, n. 10393, Monteverda c. Di Primio), in Giur. it., 1992, I, 1, 1326.

D'Auria, M., Deposito merci nel porto ed incendio: la responsabilità dell'ente portuale—Cass., 7 luglio 2010, n. 15988—CC. art. 1411, in Fonti del diritto—Agg. Cod. civ. di P. Rescigno, 2011, 3.

Di Bella, D., Deposito, custodia e responsabilità delle officine di autoriparazione, in Nuova giur. civ., 1997, I, 42.

Gardella Tedeschi, B., Deposito—Comodato—Mutuo, in Riv. dir. civ., 1995, II, 633.

Martellino, G., Il deposito: un contratto in bilico tra gratuità ed onerosità, in Nuova giur. civ., 1993, I, 884.

Natale, A., In tema di deposito per la conservazione di merce deperibile, in Contratti, 1997, 141.

Petricone, F., Cassette bancarie di custodia e deposito in albergo, in Nuova giur. civ., 1996, II, 185.

Salomoni, A., La responsabilità del custode per la perdita della detenzione del bene ricevuto, in, Resp. Civ. e Prev., fasc.5, 2014, 1435B.

Tassoni, G., Contratto dicampeggio ed obblighi del gestore, in Giur. it., 1994, I, 1, 1827.

Specific Contracts: Gaming and wagering

Balestra, L., Il giuoco e la scommessa nella categoria dei contratti aleatori, in Riv. trim. dir. proc. civ., fasc.3, 2011, 665.

Crismani, A., Gioco del poker e disciplina sportiva, in Foro amm. CDS, fasc.1, 2009, 307.

D'Acquino, F., Il rischio-scudetto: assicurazione o scommessa?, In Riv. dir. sport., 1995, 745.

Merone, A., L'esercizio abusivo di attività di giuoco e di scommessa, in Rass. trib., 1991, fasc. 3, 13.

Migliorelli, G., Bookmakers stranieri: un tentativo di invasione fallito?, in Riv. giur. polizia locale, 1996, 571.

Pollari, N., Senatore, S., Le scommesse sulle corse dei cavalli, in Impresa, 1996, 1564.

Simone, S., Totocalcio: conclusione del contratto e clausole vessatorie, in Giur. pugliese, 1995, 50.

Tusset, A., Sulla causa e prova della scommessa, in Giur. it., 1995, I, 1, 73.

Zanotti R., Sulla illiceità delle scommesse con allibratori stranieri, in Riv. dir. sport., 1994, 464.

Specific Contracts: Sale of Goods

Cartella, M., Concessione di vendita—Franchising [voce aggiornata 1997], in Enc. dir., Giuffrè, Milan, 1997, I, 327.

D'Alessandro, L., Concessione di vendita: descrizione del fenomeno e profili sistematici, in Giust. civ., fasc.2, 2002, 71.

Ferrari, F., Princìpi generali inseriti nelle convenzioni internazionali e diritto uniforme: l'esempio della vendita, del factoring e del leasing internazionali, in Riv. trim. dir. e proc. civ., 1997, 629.

Scarpa, A., La vendita dei beni di consumo: la conformità al contratto e i diritti del consumatore tra codice del consumo e codice civile, in Giur. merito, fasc.11, 2008, 3038B.

Specific Contracts: Lease

Bellini, F., Alcune notazioni sul negozio di locazione finanziaria di beni detto leasing, in Riv. dir. trib., 1997, I, 179.

Bonfante, G., Nuovi orientamenti della Cassazione in tema di locazione finanziaria in Giur. it., 1990, I, 1, 379.

Branca, A., Sanzioni amministrative tributarie in materia di contratti di locazione. Principali novità e dubbi irrisolti alla luce del D.Lgs. n. 158/2015, in Riv. di Dir. Trib., fasc.6, 2015, 543.

Carbone, P., Locazione finanziaria. Natura, locazione finanziaria con scopo traslativo, in Nuova giur. civ., 199, I, 90

Clarizia, R., La convenzione Unidroit sulla loocazione finanziaria: analogie e differenze rispetto al modello italiano, in Riv. dir. impresa, 1994, 27.
Cuffaro, V., Regole e deroghe nella disciplina del contratto di locazione, in Giur. it., 1996, I, 473.
Fidone, G., Dalla locazione finanziaria al contratto di disponibilità: l'evoluzione del contratto di leasing immobiliare pubblico, in Foro amm. TAR, fasc.3, 2012, 1039.
Palisi, F., Note sulla locazione finanziaria, in Riv. it. leasing, 1991, 11.

Specific Contracts: Compromise and Settlement Agreements

Bozzola, G., Presupposti ed effetti preclusivi della transazione, in Contratti, 1994, 176.
Cerdonio Chiaromonte, G., La transazione nelle obbligazioni solidali, in Studium iuris, 1997, 798.
Delfini, F., Obbligazione solidale e transazione (nota a Cass. sez. III, 3 marzo 997 n. 1873, Valente c. Tosi)', in Contratti, 1997, 485.
Fiumara, O., Decisione giudiziaria e transazione giudiziaria nella convenzione di Bruxelles del 27 settembre 1968, in Rass. Avv. Stato, 1994, I, 275.
Galletto, T., La transazione: complessità dell'istituto ed attualità della funzione, in Riv. Trim. di Dir. e Proc. Civ., fasc.4, 2013, 1379.
Moretti, M., Contratto di transazione e rapporti di diritto familiare, in Contratti, 1996, 523.
Moscarini, L.V., CORBO, N., Transazione (diritto civile), in Enc. giur. Treccani, Roma, 1994, vol. XXI.
Vecchioni, F., Nota sul contratto di transazione, sulla definizione transattiva del danno e sull'atto di quietanza, in Arch. civ., 1996, 1345.

Specific Contracts: Loans

Carbone, V., Mutuo: traditio rei e strumenti alternativi alla consegna, in Corriere giur., 1992, 1329.
Gallo, P., Mutuo in diritto comparato, in Digesto IV, Turin, 1994, vol. XI, 580.
Gardella Tedeschi, B., Deposito—Comodato—Mutuo, in Riv. dir. civ., 1995, II, 633.
Gazzara, M., Crediti speciali, prestito a consegna differita e consensualità del mutuo, in Banca, borsa, 1995, I, 335.
Giomaro, A.M., Morosini, P.G., Mutuo nel diritto romano, medioevale e moderno, in Digesto IV, Turin, 1994, vol. XI, 584.
Godio, F., La prescrizione del diritto restitutorio nel (deposito e nel) mutuo senza termine, tra interessi delle parti e tralatizie posizioni giurisprudenziali, in Resp. Civ. e Prev., fasc.1, 2018, 316.
Viotti, S., I nuovi strumenti giuridici di modifica dei contratti di mutuo, in Giur. merito, fasc.12, 2008, 3084B.

Specific Contracts: Government Contracts

Bortolotti, D., Contratti dell'amministrazione pubblica, in Digesto IV, Turin, 1989, 37.
Battista Bisogni, G., La struttura amministrativa della società per azioni tra diritto comunitario e disciplina della public company, in Giur. comm., 1996, I, 954.

Cappai, F., Le fonti normative dei contratti della pubblica amministrazione: uno sguardo d'insieme, in Resp. Civ. e Prev., fasc.4, 2017, 1138B.

Specific Contracts: Partnerships, Company Law

Bartolacelli, A., Nuove esperienze europee in tema di costituzione "semplificata" e "a basso costo" di società con responsabilità limitata, in Giur. Comm., fasc.2, 2015, 382.
Bovesi, M., La dodicesima Direttiva CEE sule società unipersonali a responsabilità limitata ed il suo recepimento da parte dell'Italia, in Dir. scambi internaz., 1994, 477.
Cagnasso, O., Irrera, M., Società a responsabilità limitata, in Digesto IV, Turin, 1997, 183.
Carbonara, U., Elementi organizzativi e forme decisionali extra-assembleari nella società a responsabilità limitata, in Giur. Comm., fasc.6, 2017, 987.
Cimei, F., Società a responsabilità limitata, in Gius, 1995, 1137.
Corsi, F., Società in accomandita per azioni, in Digesto IV, Commercial Law Section, Utet, Turin, 1997, 234.
D'Antino, M., Deloga di poteri e responsabilità degli amministratori delle società per azioni, in Arch. Civ., 1997, 353.
di Belmonte di Tarsia, F., La società a responsabilità limitata con unico socio, in Riv. not., 1996, 793.
Galgano, F., Contratto e persona giuridica nelle società di capitali, in Contratto e impresa, 1991, 1.
Marasa, G., Spada, P., Cotting, G., Covelli, M.R., Contratto di società, in Enc. giur. Treccani, Rome, 1993 XXIX.
Racugno, G., Società a responsabilità limitata, in Giur. comm., 1996, I, 157.
Spezia, F., Il divieto del patto leonino nel contratto di società, in Arch. civ., 1991, 993.
Spolidoro, M.S., Una società a responsabilità limitata da tre soldi (o da un euro?), in Riv. delle Soc., fasc.6, 2013, 1085.
Various Authors, Trattato delle società per azioni, Utet, Turin, 1996.
Weigmann, R., Società per azioni, in Digesto IV. Commercial Law Section, Utet, Turin, 1997.

Selected Bibliography

Index

The numbers refer to the paragraph numbers.

Index

www.ingramcontent.com/pod-product-compliance
Lightning Source LLC
Chambersburg PA
CBHW071345230926
51846CB00002B/450